TOTAL INSECURITY

Also by Carol Brightman

Venceremos Brigade (co-edited, 1971)

Drawings and Digressions (with Larry Rivers, 1979)

Writing Dangerously: Mary McCarthy and Her World (1992)

Between Friends: The Correspondence of Hannah Arendt and Mary McCarthy (edited and introduced, 1995)

Sweet Chaos: The Grateful Dead's American Adventure (1998)

TOTAL INSECURITY

The Myth of American Omnipotence

CAROL BRIGHTMAN

VERSO

London • New York

First published by Verso 2004
© Carol Brightman 2004
All rights reserved

The moral rights of the author have been asserted

1 3 5 7 9 10 8 6 4 2

Verso
UK: 6 Meard Street, London W1F 0EG
USA: 180 Varick Street, New York, NY 10014-4606
www.versobooks.com

Verso is the imprint of New Left Books

ISBN 1-84467-010-4

British Library Cataloguing in Publication Data
A catalogue record for this book is available from the British Library

Library of Congress Cataloging-in-Publication Data
A catalog record for this book is available from the Library of Congress

Typeset in Fournier
Printed in the USA by R. R. Donnelley & Sons

"It is easy to go down into Hell; night and day, the gates of dark Death stand wide; but to climb back again, to retrace one's steps to the upper air—there's the rub, the task."

VIRGIL, *Aeneid*

In memory of C. Gordon Brightman, Jr.

CONTENTS

	PREFACE	xi
	ACKNOWLEDGEMENTS	xvii
1	STARTING OVER IS NOT AN EASY THING TO DO	1
2	HOW IT WAS	30
3	SECURING THE REALM	45
4	MAKING WAVES	75
5	MOUNTING WAR	99
6	VIETNAM REDUX	120
7	THE POLITICAL ECONOMY OF DEATH I	165
8	THE POLITICAL ECONOMY OF DEATH II	180
9	THE POLITICAL ECONOMY OF DEATH III	195
10	THE *CONSIGLIERE* IS BACK	220
	EPILOGUE	229
	NOTES	243
	INDEX	259

PREFACE

This is a story about how the United States lost its way. A powerful nation, though not wise, its military forces stood alone in the world. No one attempted to challenge it—certainly not its peers in Europe, or in Russia and China, who had more to gain from economic cooperation and competition than from combat. Besides the US had become the world's supercop, and global security was generally left to its armed forces and its arms sales. Only Vietnam stood up to America, and that was a long time ago, twenty-five years before the end of the Cold War. Vietnam was a poor country, a midget compared to the US, but it had defended itself against more powerful invaders for centuries, most recently the French, and knew how to do it. After a ten-year war, and over 58,000 American deaths, the US was defeated. It was chased out of Saigon, literally, over a week in April 1975, and never looked back. Or it tried to look back, and didn't learn the first lesson—which is never to wage war against a people.

"History advances in disguise," Régis Debray wrote in 1967; "it appears on stage wearing the mask of the preceding scene, and we tend to lose the meaning of the play. ... The blame, of course, is not history's," he said, speaking of the Cuban Revolution, "but lies in our vision, encumbered with memory and images learned in the past. We see the past superimposed on the present, even when the present is a revolution."[1] The resistance in Iraq is not like Cuba's or Vietnam's, although each country in its fashion has outwitted the United States, and Iraq is on its way to outwitting Washington. We have heard a great deal about Iraq's parallels with Vietnam: about the illusion that "we will be greeted as liberators," in Vice President Dick Cheney's words, so much like the belief that US nation-building efforts would win over the Vietnamese; or the notion that democracy in Iraq will spread throughout the Middle East, thereby turning it into a bulwark against terrorism or a friend to Israel, like the idea that a victory in Vietnam would transform Southeast Asia into a bulwark against China; or that the US is in a quagmire because it can't win and it can't get out. The events of April and May 2004—the loss of Fallujah and the rise of the Shi'ites—recall the Tet Offensive of February 1968, a brilliant military campaign that cost the enemy many lives, but it humiliated an ignorant and over-confident America and began to destroy the war's political support at home.

That much we have seen before. But conflict with Iraq is always about oil, and always has been, even during Saddam Hussein's war against Iran from 1980 to 1988, backed up by the US in 1984, in part to punish Iranian clerics for the overthrow of the Shah. In 1990, when Saddam got an okay from April Glaspie, the American ambassador to Iraq, to invade Kuwait ("we have no opinion on the Arab–Arab conflict, like your border disagreement with Kuwait ... Secretary [of State James] Baker has directed me to emphasize this instruction"[2]), America's first war against Iraq began. After the long fight against Iran, Iraq's economy was depleted; Kuwait had prevented OPEC from raising the oil price; Iraq, a nearly landlocked country, coveted Kuwait's access to the Persian Gulf, and so on. Saddam invaded. And the US was waiting for him. How the first President Bush assembled American forces without Saddam Hussein's notice, when it took over six months for his son to mobilize the invasion forces in Kuwait and the Gulf in 2002 and 2003, is a mystery that has not been addressed. In any event, Gulf War I was over almost before it began; and by imposing the sanctions, with the Oil for Food program, in particular, the US gained some control over the distribution of Iraqi oil—the first step, one might say, in gaining direct access to that oil. With the start of US and British bombing of the no-fly zones in 1992, Gulf War II, in a sense, had begun.

Americans knew little about Vietnam until the Marines hit the beach at Danang in the spring of 1965. They know less about the Middle East and Iraq, even now. It's part of American culture that its citizens remain uninformed about the larger world, and specifically about the nations with whom its leaders are at war. As the occupation of Iraq shows, this ignorance now extends to the leadership itself. US interests, as defined by George W. Bush's administration, are institutional: they're defined by the well-being of the oil and defense industries, and their partners on Wall Street, in alliance with America's chief ally in the Middle East, Israel.

Alas, there is no Dean Acheson or Clark Clifford to tell President Bush that the jig is up, and that the costs are far too high to justify staying in Iraq—that the scattered acts of violence with which the resistance began have become organized attacks across the nation, accompanied by what, even before the exposure of torture at Abu Ghraib, had become a massive popular rejection of the United States. Former national security adviser Brent Scowcroft or one-time secretary of state Zbigniew Brzezinski have no influence over Bush, and in any case their multilateralism does not furnish them with a critique that takes on the foundations of the president's war policy. Today's Democratic Party leaders are nearly as involved in the premises of America's National Security Strategy—in American "exceptionalism" and the first-strike policy—as the Republicans are. In fact, the criticism that has broken out across the land against the occupation of Iraq is led by Republicans, such as Senator Pat Roberts (R-Kan.), the conservative chairman of the Senate Intelligence Committee, who says, "We need to restrain what are growing US messianic instincts, a sort of global social engineering where the United States feels it is both entitled and obligated to promote democracy, by force if necessary … Liberty cannot be laid down like so much Astroturf. Law and order must come first." This touches on another problem, which is the centrality of the transitional government to be chosen by UN envoy Lakdar Brahimi—something the US can engineer—rather than "law and order," which it can't. "We are in a desperate state there," says Phebe Marr, an Iraq expert formerly at the National Defense University; "[we] don't have any security in the country," and thus "the big agenda," democracy, "has to be jettisoned"—as if democracy ever mattered, or the Iraqi people cared. They want stability.

When Defense Secretary Donald Rumsfeld and his deputy, Paul Wolfowitz, testify before a Senate committee, they are as likely to be blasted by high-ranking members of the military, not only Retired General Anthony Zinni but Army Major General Charles H. Swannack, commander of the 82nd Airborne Division in Iraq, and Army Colonel Paul Hughes, who directed strategic planning in Iraq in 2003. Both have challenged Rumsfeld and the chairman of the Joint Chiefs of Staff, General Richard B. Meyers, to demonstrate how the war has not already been lost strategically. "I believe we are absolutely on the brink of failure," Retired Marine General Joseph P. Hoar, a former commander, like Zinni, of US forces in the Middle East, told the Senate Foreign Relations Committee. "We are looking into the abyss. We cannot start soon enough to begin the turnaround."[3] These voices only begin to express the anger building up within the Army, whose in-country morale plummeted after the revelations that US soldiers were torturing Iraqi prisoners.

The Army War College Strategic Studies Institute long ago pronounced the Iraqi war "unnecessary," and called the war on terror "unfocused." The White House never had an exit strategy, it charged, and used the war to "establish a large American military presence in the region" without a clear purpose.[4] It was a Marine commander, acting on the advice of the Iraqi Governing Council, who turned Fallujah and Samarra over to the Iraqi Revolutionary Guard and the Sunni insurgents, and thereby secured a modicum of quiet in the tumultuous central triangle while the US military went after the Shi'ite army under Moqtada al-Sadr. One suspects that in Iraq the military has a plan—which will not work because it's based on separating the Sunnis and the Shi'ites—and the White House has none.

When former Henry Kissinger associate L. Paul Bremer was asked on NBC's "Meet The Press," on April 11, to whom the US would turn over Iraq on June 30, he gave the appropriate answer: "It's a good question." Washington knew that Brahimi would no more be able to pull an interim Iraqi government together out of the chaos of Iraq than the Iraqi army administrator already in place in Samarra would get his leader back. "We can't deny Saddam is our President," said the mayor's assistant in this old Ba'ath Party stronghold (his salary paid by the US). "We want him back."[5] Actually, Saddam Hussein has as much of a chance of returning to Baghdad as the Bush administration has of choosing the next government. An incredible thought: the war come full circle, with all the troops, matériel, military advisers, commercial holdings, contractors, spies and lies, wasted—and Saddam, or someone like him, back in power. But that won't happen, at least not in the short term in which this extraordinary war is playing itself out. In the long term, who knows?

"An Iraqi democracy is emerging," said Bush on May 24, in the first of six speeches planned to reassure the American people about his conduct of the war. The speech was not about Iraq or the Middle East; it was about November 2, and the president's efforts to stop his inexorable slide in public opinion polls. The American antiwar movement, too, is caught up in the presidential elections, decrying Ralph Nader's entrance into the race, wishing John Kerry would say something, anything, signing petitions and protests and swapping news on the Internet. It does not communicate with American soldiers in Iraq.

Meanwhile, if the grant of sovereignty at the end of June is postponed, the resistance will acquire the legitimacy of a national liberation movement, but with support from its complicated friends throughout the Middle East. To prevent this from happening, America will have to give up the idea of holding on to strategic bases in Iraq. It must surrender the belief that corporate investors will have a major role in Iraq's economy, and that it will influence oil prices through leverage over a new Iraqi government. One thing will be absolutely necessary: it must set a deadline for US military and political withdrawal, and begin the withdrawal now.

May 2004

ACKNOWLEDGEMENTS

This book grew out of an e-mail exchange with Tariq Ali in the spring of 2002. I was reviewing a book about Vietnam for the *Los Angeles Times*, and complained about the author's effort to seek "closure" (a word on everybody's lips)—meaning denial of the past, of conflict. There was a patch of purple prose about the terrible Sixties; like a slug in a print shop, it popped up readymade in many a book. And Tariq, Verso's editorial director, said, "Why don't you write about that? Why don't you make a strong defense of the tradition of dissent in the US?" I was working on a novel, my first, inspired by the experiences of my Brightman ancestors in nineteenth-century Alaska, but had an eye cocked on the coming war. The political climate was rapidly changing. September 11 had happened; Bush had gone in and out of Afghanistan, and was already getting ready to invade Iraq, though we didn't know when. Soon Vietnam would be back in the news, as if the war had never really ended, which in a way it hadn't.

It wasn't hard for Tariq to persuade me. "You write. I'll publish," he said. Then the book shifted focus on to the new National Security System, which put an end to containment and deterrence and the web of non-proliferation treaties, and advanced the ideas of US exceptionalism and of preemptive war. The book about dissent gave way to one about the myth of American omnipotence, and the global insecurity that was bound to result from cutting off US ties to the West, and from the loss of the "safe harbor" foundations of a strong dollar.

Paul Seminon, author of *American Monster*, and one of my trusted readers, was the first who picked up on the change, and wrote that he thought there should be more emphasis on the "psychology of insecurity that motivates the Bush administration and the fundamentalists." They know they are "extremists," he said, and "their reliance on military power rather than diplomacy or economic power reflects this sense of their weakness. Without 9/11 and the so-called war on terrorism they would be in big trouble." Historian Dan Rosen turned me on to military websites, and first introduced me to the stories that opened up the workings of the petrodollar crisis in the Middle East. He read nearly every chapter, and was a source of constant support. Marilyn Young, professor of history at New York University, and author of *The Vietnam Wars, 1945–1990*, gave me a critical reading and many helpful suggestions for Chapter Six, "Vietnam Redux." William Tabb, professor of economics at Queens College, and author of *Unequal Partners: A Primer on Globalization*, who read "The Political Economy of Death," I, II, and III, and Chapter Three, "Securing the Region," also made useful suggestions.

I am indebted to Frances FitzGerald, who wrote *Way Out in the Blue*, for discussions about Iraq, and to Danny Schecter whose weblog, the News Dissector, kept me apprised of back channel information about the media. In Maine, I am grateful to Jim Algrant, whose Maine World News Service is a first-rate compendium of online clippings, and Henry Myers, whose Casco Bay Observer kept me abreast of US newspapers; and with Truthout, AlterNet, Information Clearing House, the *Wall Street Journal*'s Opinion Journal, and other Internet sites, I managed to write this book without going to Iraq, a mixed blessing. Thanks also to Janii Laberge, who knew when to get out of the way but was there when it mattered.

At Verso HQ in London, I am grateful to Tim Clark, Gavin Everall, Jane Hindle, Andrea Stimpson, and Andrea Woodman for ensuring a smooth production; and, in the New York office, to Niels Hooper and to Amy Scholder—whose suggestion it was to run the last chapter, "Starting Over Is Not An Easy Thing To Do," first, and thus to bring the wake-up call for a new kind of dissent to the front of the book.

In the course of writing *Total Insecurity*, I did a number of OpEd pieces, which are here placed between the chapters—together with a White House Press Conference, a letter from Texas, and a fragment from a 1967 Vietnam journal—a little like the newsreels between the stories in John Dos Passos's *USA Trilogy*.

I

STARTING OVER IS NOT AN EASY THING TO DO

Show always
What still remains,
What already has come.
The new against the old
Also rages in the heart.

BERTOLT BRECHT's advice to actors

The oil barons in Washington set out to play the great game of empire alone; a momentous undertaking, which pundits at home and abroad generally defended until Afghanistan and Iraq took the starch out of the uniforms of the US armed forces. Meanwhile, the underpinnings of economic well-being on which US guarantees of global security ultimately rest are unraveling. The crash of the giant telecoms cost the US over a trillion dollars in 2002, *one-fifth* of the GDP. This is the larger significance of the criminal accounting practices uncovered at Enron, WorldCom, Global Crossing, Merck, Rite Aid, Bristol Myers, Squibb, and Halliburton—

which is currently under investigation for fraud and bribery allegations on six fronts. These corporate scandals have undermined the dollar, and alarmed America's allies, but they have not come close to US military failures in their ability to rock the foundations of the post-Cold War order.

It's a dangerous paradox, the mix of unchecked power, corruption, and vulnerability at the top. When it's joined, as it has been, by failure in Afghanistan, bungling in Iraq, and a somnolent disregard for the escalating Israeli–Palestinian conflict, the hatreds that inspired the World Trade Center attacks can only increase. And with them grows the fear with which the Bush administration squabbles over what to do in Iraq before a civil uprising begins—or before Bush loses the election. Which brings us to another paradox: if there was ever a time when conditions appear ripe for the rebirth of dissent on a broad scale—for a willingness to stand up to this Trojan horse called the War on Terrorism, and empty its contents on the ground—it is now. And yet Americans, who are presently caught up in the drama of the presidential campaign, are missing the opportunity that stands before them, which is to cut the cord that ties the republic to the iron triangle: to the domination of a military–industrial–congressional complex which has yielded almost nothing but defeat.

But how? How to sever relations with America's ancient trust? "The fact of America's place in the world is one in which unparalleled primacy coexists with a powerful sense of its unique vulnerability," writes the conservative columnist Philip Stephens in the *Financial Times*. "That will never be comfortable for everyone else."[1] But our challenge is to lay bare that vulnerability: to contest the supporters *and the critics* who grossly exaggerate the power of the American empire. They include neoconservatives such as Paul Wolfowitz and Douglas Feith who believe that only American hegemony can safeguard the world; and extend to traditional Republican and Democratic realists like Brent Scowcroft and Zbigniew Brzezinski, who see the Bush administration as squandering American power and needlessly antagonizing its allies. And they also include important critics such as George Soros, who discerns a "supremacist ideology" in Washington that is redolent of the Nazi era, and who has dedicated himself and his funds to the defeat of George Bush; and even Arundhati Roy, that most eloquent of anti-imperialist writers and speakers, who warns that for the "first time in history, a single empire with an arsenal of weapons that could obliterate the world in an afternoon has complete, unipolar economic and military hegemony."[2] Such formulations are probably not meant to be taken literally but to arouse and provoke; and they do, although they contribute to an underwhelming sense of helplessness that dampens our resistance.

We are in thrall to voices whose special forte is their ability to expose the horrors of the state. No one does this more brilliantly than Noam Chomsky, who always shows how the power system works; teaching us, correcting errors of assumption, but rarely focusing on the weaknesses of the system, or on the circumstances that might bring it up short. The fatal flaws remain unknown, untested. We're in the midst of an unraveling now, and will be farther along it in a few months, no matter who wins the presidential elections—though we may have undergone another terrorist attack. The marches on the one-year anniversary of the war were impressive, especially in Rome, where a million demonstrators filled the streets. But the decisive action was the terror bombing of Madrid, and the spiraling effects which included not just the election of a socialist government and the pledge to recall Spanish troops from Iraq, but the effect on the European Union.

France and Germany now have a new ally from "Old Europe," which augurs well for completing the EU's beleaguered constitution in Brussels, and hammering out a stronger foreign policy statement that is independent of the United States. The EU, whose currency is the euro, and whose domain has become immense with the arrival of ten new member states from "emerging Europe," is important now in ways it wasn't before Iraq. A compelling argument for keeping oil pricing and payments in dollars has long been that the US remains a large importer of oil, despite being a substantial crude-oil producer itself. But looking at the statistics for crude-oil exports, one notes that even in 2002 the euro-zone was a larger importer of oil and petroleum products from the Middle East than the United States.[3] The continued growth of the EU, during a period of rocketing American deficits and a faltering dollar, offers the world the opportunity to establish the euro as a second international reserve currency. OPEC will no doubt await the decision of the UK to adopt the euro, which is likely to happen before the decade is out, and then it will almost certainly drop the dollar.

Meanwhile, Richard Clarke, the former top White House counterterrorism official who has said that President Bush ignored the warning signs of a possible terrorist attack in 2001, and that his decision to invade Iraq has strengthened international terrorist groups, has wounded the president, and the security system he oversees, irrevocably. The murder of Hamas Sheik Ahmed Yassin on March 22 in Gaza City, by rockets from an Israeli helicopter—a signature assassination, in the manner of Donald Rumsfeld's "man-hunting" by Predator drone—was condemned by nearly every government except the US government. And quite unexpectedly, that has contributed to the unraveling, too.

As the world saw it, an Israeli Goliath killed a frail old David, and did so prior to Sharon's supposed withdrawal from Gaza. Sharon's idea is to "decapitate" the Hamas leadership, to render it incapable of initiating further suicide bombings; a "housekeeping" chore prior to departure. But he went too far; and a dangerous new page was turned, not only in the Israeli–Palestinian conflict, but in America's "Greater Middle East initiative." A loss in the propaganda war of this dimension may cost Israel far more than whatever Yassin personally added to the bloodletting that Hamas will continue to carry out. For one thing, it may elevate Hamas over the PLO; which, whatever else it is, is a secular and nationalistic force. Under Hamas, which is pan-Islamic, in the tradition of the Muslim Brotherhood from which it sprang, the Palestinian movement will be linked more tightly to Islamic religious radicalism throughout the Middle East.

As for Washington's Middle East initiative, the grand vision had already fallen on hard times when the London-based daily *al-Hayat* presented a leaked copy of the proposals to be unveiled at the G8 summit in June 2004, and Egyptian president Hosni Mubarak told the US the region would "not accept" reform being "imposed on Arab and Islamic countries from the outside." Stability first required Washington's attention to "crises," namely the Israeli–Palestinian conflict and Iraq.[4] Not much new there; but after the assassination of Yassin, Arab countries have redoubled efforts to set forth their own reforms (not so different from America's) to fend off Islamist opposition movements. Recent elections in Jordan, Morocco, and Kuwait have shown that Islamist parties now comprise the largest opposition to government, while the Pew Research Center finds overwhelming majorities in Jordan and Morocco, and 34 percent in Turkey, who justify suicide attacks against Americans and other westerners in Iraq. Human rights defenders in Arab countries say that new antiterrorism laws are being used to suppress freedom of expression. A familiar charge; we've heard it at home. Richard Perle expressed it on national TV when he called Seymour Hersh a "terrorist" for what he wrote about him in the *New Yorker*. It's the war-on-terrorism franchise, Naomi Klein's built-in "opposition-cleanser."

Meanwhile, the US lines up with Tunisia and Algeria, the most unsavory regimes in the greater Middle East, in its antiterrorism campaign. But the high sign that the murder of Sheik Yassin brought trouble were the tumbling stock markets, which now fear terrorist attacks everywhere and the strain this will place on giant insurance companies—not to mention on tourism, which is, I'm reminded, "a vital element in the globalization strategy." Writing from Spain last summer, Paul Seminon (known as Violet Ray in the '60s and '70s) calls the T-war the "War on Tourism." He's begun to wonder if we're not at the beginning of World War III, "only this time instead of large industrial states battling each other, it's a descent into anarchic conflicts pitting militarized gangs in different countries against each other and the United States." This, in fact, is where Israel under the Likud Party has gone; Hamas fights back, is decapitated, which provokes further violence from Hamas or other groups. UN Ambassador John Negroponte lines up the usual suspects—Australia and Eritrea—to veto a

Security Council resolution condemning the assassination. And the extra-judicial killings go on.

Far from controlling the globe, the US struggles by hook or by crook to maintain its footing in Iraq. A year ago, on March 20, 2003, cruise missiles hit the presidential palace, the same pile where Paul Bremer, fresh from his job with Henry Kissinger, came to work as proconsul over what British journalist Robert Fisk calls "the Anglo-American Raj." The "illusions," Fisk says, "are more awesome now than they were at the time." And that is true, although he doesn't wrestle with the chief illusion, which is that the US administration would take the dollar-based Iraqi oil gusher and turn it into a model for the rest of region, some of whose governments (Iran, for example) are moving their oil sales toward the euro. The dream has become a nightmare, with traders revising the potential for oil exports from Iraq downward following continued sabotage of the northern pipeline and questions about when the southern port of Khor al-Amaya will return to full capacity. US Energy Secretary Spencer ("Big Buddy of Big Oil") Abraham continues to route Middle East oil imports to emergency stockpiles "due to security concerns," despite frantic calls from politicians and lobbyists to route them through the market to ease rising prices.[5] This is spring, when prices usually flatten out before a burst in the summer driving season, and gas prices are very high in the US. Imagine where they will be in August. But Secretary Abraham has "made clear we're not going to beg for oil" from OPEC—how could he, given America's original plans for undermining the cartel?—which cut production even further on April 1, 2004.

In Iraq, Fisk follows the battlefield "narratives" which have shifted as resistance to the occupation has intensified—starting with how the insurgents came from only a few Sunni cities "previously loyal to Hussein"; when the resistance moved north and south to Nassariyah, Karbala, Mosul, and Kirkuk (and there were up to sixty assaults a night), word went out that al Qaeda was sending in fighters from Iran and Saudi Arabia. "Foreign fighters" were supposedly the menace, when most of the foreign fighters were wearing American uniforms.[6] Of some 10,000 men the US has arrested for assault on coalition troops, fewer than 150 are non-Iraqi Arabs.[7]

Which brings us to another suspect narrative, the danger of civil war. I have bought it myself, it's so easy to contemplate when reading about Iraq from afar. The devastating insurgent attacks on the Kurds in Arbil in February, and the Shi'ites on March 2, seem aimed at forcing these communities to rely on their own militias and intelligence, and to give up the federal project. If the Shi'ites are forced by repeated provocations to depend on their own security, would this not unleash a dynamic that points to the breakup of Iraq? The Kurds would fight for the three provinces that make up Kurdistan; the Shi'ites will take over the south; and the Kurds and Shi'ites and Sunnis will go after greater Baghdad. But Fisk asks why no Iraqis have been heard demanding a conflict with their fellow citizens. "Who actually wants this 'civil war'?" He drops it there; and leaves me wondering. Is it the Americans who want this conflict? Is it their ace in the hole?

Naomi Klein writes from Baghdad that right after the bombing of the Mount Lebanon Hotel on March 17 the rumors began to fly: "it was the US, the CIA, the British." Amazing. "If these conspiracy theories have traction," she thinks, "maybe it's because the occupying forces have so brazenly taken advantage of the attacks to do precisely what they accuse foreign terrorists of doing: interfering with the prospect of genuine democracy in Iraq."[8] We have to remember that US soldiers have been largely pulled out of the center of Baghdad, Fallujah, Baqubah, Mosul, Basra. Occupation targets are not being hit quite so often by the guerrillas—though a new stage opened on March 31, when four Americans were killed and mutilated in the center of Fallujah, and five GIs were killed in Ramadi. Now that the targets in Baghdad include Iraqi civilians, foreign-aid workers, and journalists, the White House is trying to make Iraqis appear hopelessly divided by religious and ethnic hatreds. They are incapable of governing themselves, and so *presto* an interim government is being installed that is fully controlled by the US. The Governing Council (or "governed council," as the discredited body is called) will simply be expanded; and the new constitution, rushed in after the March attacks on the Shi'ites at the festival of Ashura, states that "the laws, regulations, orders, and directives issued by the Coalition Provisional Authority ... shall remain in force," including Bremer's infamous Order 39, which allows foreign companies to own 100 percent of Iraqi assets (except in natural resources), and to take 100 percent of their profits out of country, paving the way for privatizations. But within a week of the US siege of Fallujah, the twenty-five-member Governing Council began to disintegrate, with multiple resignations.

In January, 100,000 Iraqis marched in Baghdad and Basra to reject the US plan to appoint an interim government through a system of regional caucuses, and to demand direct elections instead. Bremer was forced to scrap the caucus plan, and Klein says that briefly it looked like Bush's hollow words about bringing democracy to Iraq might become a reality. Now after three months of terror and steady assertions from "experts" that Iraq is on the verge of civil war, she reports that this was before Fallujah, which has led to a de facto imposition of the military draft, with some 30,000 American troops being held in Iraq for another three to six months. Meanwhile, a substitute regime for the Governing Council has been hastily negotiated with an uneasy UN.

Klein concludes that the occupation "will simply be outsourced to a group of hand-picked Iraqi politicians with no democratic mandate or sovereign power"[9]—which is a pretty fair description of UN envoy Lakdar Brahimi's transitional government. It's a wafer thin stand-in for the "transformation" of Iraq that Washington hoped to engineer out of the invasion so many months ago. But the transformation was another illusion. Only the Israeli–American alliance is stronger than ever. The *Financial Times* editorializes that it's in "all our interests to ask ... whether the tail is wagging the dog in this relationship." And of course it is. For in Washington's embrace of Sharon's Israel—whose outlines can be found in the document prepared for Netanyahu's Likud Party in 1995 by Richard Perle and Douglas Feith, entitled "A Clean Break: A New Strategy for the Realm"*—one sees a perfectly functional relationship. The bloated American leviathan, bristling with weaponry ill-suited to asymmetric warfare, but still endowed with diplomatic authority, empowers the military state of Israel to be its "second" in the crusade against the Arabs.

There really is a psychology of insecurity that underlies American geopolitical strategy in the Middle East; and its dependence on military power rather than on economic leverage or diplomacy reflects it. Without September 11, and without President Bush's insistence that it was an attack from the blue, there would have been no Afghan campaign or war in Iraq. This is why Richard Clarke's testimony before the September 11 Commission was important, for it strikes at the very heart of the problem—which is the use of the terror attacks as the *raison d'être* for two wars that have little to do with terror. The fact is that Bush didn't take al Qaeda seriously before or after the fateful day; a little less seriously before than Clinton did, and afterwards, except for the lumbering Homeland Security and the dangerous Patriot Act, not very seriously at all.

The US national security strategy reads like a Marxist take-off of the Last, Deadliest Stage of Imperialism. *Item*: "The president has no intention of allowing any foreign power to catch up with the huge lead the United States has opened up since the fall of the Soviet Union." *Item*: American "forces will be strong enough to dissuade potential adversaries from pursuing a military build-up in hopes of surpassing, or equaling, the power of the United States." *Item*: "We will not hesitate to act alone, if necessary, to exercise our right to self-defense by acting preemptively." Finally: "What

---

* This study called for a break from the Oslo Accords, and upheld "the *right of hot pursuit* for self-defense." The way to ensure Israeli security for the long-term was to reshape Israel's "strategic environment" to eliminate future threats.

is at stake today is not control of a particular part of the planet ... putting at a disadvantage but still tolerating the independent actions of some rivals, but the control of its totality. ..." This last, from *Socialism or Barbarism* by Marxist economist Istvan Meszaros, slips into place without a wink, though it lacks the plain-spoken English favored by the "boys in Lubbock." As for the three items, the first two are intended to justify huge military spending, while the third has already been partially remanded.

In *On Violence*, written in 1969, Hannah Arendt develops a theory that bears thinking about in connection with the US estimate of its post-Cold War status. "[E]very decrease in power is an open invitation to violence," she says, "if only because those who hold power and feel it slipping from their hands, be they the government or ... the governed, have always found it difficult to resist the temptation to substitute violence for it."[10] A large generalization, it is one that hardly seems to apply to the American military doctrine of "full spectrum dominance," and its subsidiary strategy of preemptive war, which Pentagon neocons have been working to install since the fall of the Soviet Union. But the fact is that Washington perceives the unipolar world as fraught with dangers unknown during the Cold War.

In the inverse relationship between power and force, one finds the crack in the American Gibraltar. "Violence appears where power is in jeopardy, but left to its own course it ends in power's disappearance. ... Violence can destroy power," Arendt continues; "it is utterly incapable of creating it."[11] In neither Afghanistan nor Iraq has the injection of huge amounts of US military force brought us any closer to the power we need to reshape their destinies.

A forty-year-long global expansion and reintegration of US capital has stalled, partly for lack of competition within and without the Fortune 500. The concentration of economic power in a handful of behemoths overseeing energy, defense, telecommunications, and information technologies has grown top-heavy, and fuels what Federal Reserve Chairman

Alan Greenspan, in an uncharacteristic moment of candor, has called the "outsized increase in opportunities for avarice." It has also helped shape a submissive Congress, which, when confronted with genuine emergencies, is incapable of independent action. We have entered a time of danger, real and imagined, which is fed by the decoupling of government regulation and business that began under Jimmy Carter, increased with Ronald Reagan, continued with Bill Clinton, and runs riot under Bush, Jr. It was under Carter, not Reagan, that the regulatory arm of government commenced its retreat. Similarly, it was Carter who declared the Middle East a "vital interest" to the United States, which of course it is; though the Middle East is far less secure today than it was before the US invasion of Iraq.

It was in the late 1970s that the long, slow free-fall of liberalism began; and the rise of neoliberalism, armed with a conservatism rooted in the sectarian left movements of the '30s and '40s, followed. If the Bush administration succeeded in rolling back public interest regulations and legislation on front after front, it was for a reason not dissimilar to the ease with which it has been able to move its military forces across continents without upsetting the status quo of another superpower. It faced no serious resistance from any other center of political gravity capable of forcing it to share power, not in the Republican Party and not in the Democratic Party either. And outside the party system, there was little organized resistance to the mowing down of environmental controls, the dismantling of social service institutions, and the speed with which prisons have been thrown up.

At home, the principal accomplishment of the war on terrorism has been the partial militarization of the federal bureaucracy. Homeland Security Secretary Tom Ridge, speaking at a confirmation hearing in January 2003 of the need to harness twenty-two federal agencies to the goal of protecting Americans from terrorist attack, stressed the "hate-filled, remorseless" nature of an "enemy that takes many forms, has many places to hide and is often *invisible*" (emphasis added). Terrorism's invisibility, in particular, gives security officials the license to monitor the population's private and public affairs. Armed with the enabling legislation provided by the Patriot Act, investigators are free to wiretap without judicial review, deport lawful permanent residents, visitors, and undocumented immigrants without due process, scan e-mail, seize library hard-drives, fingerprint teachers, and profile male travelers above the age of sixteen from the Middle East, Afghanistan, Bangladesh, Eritrea, Indonesia, and North Korea by registering and fingerprinting them on their arrival to the United States.

Under a classified surveillance program started in December 2002, countless Arab-Americans have been electronically monitored for possible ties to terrorist organizations, while thousands of Iranian citizens and immigrants have been held for questioning in California. On January 25, 2003 the US began the round up of 50,000 Iraqi-Americans for questioning. And looming over it all, like a bad dream, is Guantanamo, where 600 "unlawful combatants" from forty-four countries are held without charge, many of them turned in by Afghan bounty hunters. Every prisoner has been interviewed dozens of times by US intelligence and antiterrorism agencies, and who knows how many have been stripped, hooded, and abused, yet not a single man has been put before a military tribunal—very likely because the legal proceedings would reveal that most of the so-called Taliban and al Qaeda captives were only of low to middling importance. A few have been released to home prisons, but the rest may be held indefinitely.

Because this is war, with no end-point in sight, such actions can proceed without Congressional approval. One by-product of Homeland Security decisions is to countermand the authority of the once strong civil service unions, while chipping away at the civil rights and liberties which are the bedrock of American democracy. If Homeland Security succeeds, and it is by no means clear that it has, the new apparatus will cut through what Republican Senator Robert Bennett, speaking at the Ridge hearing, happily calls "the inertia of the old way of doing things." By this, the Senator from Utah means the leftover clout of labor and civil rights defenders, the "habeas corpus people," whose interests are to be swept aside.

Critics worry over how the unchecked police powers will transform American political institutions. They point to the breakdown in the separation of powers which obtains when Congress, the Judiciary, and the Executive are roped to the same political horse. Or when traditions of free speech and a free press are invoked not by journalists but by then media CEOs such as CNN's Walter Isaacson, who defended the Pentagon plan to "embed" reporters with US troops in Iraq so that the public would get a "full, independent chronicle" of the war. Such warnings miss an important point, for the transformation has already taken place. The wearing down of political institutions that opened the stage door to the disconcerting Mr. Bush and his posse was not opened by Mr. Bush, or his father, but were in the making for over thirty years.

It's a multilayered transformation of American political life and culture that began in the mid-'70s, when observers took note of the rise of a grassroots conservative movement, not a backlash to the social and political radicalism of the 1960s and early '70s, but not unrelated either. For example, it formed around women who took their opposition to the ERA (Equal Rights Amendment) and to "abortions on demand" out into the streets. It had nothing to do with the rise of neoconservatives, which happened under Reagan, with men like Wolfowitz and Perle and Feith and Adam Schulsky, some of whom, like Wolfowitz and Schulsky—a member of the Pentagon's former Office of Special Plans—were students of the political scientist Leo Strauss at the University of Chicago in the 1960s. Strauss was an acquaintance of Hannah Arendt in Berlin in the early 1930s, and had made an effort to court her, becoming angry when he was rebuffed for his conservative political views. The bad feelings grew worse when she turned up at Chicago in the '60s; for he was haunted by how she had judged his assessment of National Socialism. Arendt had pointed out the irony of the fact that a political party advocating views that Strauss appreciated could have no place for a Jew like him.[12]

Some of the neocons were still liberals, except on the subject of Israel. Like Norman Podhoretz, who was editor of *Commentary*, they nurtured a "dirty little secret," which was their fascination for "making it"; though it was the intellectual establishment they aimed for, not state power. Perle had hooked up with Democratic hawk Senator Henry "Scoop" Jackson of Washington, and quickly indentured himself to the nuclear weapons strategist Albert Wohlstatter (marrying his daughter). He seems to have known where he was going from the start, but it took the others longer, until one by one, over the years, they pulled themselves into the Pentagon.

Yet the United States, "no longer even remotely the last best hope of the world," in Gore Vidal's words, did not become "merely a seedy imperial state whose citizens are kept in line by SWAT teams."[13] Not yet. There were too many new people who were aroused by Iraq, brought into play by the Internet, by MoveOn, and by Howard Dean. Brief as the lifespan of his Democratic candidacy was, Dean's elimination at the hands of the media was a lesson in how party politics works, a lesson that will be hard to forget. It was Dean who fired up the democratic process, by mobilizing hundreds of thousands of citizens who were shocked by the war but detached from the political process. As a result of their mobilization, it is likely that the resort to domestic repression by a tainted government that has lost its ability to deliver the goods will backfire, and that SWAT teams will not be in evidence any time soon. America's legacy of resistance to arbitrary power and oppression may find its voice once again.

But let's not fool ourselves. The obstacles to a resurgent activism in the US are all the more formidable for being hard to see. The very idea of resistance over any length of time has been leached from American soil. A funny thing happened to our belief in political change over the past three or four decades. To most Americans "politics" is still a game played by politicians who are hired by special interests to put something over on the public. Politicians are "corrupt" except during an election year, when the candidate of the moment is not. Underneath the often well-deserved cynicism lingers a deeper skepticism for those who work "outside the system" or try to change things through direct action. In the nation's memory banks, the political activists of the 1960s—who fought inside and outside the system for civil rights and an end to the war in Vietnam—are safely filed under *h* for *hippies* (as in "my mom was a hippie"). Everybody knows only vigilantes and kooks live outside the system.

Behind the withering away of American traditions of dissent lies the withering away of the idea of change. And with it, for many, has fled hope, even interest, *even belief*, in the future. Change, other than personal change or legislative adjustments, has lost its social agency and been replaced in the popular mind by force or accident. Change *happens* by way of the unexpected, like the attacks on the World Trade Center or the Enron collapse. Such actions follow upon intricate chains of events that are either ignored or inaccessible to the watchdogs of security. Thus they appear like the hand of God (or the Devil) and remain, in a practical sense, unaccountable and uncontrollable. So it was until the end of George W. Bush's first term.

It's hard to underestimate the thoroughness with which the United States set about ridding itself of the legacy of 1960s radicalism. Sixties bashing began almost immediately, and never stopped, having become over the decades a subset of the demonization of liberalism, which is only now coming up for air. Young activists aided the process by slipping back into the workaday world with a speed historians mistook for lack of seriousness. And few tried to tell the story themselves. The endgame began in 1970, when in April Nixon bombed Cambodia. A few days later, with 30 percent of the nation's colleges on strike, the National Guard fired at protesting students at Kent State, Ohio, killing four, while state troopers killed five black students at Jackson State in Mississippi. The year was a cyclone of violence and death. In March, two black civil rights organizers were killed by a car bomb in Maryland. Three Weathermen blew themselves up while making bombs in Greenwich Village. A few days later grenades went off in two corporate headquarters in New York, killing no one. An armed underground was forming inside the belly of the whale, a fantasy out of Carlos Marighelli and John Brown, but real.

If you were away for a few months (as I was when I went to Cuba to cut sugar cane with the Venceremos Brigade), the country you returned to was not the one you left. Airports and train stations were patrolled by National Guard and police on walkie-talkies. Communes that ran alternative presses, community gardens, or day-care collectives were busy training for self-defense. Except for the noisy MAYDAY march on Washington the following year (*"If the government doesn't stop the war, we'll stop the government!"*), the demos were over, along with electoral peace campaigns and the heyday of a genuinely countercultural press. Mainstream newspapers started calling radicals "revolutionaries" without the adjective "self-styled." Mississippi Senator James Eastland proclaimed the cane-cutting in Cuba a cover for guerrilla training, and called us "missiles in human form which have been fashioned on the Communist island and fired at America." We laughed, but it seemed as if the country had tipped on its axis, and anything was possible. "Wholly unorganized and utterly undirected, the revolutionary movement exists," wrote former journalist Andy Kopkind, "not because the left is strong but because the center is weak."[14]

He was right on both counts. Despite stepped up harassment of black power and antiwar movements under COINTELPRO, and the "Vietnamization" of the war, officials in and out of government found their authority compromised. Rebellion rippled downward into high schools and outward into the professions, exacting reforms in governance and curriculum. But the "revolutionary movement," which had cut itself off from organizing projects in the South, the inner cities, and on campuses, as well as from debates on the "politics of resistance" and the "new working class," was disintegrating. For a few leaders, there was nowhere to go but deeper into violence, which was what remained of the revolutionary dream.

In 1971, the country's tolerance for chaos found its limit; and both sides pulled back from the brink. Henry Kissinger traveled secretly to China to arrange for Nixon to meet Mao. A few years later, some of us darkly quoted Kissinger's theory of change: "If you act creatively you should be able to use crises to move the world towards the structural solutions that are necessary." Today he might point to September 11. Despite massive B-52 raids against Cambodia, Laos, and North Vietnam, the war was winding down; the draft had ended, and the troops were coming home. The US military had taken to the air, using maximum force to strike questionable targets—just as in Afghanistan—to escape American casualties and the prying eyes of the press.

Of the Vietnam era, a US correspondent whose beats included Berkeley in 1965, Saigon during the war, and Hanoi in recent years, presents the prevailing view.

> That era challenged the standards of World War II—the yardstick against which we had judged heroism and the rightness of battle—and turned society topsy-turvy in a social and political upheaval of drugs, free love, political scandals and assassinations, interracial strife, protest demonstrations, and the cry: 'Hell, no! We won't go!' [15]

What's missing is the sea change in political thought and action that cut the 1960s (give or take a few years) off from the 1950s. It's hard to chart the rising wave: 1956, when Rosa Parks refused to go to the back of the bus in Montgomery, Alabama? 1959, the year of the Cuban Revolution? 1960, when thousands of students visited Cuba; black students staged the first sit-ins; and Bay Area youth demonstrated against HUAC (House of Un-American Activities Committee)? 1962 saw the arrival of the Port Huron Statement, launching Students for a Democratic Society's vision of "participatory democracy." 1963 was the year SNCC (Student Nonviolent Coordinating Committee) expanded voter registration projects throughout the South, and Martin Luther King led the Civil Rights March on Washington. In 1964 came Mississippi Summer, the Harlem riots, and the Free Speech Movement, which shut down the University of California in Berkeley. In 1965, the Vietnam Day Committee blocked troop trains in nearby Oakland; antiwar teach-ins began, followed by the (annual) march on the Pentagon.

This was the movement's heroic period, its Bronze Age, when young activists hurled themselves at a system that had defended itself with all its might. The word *Movement*, spoken with a capital *M*, still embraced the separate strands. The period was dominated by single-issue reform politics, integration being the leading call; and the New Left served, in effect, as the shock troops of liberalism (a point one-time SDS president Carl Oglesby makes) whose humiliation arrived in 1968 at the Chicago Convention at the hands of Mayor Daley, and a triumphant Nixon. Underneath the civil rights and anti-war demands, however, an awareness was growing of the structural maldistribution of wealth and power in America, and a sense, intensified after 1965, that it wasn't going to be corrected by the abolition of Jim Crow alone or by bringing the troops back from Vietnam. For SDS, the recognition led to an experimentation with Marxism-Leninism in all its varieties which culminated for a self-proclaimed vanguard in the experiment with armed struggle. Before that the student movement rocketed from pro-peace to antiwar to pro-NLF to anti-imperialist (the last two, sometimes reversed) to pro-Third World revolution to anti-capitalism to pro-socialism (where some older comrades began), and then, with more twists than this synopsis suggests, to anti-peace (i.e. no "co-existence") and anti-democracy ("bourgeois jive"). It's no wonder that the anti-imperialist women's liberation movement burst like Ho Chi Minh's dragon out of the prison of the factions; and when street-fighting began in 1969–70, it was women who led the pack. I remember, because in 1971 in Berkeley I was one of them.

For the larger movement, direct action led to the formation of communities of dissent, not unlike the dissenting or "nonconformist" sectors of Christianity in seventeenth-century England. Like them they created new institutions—Free Universities, GI collectives, magazines, theater troupes, healthcare collectives—a few of which continue. When the communities melted away, so too did a collective vision of a flawed society and of a wrongheaded war policy, still open to reform. Perhaps such a society no longer existed, or was no longer susceptible to the influence of citizens organized independently of vested interests. For corporate America had changed too. Old-line family firms, like my father's Jahn & Ollier, Engraving Co., were being bought out by conglomerates like Beatrice Foods, who were building up their portfolios. US conglomerates were heading overseas, to England primarily where they bought up older firms short on capital. Their take-off and our meltdown were not unrelated; for we had completed a piece of our task—our fathers (figuratively speaking) were in the way, and we had helped clear the deck. We had pilfered their files, published their secrets, occupied their offices, and done without them. (Columbia 1968.) We were a youth movement, with the nerve of our years and a vision that was ageless.

The political movement that followed was called "identity politics," succeeded by the politics of victimization. The government's game changed too, from trying to prove in Vietnam that the US could lead the Free World's postwar fight against Communism, to trying to rule the world. The "center" is both stronger and weaker than it was thirty years ago; stronger because so much military might is concentrated in the hands of one nation, and weaker for the same reason—because American strength is now equated with military dominance, which has been tested and found wanting. The military and political costs of defending US interests have mounted by the day. The poor get poorer and more numerous; the fanatics more fanatical; our friends less friendly; while back on the homefront, the people who seemed safely drowned in a sleepy lethargy, as if drugged, are waking up.

The '60s slipped back into American culture in the 1980s by way of movies like *The Big Chill*, forerunner of *Friends* and *Sex in the City*. The "movement" became a gang of loopy singles hanging out. The music was wrong, but that was fixed later in the decade by the merchandising of Classic Rock 'n' Roll, and by the revival of the Grateful Dead (who had never stopped touring) on MTV, of all places. The Dead scooped up a new generation of kids, who found and disseminated the old drugs and the patchwork fashions of Woodstock. There was a promise of escape from the boredom of high school and dead-end jobs, and a fresh feeling of camaraderie, but it burnt out after a rash of teenage shootings in the 1990s showed that it was dangerous just to be young.

The true market for a sanitized '60s was the boomer generation, whose early brush with history was enshrined in nostalgia. It was the soft sell of sex, drugs, and rock 'n' roll, along with "Sixties idealism," that turned off many students like my daughter Sarabinh, who looked around at the brave new world of corporate America and wondered what their parents had accomplished. By the 1980s, the word *revolution* was safely repositioned on the right, viz. "the Reagan Revolution" and the "Newt Gingrich Revolution," or attached to personal care products, autos, and fashion statements. A frightened liberalism reemerged, after a sojourn with the trickle-down theorists of the Chicago School, as neoliberalism, the hard-nosed credo for the global economy. The '80s had a "retro" feel, like the Dulles years, Andy Kopkind thought: "Rebellion, utopias and tender-mindedness are out; conformity, realism and hard-heartedness are in."[16]

A reframing of discourse in literature and politics led critics to position themselves in relation to soliloquies on "truth" and "identity," when not policing gender hierarchies or "stabilizing the canon." To a history-minded person like myself, it was as if there was no longer a real world out there with real people in it, but a desert inhabited by voices spouting "texts." *Luftmenschen*, Hannah Arendt might call them: *air people*. There was no popular discourse for tracking the gathering storm in the Middle East in the 1970s and '80s, or Iraq's invasion of Kuwait in 1990, in which US and Allied soldiers defeated the Iraqi Army in a 100-hour battle (origin of the quick-fix preempt scenario for crushing Iraq), but left Saddam alive, and turned away when the Kurds and the Shi'ites revolted. Nor was there a popular discourse for understanding the importance of oil, and of "Peak Oil," and how the dollar-based global oil trade gives the US carte blanche to print dollars without causing inflation; or for tracking the streams of capital emanating from new consortia of banks and businesses. There was little said about the continuing breakdown of legal and national barriers to the free flow of money around the world; or the meaning of downsizing, restructuring, and outsourcing, until it was too late; or about the growing tug of war between the dollar and the euro.

New discourses were crafted which include the staples of government and corporate handouts: "*aggressive accounting*," using offshore companies to cook the books and evade taxes; "*transparency*," supplying banks and brokerages with accurate figures on profits and losses, except in the US. And all-purpose words like *Independent*, as in "he's running as an *Independent*," i.e. a pro-business candidate going after Democratic votes; or "*independent* auditors," like Arthur Andersen; or "*independent* directors," meaning outside directors in bed with the company's board. An up-to-date Devil's Dictionary would include the mutant verbs, *impact on*; *contextualize*; *weaponize*, as in "The FBI is investigating whether the anthrax spores used in last fall's attacks could have been grown secretly inside an Army lab and then taken elsewhere to be *weaponized*." Problematic events are "*issues*," as when a plane flying from Chicago to Dallas can't take off because it has "*mechanical issues*"; or somebody doesn't say they're sorry because they have "*apology issues*." But the million-dollar word, the one hand-crafted in mental health clinics to sanitize conflict and neutralize collective memory, is *closure*.

Closure: *the condition of being closed* (Webster's) perfectly evokes the culture of compliance into which Americans had slipped before the war in Iraq woke them up. "A bit of closure" is media slang for someone who's found respite from suffering or anger. Vietnam haunts the formula. "The problem was that Vietnam left Americans with nothing to celebrate. ... And if there is nothing to celebrate," writes a *Los Angeles Times* correspondent, "[y]ou continue to mourn. You go back to the Vietnam Veterans

Memorial over and over again. But everything that helped heal, like the wall, also ensured that the wounds kept festering and denied us closure."[17] Today it's "*9/11*," and the news that the White House had clues from both the CIA and FBI that al Qaeda was planning to hijack airliners, and did nothing, that rattles the national psyche. More and more people suspect a conspiracy. In May 2002, relatives of Pentagon and World Trade Center victims assembled to protest the mishandling of clues, and to call for an independent investigation. "I believe the whole government let people down," one says; others agree; but the reporter ends with the woman who insists, "It's time to put aside the anger … it's time to start the grieving process properly so that we can find closure."

The rush to closure, and its opposite, the national fascination for narratives of personal abuse—sexual, mainly; never economic—suggests something has gone awry. An ambient sense of powerlessness pervades the land of silk and money, and manifests itself among the better-off as a terror of ageing and disease. As in Shakespeare: "And so, from hour to hour we ripe and ripe, / And then from hour to hour we rot and rot, / And thereby hangs a tale." And beneath the fear of loss, a variation on the fear of change, lies a wound about which the therapeutic discourse says little.

This is the dwindling away of the essence of democracy, which is the capacity for self-government. Until 2003, Americans by and large no longer behaved as if they had the authority to be in charge of anything beyond personal goals. They did not display the attitudes and demeanor of sovereign citizens but of consumers loyal to brands or corporate citizens loyal to a firm. In their overall submissiveness to authority, citizens had lost much of the ground for which the American Revolution was fought. The Bill of Rights had atrophied from disuse, leaving behind an abundance of rhetoric. Civil rights are always contested and must be fought for, something we knew in the '60s and must relearn again. Corporate lawyers have always known it—ever since corporations were declared "persons" in 1886, and the Supreme Court accorded them Fourteenth Amendment protections of due process (protections originally intended for freed slaves). In recent years business has won Fourth Amendment protections from "search and seizure" which effectively limit health law and workplace safety. Environmental regulations have been blocked on the grounds that they encroach on corporate "property rights." Like the laws that allowed Enron to pick candidates and bankroll them into office, shape energy policy, hide debt in ghost entities called partnerships, buy and sell fictional "derivatives," hide profits in tax-free offshore banks, they are all "legal." But they may sometimes kill the goose that lays the golden eggs, as Halliburton is learning.

Such matters are more important now than before because corporations are more powerful and have usurped many of the functions of government, not to mention politics, the press, entertainment, education, religion, medicine, and law. The extension of corporate controls, however, has not been accompanied by a larger and more flexible vision of human potential. On the contrary, the more concentrated the command mechanisms of global capitalism, the more remote they are from local conditions—and the more vulnerable they are to challenges from outside their spheres of influence.

It's a lesson anti-globalization activists have learned and turned upside down to apply to themselves, and it has spread to the contemporary anti-imperialist movement. Anti-globalists have found strength in decentralization, in fluid horizontal networks, leapfrogging borders and languages with the aid of the Internet, and deploying themselves in unexpected settings with unexpected partners. After "de-arresting" someone seized by police at a Strasbourg rally in France in the summer of 2002 (site of the European Court of Human Rights), demonstrators split over the conflicting tactics of the black bloc, known for its confrontational tactics, and the pink-silver bloc, a samba band. Whenever the former embarked on a graffiti raid ("subvertising") the dancers surged nervously ahead, until the two reached a compromise in which the samba drums beat out the *"No Border, No Nation!"* slogans of the black bloc, and the black-blockers clapped and danced to the rhythms of the band.

In the 1960s, a similar split existed between Ken Kesey's Merry Pranksters and antiwar radicals in the Bay Area, which never healed. The Yippies came closest to injecting humor and fun into the student movement, but the huge vertically organized mobilizations of the Vietnam era snuffed out elements of play. They provided the media with a setting that promoted leaders, which could be picked off and celebrated, until the leaders were more responsive to the media handlers than they were to their own people.

Today there are still splits that divide anti-imperialist and environmental and Palestinian solidarity movements in the United States. Some have the odor of old schisms between community and antiwar organizing, while others turn on the touchier confusions of criticizing Israel and anti-Semitism. One and the same, thunders Ariel Sharon, while at the opposite extreme, no connection is conceded. There's something old about this as well, with certain contingents in Palestinian solidarity ranks, waving their banners, evoking the horror of the red and blue flag-waving Vietcong supporters who turned up at peace parades: *No, no, not them!* But the answer was Yes. They're here because they're there. It was all about them.

Dissent flourishes whenever the moment has come to break up a hegemonic power that has outlived its time. So it was in the 1960s, when the power was concentrated in Vietnam, and so it is now. A phenomenal change has already taken place in just two years. It began with what some call (wrongly) a coup d'état, which was the emergence of a powerful new constellation of forces: hawks like Cheney and Rumsfeld, with ties to neoconservative foundations, but with more important service in previous administrations; Christian fundamentalists like George W. Bush who is linked to roughly 18 percent of the electorate, mainly in the South; and the neocons. Behind them all extends the tender embrace of the corporate big spenders: the financiers of the American government.

The Christian Coalition is a passionate defender of the expansionist policies of Greater Israel ("And I will make of thee a great nation. And I will bless them that bless thee and curse them that curse thee"). They believe that the Second Coming will arrive only when Israel is in possession of all the lands given to them by God. Then the Jews will be converted— this is the "Rapture," celebrated in the best-selling novels of Tom LeHaye and Jerry Jenkins, and quietly discounted by the Jewish leaders in the United States and Israel who welcome Christian support. It's the big spenders, however, who exercise the greatest influence. They've been at it since almost the beginnings of American history; but "the lethal combination of money and power on a vast scale that can control elections and national policy," as the critic Edward Said put it, hasn't been seen before, and certainly not in Europe.[18] It raises the tired issue of money, but money on such a scale—Bush is spending $200 million to defeat John Kerry, twice as much as in 2000—as to boggle the mind. Except that it doesn't; for MoveOn has initiated a national TV ad campaign, thereby shocking the Republican National Committee, which has tried to block its ads by blanketing news stations with threatening letters from counsel charging MoveOn with violating campaign finance laws.

As a result, the 2004 campaign started out as a battle of TV ads; and the Republicans have been caught by surprise by the negative response to ads that yoke the president to 9/11. Times have changed since the bottom fell out of the WMD arguments for Iraq. Now it's not only Democrats who say that Bush has dodged the investigations into 9/11. Bush has mistakenly cast himself as a "war president," and is touting "steady leadership," despite the fact that 771 American GIs have been killed in Iraq,* and over 3600 have been wounded in a war without logic. According to Pentagon adviser Anthony Cordesman, casualties could rise to at least 1000. "One thousand or more dead in Iraq is hardly Vietnam," Cordesman says. "But

---

* As of May 19, 2004.

it must be justified and explained, and explained honestly";[19] and nobody can. Meanwhile, economic uncertainty has darkened Bush's reelection prospects, and jobs are the number one issue in the polls.

Sixty percent of Americans think the US is on the "wrong track"; 21 percent of probable voters are afraid of losing their jobs in the next twelve months, and the proportion is *higher* among people earning more than $75,000 a year. Support for free trade has fallen from 57 percent five years ago to 28 percent, and Bush has defended free trade in Ohio of all places, where unemployment figures (3.9 percent in 2000) have risen to 6.2 percent. All the battleground states: New Hampshire, Wisconsin, Minnesota, Michigan, Washington, New Mexico, have experienced rising unemployment; and the one state to achieve job growth is Alaska, where Bush had a 31 percent lead in the last election.[20] The loss of jobs plays across the political landscape like a giant kleig light, independent of the spin from the White House. Of the 290,000 private-sector jobs created since April 2003, most of them (215,000), have been temporary. No wonder Democrats are asking the question Ronald Reagan asked: "Are you better off today than you were four years ago?" and the answer is clearly no.

The stock market, which climbed by about 1000 points over the past six months, was an exception to this picture, until it dropped temporarily with the murder of Sheik Yassin. If Bush is right in calculating that two-thirds of Americans have stock investments, and that they will treat him more favorably now than they did in the mid-term elections when the stock market was down, the picture becomes less bleak for the president. But the failure to generate jobs—Bush has seen 3.2 million jobs disappear in the course of his tenure—is an unwelcome reminder of the reelection defeat of the last incumbent Republican president, George H. W. Bush.

The mantra of John Kerry's stump speech, that the Bush administration "has run the most arrogant, inept, reckless, and ideological foreign policy in the modern history of our country," remains the brief that can bring the president down, for it will continue to be bolstered by events. While Bush's Iraq policy has not redrawn the political map of the Middle East, it has certainly done so in Europe, where the terrorist attack in Madrid was followed by the defeat of Bush's Iraq ally Jose Maria Aznar. The socialist prime minister-elect has stated that "the war has been a disaster, the occupation continues to be great disaster. ... You can't bomb a people 'just in case.'" The unexpected reelection victory of antiwar German Chancellor Gerhard Schroeder in September 2002 was the first European election decided by the unpopularity of the war; Spain is the second, and the post-mortem analysis has been keenly examined in Washington, London, and Tokyo.[21]

Asked at a recent Congressional hearing why the costs for Iraq were not included in the Bush administration's budget, Pentagon comptroller Dov Zakheim replied: "Because we simply cannot predict them." There was an awkward truth to the answer. "The White House plays hide and seek with the costs of war," as Senator Robert Byrd has said. The Pentagon refused to estimate the cost before the war on the grounds that it didn't know how long it would take, and a few days later the defense secretary asked for $63 billion. In May 2004 the White House asked for $25 billion. And today the hesitation starts with whether the "interim" government promised by June 30 will allow the US military to stay,[22] or whether there will even be a new Iraqi government.

It's no surprise that the Council on Foreign Relations, citing polls that show American support for the war slipping, has urged the leaders of both parties to publicly commit themselves to a multibillion dollar program over the next several years, and to outline "the magnitude of resources that will be necessary."[23] That is because the American presence in Iraq—despite the fact that it was planned to validate American unilateralism and the first-strike doctrine, neither of which worked—is viewed as essential to global American predominance. Control of the Middle East requires US bases in Iraq, not just to keep Iran from developing nuclear weapons, or Syria from supporting Hamas, but to lay claim to the distribution of Iraqi oil, and to make sure that no other Middle Eastern country switches from the dollar to the euro as the medium of oil exchange as Iraq did in 2000.

The stability of "petrodollar recycling" was set in place in 1974, when Nixon negotiated assurances from Saudi Arabia to price oil in dollars only, and to invest surplus oil proceeds in US Treasury bills, while in return the US would protect the Saudi regime (a protection which has been largely removed). The arrangement promoted a healthy subsidy to the US economy which was based on America's flexible market, the free flow of trade goods and trade surpluses, high worker productivity, government oversight (the SEC), total cash flow and profitability, and of course superior military power.[24] Over the last two decades we have seen a sharp dilution of these "safe harbor" fundamentals, such as an increase in the national debt to $6.021 trillion against a gross domestic product (GDP) of $9 trillion,[25] and decreasing worker productivity. All indications are that the war in Iraq is, among other things, a way "to deliver a deadly preemptive warning to OPEC ... not to flirt with abandoning the Petrodollar system in favor of one based on the euro."[26] The security of the dollar ranks next to national security as an issue that cuts across party lines. That it's in grave danger is no longer in any doubt.

Kerry, who supported the Senate war resolution in October 2002, but didn't support the first Gulf War, which was all about oil, has not signaled any radical change in foreign policy. He has met with Jewish groups in New York in March, and offered a strong defense of Israel. He has promised to prosecute the war on terrorism; indeed, a key plank in his platform comes from Rand Beers, who joined Kerry in 2003 after quitting his job with Bush, because he was concerned that the military action against Iraq would divert resources away from terrorism. Beers has assembled a loyal crew of former Clinton aides. But this doesn't mean that Kerry would pull out of Iraq. Should he favor any such idea, Republican majorities in Congress would make fast work of it.[27]

Many of the totems of what Americans and Europeans see as George W. Bush's unilateralism—rejection of the Kyoto Treaty, refusal to ratify the International Criminal Court—are blunt restatements of decisions that had already been made, or would have been made, in the Senate by overwhelming majorities. For all his promises of global comity, Kerry faces a set of priorities, having to do mainly with free trade and the loss of jobs to outsourcing, which makes his pledges to save jobs ring hollow.

As events in Afghanistan and Iraq have served as a corrective to the high-flown theory of the Bush administration, Democratic and Republican formulations of US foreign policy have actually converged in recent months. Even the most hawkish of Bush's advisers no longer expect him to go after Iran or Syria or Saudi Arabia while Iraq holds down nearly half of the US army. Indeed, the Iraqi insurgency has forced the White House to rethink the role of the UN, and to invite the participation of Russia, Germany, and even France, in the divvying-up of Iraqi oil. Bush has become more of a multilateralist, and Kerry, who once declared himself in favor of the use of force only as a "last resort," is learning how to live with war.

2

HOW IT WAS

My first conscious political act took place in a TV room at Vassar College in the fall of 1960. The Nixon–Kennedy debates were underway, and dozens of seniors in nightgowns and curlers had squeezed into the narrow second-floor parlor in Main Building to watch. The air was blue with smoke and I remember being surprised by the electricity in the room. The debates were a sham, I thought. A publicity stunt. What was all the excitement about?

It was the night the swarthy, shifty-eyed Nixon announced, in answer to a question about agricultural policy, that he would "kill the farmers." In our dorm the slip went almost unnoticed. "Did you hear that?" I said, astonished. "He spoke his mind!" The Republicans in the group, surely the majority, were already leaning toward the handsome Irishman; Nixon's gaffe had clinched it.

John F. Kennedy's star had soared that night. I found myself strangely agitated. I was supposed to feel vindicated. After all, Kennedy was a Democrat and so was I. He was a Catholic, and until my last Marymount retreat, two years before, I was too. But all of a sudden I was denouncing him. "He's a phoney. I don't trust him," I declared. And nobody could convince me otherwise.

I'm not sure what provoked me. I like to think I caught a whiff of the dangers that lay behind Kennedy's activism. All the talk about defending freedom in the far corners of the globe might have aroused my suspicions, even then. A favorite uncle who served under MacArthur in the Pacific, and watched him wade ashore in the Philippines, proclaiming "I have returned," twice, for the cameras, had inoculated me against "war heroes," which was how Kennedy was touted. Or another, younger uncle, stationed in London in the final months of the war, where he joined a Socialist reading circle (something I learned much later), may have disposed me against the New Frontier's "higher patriotism."

But probably it was simpler than that. I was put off by the mounting delirium in the room, which had struck the groveling note one sometimes hears in the I-Can-Hear-Him-Now memories of Cold Warriors from my generation. Anthony Lake, for example, who recalls, in a 1975 memoir, standing "briefly next to Senator Kennedy's open car as it forced its way through the election eve crowds in Boston. His confident smile and the almost hysterical adulation of the people (which I shared) produced an incredible sense of power—and the feeling that it could be harnessed to serve great purposes. As the car moved off," he writes, "I desperately wanted to follow it." From this encounter, Lake traces his decision to join the Foreign Service and go to Vietnam, about which he knew nothing. Partly it was ambition; but more, "it offered a chance to serve, to take part in an exciting national effort."[1]

Something of the same hysteria had gripped the Vassar girls, whose chance to serve would more likely come in the form of marriage to a Foreign Service officer than in the Basic Foreign Service Officers Course, which included, Lake recalls, a session in "Counterinsurgency Tactics: the Peace Corps." Remembering that evening in Main, and the separateness I felt—which had no real consequences, not yet—I am reminded of another defection, much earlier. It was in the wet spring of 1951, as I stood shivering on Sheridan Road in Winnetka, Illinois, in a mob of children from Saints Faith Hope and Charity school, who had been let off to see the

Old Soldier himself.

Truman had just pulled General MacArthur out of Korea, thereby endearing the president to my father, who in this instance couldn't agree more with my Uncle Junie's opinion of his commanding officer. My parents used to frequent the Belvedere Hotel in Baltimore during the late thirties, where they often saw Douglas MacArthur, who was in-between wars, holding court at the bar. He kept a room at the hotel, where it was said of him that "he would go upstairs to curl his moustache" (which he didn't have, but that wasn't the point); he was considered a show-off, even then.

In 1951, the General, who had won the big war in the Pacific and bungled the smaller one, was making a comeback tour through the heartland. Visions of the presidency danced in his head, but it was Eisenhower the Republicans wanted, not this Hotspur. In any event, there he was, bigger than life, like a dictator in a Marx Bros. comedy, standing tall in a trench coat and braided hat, in the back seat of a gun-metal gray Lincoln convertible, right arm raised in salute; while beside him sat a tiny woman wrapped in furs and a boy around my age with dark crinkly blond hair.

Everybody shouted and waved. I stood on the curb in stony silence, glaring, my fists shoved deep in my pockets. I hated MacArthur, I explained to whomever was near, but of course I was only a child; it didn't matter.

By 1960, my estrangement from the rituals of American politics had been informed by a more direct encounter. This took place in Chicago ("the cosmopolitan colossus of the midlands," the Democrats' program called it), where I had signed on as a page at the Democratic National Convention in 1956. I was sixteen, old enough to be propositioned by a Missouri delegate, but young enough to roam the back halls and service elevators of the Conrad Hilton with my high school buddy, Prudy King, whose father, the hotel manager, had more than once given us the keys to his dominion.

Prudy, who had a crush on the Boulevard Room drummer, was also working for the Democrats that summer. In fact, she had gotten her job first, a real one, with pay; and wrote me in Cape Cod—where my mother, sister and I had gone to visit Uncle Junie and our Grandmother Hancock—about her interview with the assistant convention manager. Miss Forsling was "striking looking," at thirty-five: "tall, beautiful figure, steel gray hair—but looks very young, and the most beautiful clothes. ..." A character out of a Preston Sturges movie, she became my boss too.

Miss Forsling was worried that Mr. King's daughter might be shocked by the professional convention workers, girls in their twenties who "swear like mad and sleep with different men every night," Prudy reported. "She doesn't want to have to baby sit for me," she added; but her father had assured Miss Forsling "that I wouldn't be shocked by anything. This is going to be an education," she exclaimed. "Dad says I will meet everyone from the presidential candidates down to the loading men. It is going to be the biggest thing that ever happened to me and I can't wait!"

Naturally, when my father, who was rooting for Adlai Stevenson that year, as he had in 1952, urged me to volunteer my services after I got home from the Cape, I agreed. And soon I was milling about with the convention girls in the busy eighth-floor lakefront suite that served as Democratic Headquarters. But it was not the education that Prudy or my father anticipated.

She had been put to work in the purchasing department, which was reached by a service elevator bulging with linen; and then moved on to the mimeograph room, where she helped crank out press releases. I was sent to the Ways and Means Committee, which was where the lonely Missourian accosted me. There I stood in the back of a half-empty meeting room, awaiting my orders to run downstairs for chewing gum or Coke.

"The Party for You—Not Just the Few," was the watchword. In 1956, a recession year, the Democrats were "the People's Party." Big business was the villain; an argument party speechwriters underscored by noting that in 1955, under the GOP, "General Motors had made a billion and farm income dropped a billion. GM's profits rose five times as much as autoworkers' pay . .... The rise in corporation profits as a whole was seven times greater than the rise of the average American's income."[2]

A Bill Mauldin cartoon in the Convention program caught the drift. A wife kneels behind her farmer husband (tractor in the distance) who winces over a pinprick from the needle she plies to sew another patch on the seat of his overalls. "Sorry I'm so awkward, dear," she says. "You get out of practice in 20 years." Twenty years. That would be 1936. The Depression. Of course, such allusions passed me by in 1956.

I was more curious about the alcohol fumes that permeated the Ways and Means room when I picked up paper cups and wrappers after an afternoon's meeting. The stale fumes were everywhere in the hotel; and the delegates' rumpled suits and flushed faces testified to the binding ritual of this or any other American convention, had I known it (which I didn't— I associated hard drinking with home). It was fitting that a liquor company took out the full-page ad in the program, proclaiming, "*Once again the world watches.*" Addressing the delegates with marmoreal morning-after piety, the ad said: "As you come together to select your candidates, and to set forth your beliefs and objectives, we greet you with honor and respect. May your deliberations ... reaffirm the faith of the free world in the American system of elections by the voice of the people." Signed: "Department of Public Relations, National Distillers Products Corporation."

"... [B]y the voice of the people" was dropped, I suspect, for the Republican program. But no one could outdo the Democrats when it came to sniffing out threats to the "free world." And it is interesting to find in the party's 1956 warning that "confusion and drift [had] mounted as the result of such Republican inventions as 'massive retaliation'," which was the germ of the charge Kennedy lobbed against the Eisenhower administration in 1960—that under the mutual destruction assured by the Republicans' nuclear deterrent, American power was helpless to resist Soviet influence in more remote regions, where the United States ached to stake new claims. As President Kennedy warned in his first major defense statement in 1961: "The free world's security can be endangered not only by nuclear attack but also by being slowly nibbled away at the periphery, regardless of our strategic power, by forces of subversion, infiltration, intimidation, indirect or nonovert aggression, internal revolution ... or a series of limited wars."[3]

In 1956, however, the Democrats' attention was fixed on the "center of world Communism," where that very spring Khrushchev had issued his denunciation of Stalin at the Twentieth Party Congress. Whether the Russians were entering a period of "protracted convulsions" or transforming themselves "into a more effective front for international aggrandizement" (as the Soviet march into Hungary later that year suggested), the authors of the convention program statement were not sure.

Already the party had waded into the twilight zones of the Cold War, where Kennedy's warriors would soon follow. Pointing to "the new economic, psychological, diplomatic and political competition that had developed" between East and West, party spokesmen warned that Communism presented "a greater, not a lesser, threat. ..."[4]

I cared not a whit about such matters in 1956; though my work for the party hierarchs had taught me a few things about American politics. Democrats, I realized, were businessmen—and women. Elizabeth Forsling and Elizabeth Conkey, the Democratic National Committeewoman from Illinois, wielded administrative power; their bosses were (male) figureheads. But altogether the delegates were not so different from the Republicans with whom my father found himself so bitterly at odds on the North Shore. As social types, that is; boosters, a generation removed from Sinclair Lewis's Babbitt, and more than a generation from the farmers and industrial workers whose interests they professed, Chicago's delegates bore little resemblance to their candidate Adlai Stevenson.

Here was something to ponder. A mismatch, if ever there was one. Like the counterset between the gentleman lawyer Joseph Welch and the rampaging junior Senator from Wisconsin in 1954, when Welch's *"Have you no sense of decency, sir, at long last?"* brought McCarthy to his heels. In 1956, the gentleman liberal Stevenson appeared estranged not only from the party he represented, but from himself. Gone was the wit and candor of 1952; now he was trying to fit in.

Watching Stevenson stumble through a speech designed to identify him with the common man, my father's spirits sank. Never before had he looked more like an egghead than when he stood on the doorstep clutching a grocery bag and discussing the rising price of butter. True, it was the early days of TV image-making; and presidential packaging smartened up later. But like Nixon's gaffe in 1960, this blunder revealed a quirky fact about public relations (to me, anyway), which is that when the effort to manufacture reality runs too far afield the facts, then the facts will out. This was years before Ronald Reagan, needless to say; and Bush II.

"Loyal Democrats, such as you, make our Party the winning Party," Miss Forsling wrote to her volunteers when the convention was over, thanking us for our "generous service during a time when every hand was needed." Stevenson had lost; but his spin on the "confusion and drift" of Republican politics was recycled with more success in 1960. "We seem becalmed in a season of storm and drifting in a century of mighty dreams and great achievements," said Kennedy, and the sentiment was picked up by the chorus of yea-sayers who promoted him: Henry Luce, Walter Lippmann, Richard Newstadt, and Hans Morgenthau—who may have regretted it (I always wondered) when he broke ranks over Vietnam in 1964.

Back home in Winnetka, for a short while in the summer of 1956 when the circus came to town, my father almost seemed to belong. A Baltimore couple who were Maryland delegates had stayed over, and the new house—new to us; we had recently moved from Wilmette—bustled with talk of the Convention. A sprawling Tudor manor, bristling with chimneys, the big house proclaimed our march up the ladder from Evanston to Wilmette to 600 Berkeley, Winnetka, with a bravado I found mortifying; and for months after we moved in, anybody driving me home was asked to drop me off a block away.

Now with live-in help, and frequent company, the house was beginning to fit. My mother was pregnant with my brother Chris that summer; my sister Candy was going into eighth grade. When our parents got home from parties it was oddly quiet: no doors slammed, no one shouted, nothing was broken; in the mornings we didn't have to tiptoe past the bedroom of the sleeping man. Over dinner, with her Baltimore friends, even my mother, a Republican in self-defense, entered into the campaign talk. And then the conservative tide rolled back in over the suburbs, and my father was left standing alone on the shore.

It was an unhappy perch for this fiercely partisan man; a photo-engraving executive who was not averse to questioning the intelligence of neighbors and colleagues when their political ideas differed from his own, especially on important subjects like Senator McCarthy, and particularly when he was drinking. Scotch forked his tongue, and gave it wings too; sometimes mixing the message, as when political invective dipped into scatology. The ad hominem attack was his forte; and so fierce were the character assassinations he leveled at his opponents that I wonder now if perhaps his deeper enmity was reserved for people, not ideas. And not just anybody, but people on whom he depended. Conflict, in any event, was invariably resolved in his case in favor of further conflict.

He was not always so bitter. Humor parried the thrust, as at summer sales conferences in Wisconsin with the men from Jahn & Ollier, the engraving company he worked for most of his life, beginning as a salesman selling letterpress and offset printing to yearbook editors in the 1930s and '40s because he liked books. In the 1950s and '60s, rising to executive ranks, his clients included *Time* and *Life*, and advertising agencies such as J. Walter Thompson and Foote, Cone & Belding, many of whose accounts he served until his retirement in 1968. He made a great deal of money, and invested none of it, not believing in stocks or real estate which had nothing to do with work. He spent what he made on his family's progress, which never seemed to satisfy him. In 1968, J&O was acquired by the giant conglomerate Beatrice Foods, and my father was shipped out to pasture, with his wife and son, on a buying tour of printing companies in Europe. His pension was later paid by Foot, Cone & Belding; and when in a few years that too ended, neither he nor his daughters, who had long ago left home, took it to court. By then, in the mid-'70s, he had followed my mother and brother to Scottsdale, Arizona, which he hated.

"He shone ... by keeping us in stitches for whole evenings of revelry," a former business associate, Jim Oldham, has written me of the early sales conferences. Oldham recalls a "session" around 1953–54, having to do with Vietnam, "in which he told us about how the 'little brown people' running about in the jungle and the rubber plantations were succeeding in separating the French from all that tin and rubber. This was serious business," Oldham adds, "but he made it so funny that we all had hysterics."

I'm not sure I see the humor in it; nor do I hear my father saying "little brown people"; but the anti-imperialist sentiment rings true. He reveled in attacks on the United Fruit Company, and American relations to the banana republics of Central America were a source of derision, so why not cheer the liberators of French Indochina? If he made it "funny" probably it was to sweeten the pill for his listeners, who, with the exception of the loyal Mr. Oldham, were mostly midwestern Republicans.

Humor kept the wolves at bay. As in some of the many letters that followed me to college, in which an obsession with the physical appearance of his eldest daughter was barely reined in by irony. "Do hope things go well with you and that you are paying some attention to the body and outward appearances," he wrote me in the spring of 1961. "It's nice to have height of spirit and depth of soul housed in pleasant surroundings. Beauty may be only skin deep, but most men are not cannibals."

For my father, John F. Kennedy's victory in 1960 was a source of genuine elation. Winnetka had voted for Nixon over Kennedy 5 to 1; "the gloom on the North Shore hangs heavy," he wrote me on November 11, "everyone is still hoping for some miracle in which a recount will reverse the whole picture ... I do my best not to gloat," he added. "To do so openly would be to invite self-destruction."

He was in an expansive mood, like the new administration; lamenting the "floundering" years, when we were caught "flatfooted by international crises. ... I feel Kennedy will take firm positions," he declared. "Our position in the world demands a solid considered course of action known to our friends and allies. Something upon which they can depend, bringing a unity of purpose to the actions of the so-called free nations."

It was as if he were part of the team, sitting up there with the best and the brightest, waving the magic words: *firm* positions, on which our allies *depend*. This was the worldview that later prevented successive US policymakers from cutting their losses in Vietnam. Instead of pulling back in the face of mounting political and military defeats, they escalated. "The integrity of the US commitment is the principal pillar of peace throughout the world," was how Dean Rusk saw it in 1965. "If that commitment becomes unreliable, the Communists would draw conclusions that would lead to our ruin and almost certainly to catastrophic war."[5]

This is how the Bush administration now sees its involvement in Iraq, with one critical exception. It is not just the Muslim terrorists who have been put in the place of Communists, while that has been said; it is the nations of the Middle East, and their protective powers—Britain, France, and Russia—who "would draw conclusions ..."

My father, Gordon Brightman, was a specimen of a classic American type: the Cold War liberal, whose nobler impulses were joined to a drive to dominate the internal affairs of any state where self-determination, much less a redistribution of wealth and power, is threatened. Truman reflected the vision, albeit loosely, when he told the Chicago delegates in 1956: "In choosing our candidates, we must select men who can lead not only the nation, but the world."[6]

With the unraveling in Vietnam of the interventionist's faith, my father, like many postwar liberals, was cut off from his more generous impulses. Thus he was horrified by my activism later in the 1960s, even while he was never an apologist for intervention in Vietnam. In the antiwar magazine I started, *Viet-Report*, he saw first an affront to basic print standards, and second, an unjustified audacity; for who was I, this disobedient daughter, who hadn't kept her room clean or her hair combed, to pronounce on foreign policy issues over which she had no authority?

Worse, the idea of a movement to transform the distribution of political rights and privileges in American society, such as I embraced, smacked of insurrection. And how he hated the word *movement*, so redolent of the bowel. He proposed instead an organization: "The Movement for the Correction of Society." Like that "obstreperousness of the household slaves," which in Trotsky's account of the conquest of St. Petersburg, "destroys utterly the stability of the family regime," this stab at political change from the bottom up struck my father in a sensitive spot. It was in domestic affairs, after all, where he had lost the most ground; where he had placed his greatest demands, and suffered the greatest rebuff.

I was surprised when some years after his death, I learned that he had been proud of me during the antiwar years. "She was way ahead of us all on the Vietnam Mess," my father wrote Jim Oldham in 1975. Strange. When Oldham saw him for the last time in his office, sometime in the mid-'60s, "he told me how proud he was of your courage." Well, he never told me.

In November 1960, I received one of those epistles a father addresses a son on the eve of war or of a promising political career: "You are certainly entering an exciting period of history," he assured me. "It should be thrilling for you to contemplate." I was approaching graduation, and had begun to look into the possibility of teaching in West Africa, or, failing that, of working with a Yale anthropologist as an unqualified assistant at a baboonery in Kenya.

Africa was in the air; both Africana studies and working in Africa, especially at Yale, where I spent a good deal of time. Nor was I immune to the zeitgeist of the new era, in which a craving for adventure—a release from the conventions of the 1950s, not to mention from classrooms—combined with a spirit of service; but I wanted to steer clear of government programs. And my father was trying to steer me back.

Under Kennedy, he ventured, "you're going to see a great increase in practical help to underprivileged or emerging nations. A large action program should develop. I should think you might like to associate yourself with this program. ..." My own plans he found "quite a puzzle," though he encouraged me to "check into everything and anything that looks interesting. "Later," he wrote, "you can sort them out."

My father was trying to relate my wanderlust to his world. Is this not what parents do? He sent me the *Manchester Guardian*, whose crisp airmail packages piled up, mostly unread, in the corner of my room at Vassar. "Too bad Mother and I did not know of this inclination [to teach in Africa] earlier," he wrote, apropos a trip to Europe they had taken on the *Queen Elizabeth*, where he had met the Nigerian consul. "We might have had a few words with him."

A Yale friend who was teaching in Bide, Nigeria, had told me about the African–American Institute, which handled the bulk of teacher-recruiting programs for the United States in Ghana, Nigeria and Guinea. He suggested I get in touch with Yale's Chaplain, William Sloane Coffin, who was, he said, "acting as the chief inspirator of the movement." There was a wave of interest in Africana studies at Yale that year, and the Rev. Coffin, it turned out, was eager to carry it to Vassar. I was advised to apply to the Institute, and at the same time to make contact with OPERATIONS CROSSROADS AFRICA, a summer program popular at Yale, in which Coffin also had an interest. Did I want him to speak about such things at Vassar? Probably not, for I see no evidence that he arrived. Instead, I made a sortie to the Nigerian consulate in New York, where a Mr. Odon dissuaded me, in the gentlest of terms, from pursuing my teaching aspirations in West Africa.

There was something fishy about the Yale projects, which were far from independent. Both, in fact, were recipients of CIA funding, as I discovered later; and I kept my distance. My interest was also stimulated from another quarter by the arrival of two partisans from the African National Congress, two men in black suits, one of whom was Oliver Tambo, who told the Vassar girls about the Sharpeville massacre. This was when the authorities shot into a demonstration, the first really large attempt to protest against apartheid, killing sixty-eight and wounding many others, and it drove the African National Congress underground. I was very moved and began to read about South Africa, and about apartheid; but in the end, chance took the lead.

I won a *Mademoiselle* contest for a short story, and became one of twenty Guest Editors at the magazine for a month in New York. After that I went to Provincetown to study art, but really to get Vassar out of my system—that's how I saw it at the time—and then to move on, which I did, leaving art behind, and going to graduate school in American Literature in the fall (as planned all along) at the University of Chicago.

To the Person Sitting in Darkness

Shall we? That is, shall we go on conferring our Civilization upon the peoples that sit in darkness, or shall we give those poor things a rest? Shall we bang right ahead in our old-time, loud, pious way, and commit the new century to the game; or shall we sober up and sit down and think it over first? Would it not be prudent to get our Civilization-tools together, and see how much stock is left on hand in the way of Glass Beads and Theology, and Maxim Guns and Hymn Books, and Trade-Gin and Torches of Progress and Enlightenment (patent adjustable ones, good to fire villages with, upon occasion), and balance the books, and arrive at the profit and loss, so that we may intelligently decide whether to continue the business or sell out the property and start a new Civilization Scheme on the proceeds?

Extending the Blessings of Civilization to our Brother who Sits in Darkness has been a good trade and has paid well, on the whole; and there is money in it yet, if carefully worked—but not enough, in my judgement, to make any considerable risk advisable. The People that Sit in Darkness are getting to be too scarce—too scarce and too shy. And such darkness as is now left is really of but an indifferent quality, and not dark enough for the game. The most of those People that Sit in Darkness have been furnished with more light than was good for them or profitable for us. We have been injudicious.

The Blessings-of-Civilization Trust, wisely and cautiously administered, is a Daisy. There is more money in it, more territory, more sovereignty, and other kinds of emolument, than there is in any other game that is played. But Christendom has been playing it badly of late years, and must certainly suffer by it, in my opinion. She has been so eager to get every stake that appeared on the green cloth, that the People who Sit in Darkness have noticed it—they have noticed it, and have begun to show alarm. They have become suspicious of the Blessings of Civilization. More—they have begun to examine them. This is not well. The Blessings of Civilization are all right, and a good commercial property; there could not be a better, in a dim light. In the right kind of light, and at a proper distance, with the goods a little out of Focus, they furnish this desirable exhibit to the Gentlemen who Sit in Darkness:

LOVE, JUSTICE, GENTLENESS, CHRISTIANITY, PROTECTION TO THE WEAK, TEMPERANCE, LAW AND ORDER, LIBERTY, EQUALITY, HONORABLE DEALING, MERCY, EDUCATION,

—and so on ...

MARK TWAIN

*

Someone once asked Mahatma Gandhi what he thought of Western civilization.

"It would be a good idea," he replied.

3

SECURING THE REALM

The psychology of weakness is easy enough to understand. A man armed only with a knife may decide that a bear prowling the forest is a tolerable danger, inasmuch as the alternative—hunting the bear armed only with a knife—is actually riskier than lying low and hoping the bear never attacks. The same man armed with a rifle, however, will likely make a different calculation of what constitutes a tolerable risk. Why should he risk being mauled to death if he doesn't need to?

ROBERT KAGAN[1]

There is George W. Bush, butt of a thousand jokes, strutting across the world's stage. It's November 23, 2002, and he's in Bucharest, in Revolution Square, welcoming another ex-Communist state into NATO. It's the last leg of a five-day trip centered on the NATO meeting in Prague which will formalize the invitation to several new fringe states to join the once venerable bastion of North Atlantic power. Afterwards the president will visit St. Petersburg to reassure Russian president Vladimir Putin that he has nothing to fear from NATO's expansion to the East. Russia doesn't need those buffer states anymore, he'll say; "America and Romania are friends to the Russian people, and so is the NATO alliance."[2]

It's raining hard, and Bush crouches on a platform high above the sea of upturned faces, protected by a bulletproof shield but exposed from above to the weather. Sharpshooters are positioned on nearby rooftops. He hasn't addressed such a large crowd since the attacks on the World Trade Center and the Pentagon, much less one so far from home, and his delivery lacks its practiced rhythms. He shouts that the Romanians know all about Terrorism because they lived under Communism. Terrorism, he says, is just like Communism or Fascism. Communism, Fascism, Terrorism: it's a trinity fresh from the briefing book, and he's not yet made it his own; not like the Axis of Evil, which came easier. Just like the Nazis and the Communists—he explains to these people who know more about both than he knows about Crawford, Texas—"the terrorists seek to end lives and control life."[3]

Bush's empire is now heir apparent to much of the resource wealth—oil most importantly—over which the former Soviet Union and Europe once presided in Central Asia, Eastern Europe, the Near East, Southwest Asia, and Northeast Africa. To police these vast domains, shot through with the tensions of territories in transition, his administration has launched a massive reorganization and extension of US military capabilities. NATO would seem to have little to do with it, having turned, in part, into what the writer Michael Mandelbaum calls "Club NATO ... a kind of support group and kaffeeklatsch for the newly admitted democracies of Eastern and Central Europe, which suffered under totalitarian rule throughout the Cold War."[4] To Washington, however, NATO's new members are significant in ways they were not before the September 11, 2001 attacks—or, more precisely, before the administration decided to establish a new beachhead in the Middle East, a decision which was in fact made before September 11.

Romania's vote, along with the votes of other new states (Lithuania, Latvia, Estonia) may come in handy when and if Washington can no longer count on the durability of an increasingly tense partnership with France and Germany. While it is not yet understood inside the United States, the latter governments have begun to fear entangling alliances with their old friend and protector for some of the same reasons that eighteenth- and nineteenth-century America kept its distance from the marauding monarchies of Europe. What makes the difference is the administration's abandonment of international treaties and security arrangements, along with the preemptive war doctrine and the assertion of unilateral rights which stand at the center of the new National Security Doctrine. It's not news that militarily the United States is top dog; the trouble comes when it's on its own, acting as judge, jury, and executioner; and the French and Germans have begun to recognize the havoc the present administration, unleashed from the constraints of détente, is capable of wreaking abroad. The Bush team, for its part, has already begun to regard the "captive nations" as a pro-American fifth column inside Europe. Distinct from "Old Europe," as Secretary of Defense Donald Rumsfeld will soon call the leaders of the European Union, Romania, Lithuania, and Estonia will follow Poland as pioneers of the US-friendly "New Europe."

Romania, moreover, mired in corruption and poverty, figures strategi-cally in the military action Rumsfeld plans against Iraq—which is no doubt why a few Romanian decontamination units were invited to join America's Afghan campaign (allowing President Bush, on November 23, to welcome Romania into the "global coalition against terror"). Romania's ports on the Black Sea are a link to the Middle East, and can supply US bases in southern Turkey, which the defense secretary hopes to have in place in a month or so, after a little more arm-twisting in Ankara. Southern Turkey is where he plans to base the 4th Infantry Division, with its digitalized Abrams tanks and Bradley Fighting Vehicles positioned to lead an advance on Baghdad from the north. Ircirlik, in particular—once a linchpin in America's Cold War strategy of containment, and for the last ten years headquarters for attacks on the no-fly zones in northern Iraq—will serve as a hub in the Pentagon's campaign to topple Saddam Hussein, if Rumsfeld gets his way.

In the Bush administration's global war against terrorism, the United States has found an elusive enemy worthy of its boundless energy for expansion; one that inhabits, in the president's phrase, "the dark corners of the world." This is a foe which, unlike Communism, can be targeted at will, nearly anywhere, at anytime, without Washington having to weigh the risks of upsetting the balance of power with another superpower. It will be a simple matter to target terrorism in Iraq, for example, where Saddam is known for having used chemical weapons against the Iranians. And al Qaeda is everywhere.

On September 20, 2002, when the Bush team issued its lengthy rationale for shifting American military strategy away from containment and deterrence toward preemptive action,* it declared that the United States would never again allow its military supremacy to be challenged in the way it was during the Cold War. A revealing statement, it could not have been made during the Clinton years, or even under Bush *père*; though the germ of the millennial vision of unlimited American military power—what the Pentagon calls *full spectrum dominance*—took root in Ronald Reagan's Defense Department thirteen years earlier, principally in the busy persons of Paul Wolfowitz and Richard Perle. Perle, who in November 2002 heads Rumsfeld's powerful Defense Policy Board, was the original architect of the attack-Iraq plan to spark regime-change throughout the Middle East, while his protégé, Paul Wolfowitz, has become the number-two-man at the Pentagon, as well as chief of the new intelligence agency. This is the Office of Special Plans, which Rumsfeld set up after the CIA and Defense Intelligence Agency (DIA) failed to provide proof of Saddam's alleged weapons of mass destruction or his links to al Qaeda. Soon it will be headed by Douglas Feith.

---

* "The National Security Strategy of the United States of America," soon to be called the Bush Doctrine.

In the fall of 2002, not many people know these names. Wolfowitz and Perle, and a coterie of like-minded men—Douglas Feith, Richard Armitage, Zalmay Khalilzad, Kenneth Adleman, John Bolton, David Wurmser, Dov Zakheim, Elliot Abrams, I. Lewis Libby, all of whom hold middle-level positions in the Bush administration—are accustomed to working behind the scenes, through front groups and "citizens' lobbies" such as the Committee on the Present Danger, which argued in the 1970s and '80s that nuclear war with the Soviet Union was "winnable." In the 1990s, terrorism supplanted the Soviet menace as the *raison d'état* for huge military build-ups—terrorism and noncompliant Arab governments who were sweet on terrorism and on Israel's enemies in particular: Hezbollah, Islamic Jihad, Hamas, and the PLO.

Position papers from neoconservative think-tanks such as the Project for the New American Century (PNAC), the Jewish Institute for Strategic Affairs (JINSA), the Center for Strategic Policy (CSP), the Center for Strategic and International Studies (CSIS), and the American Enterprise Institute (AEI), busied themselves throughout the '90s arguing the case against Iran, Iraq, and Syria as host nations harboring murderous bands of Islamic fundamentalists. The international case against terrorism was fortified by the national self-interest of Israel. But the case served other economic interests as well, about which more in a moment. And the focus on Israeli interests served to distract attention from the oil interest.

Action proposals were periodically presented to the Clinton administration, whose Middle East expert, Kenneth M. Pollack, and deputy assistant secretary of state, Ronald Asmus, saw that they got a sympathetic hearing. In 1998, the idea of preemptive action—already a code word for attacking lesser powers without multilateral consent—had crept into public discourse on the Middle East. In a February 17, 1998 speech at the Pentagon, President Clinton said the US "simply couldn't allow Mr. Hussein to *acquire* nuclear, chemical, and biological weapons arsenals" (emphasis added). Presumably, Mr. Hussein no longer possessed these weapons. Echoing his conservative advisers—especially the neoconservatives, or neocons, so-called for their different roots in American history than those of traditional American conservativism—Clinton warned against an "unholy axis" of terrorists and the "outlaw nations" that sheltered them.[5] Some of the familiar theory was in place, but it had not yet taken effect. The US was still viewed by European leaders as a self-absorbed but essentially benevolent superpower. And there was as yet no public stirred up by the looming prospect of a major war to give the larger rationale of the "unholy axis" the attention it deserved.

Soon after, Clinton authorized bombing raids against Iraq in 1998 to signal US displeasure at Baghdad's expulsion of UN weapons inspectors—though, as in Serbia and Kosovo (1999), the military action was undertaken with NATO and UN involvement. The inspectors had been ordered into Iraq in 1991 as part of the economic sanctions that followed Iraq's defeat in the Gulf War (a set-piece of multilateral support), and now Saddam Hussein wanted them out on the grounds that some of the Americans had been spying for the United States. The bombing might well have been the prelude to something more serious had not sex and Hollywood intervened. But with an impeachment scandal brewing in Washington, the attack was scorned as a clumsy presidential effort to distract attention from the Monica Lewinsky affair—a case of the movie *Wag the Dog* (about a sham war declared by a beleaguered president) come to life.

Long before the neocons emerged as avatars of evil for liberals looking for the villain of the piece, Washington insiders referred to them as "the string of Perles," after their de facto leader Richard Perle, whose moniker, "the Prince of Darkness," derived from a longtime fascination with nuclear weapons and the concept of "total war." "Wolfowitz is a second-class Beelzebub," while Perle, said a former comrade who had soured on them both, "is the primary manipulator, Old Scratch himself."[6] Throughout the 1990s, the group advanced its hegemonic views in quasi-academic forums, by way of influential media hawks like George Will, William Safire, Robert Bartley, and Michael Barone, as well as through foreign policy journals. "Toward a Neo-Reaganite Foreign Policy" (*Foreign Affairs*, 1996), by columnist Robert Kagan and *Weekly Standard* editor William Kristol, was typical of such efforts, which sliced through the placid waters of policy debate during those in-between years like shark fins at Sea World.

A braintrust of a new type, this one stands in contrast to the smooth-talking cadre of warriors who swept into Washington with the Kennedy administration in 1961, many from Kennedy's alma mater, Harvard. Nobody will ever call the Bush team's jeremiahs the "best and the brightest," or see in their radical revisioning of US foreign policy a "new frontier." Not since the McKinley era have civilian military advisers been so deeply entrenched in the lobbying and business worlds—most notably Perle, whose working relationships with Israel's Benjamin Netanyahu and Ariel Sharon have not prevented him from collecting large retainers from Turkey, or doing business with Saudi multimillionaires on behalf of his various businesses (until in February 2004 he was relieved of the last of his government posts). Nor has the intermingling of ideologues, policy wonks, and top executives in the defense industry, which took off under Reagan and flourishes now, ever been so lively.

At the same time, the neo-Reaganites, as Irving Kristol prefers to call them, share with their liberal predecessors a reckless faith in the magic of hi-tech weaponry, as well as a predilection for viewing international relations in Manichean terms, primarily as a tool for empire-building. No longer Democracy versus Communism, but not Democracy versus Terrorism either (Democracy versus radical Islam is more like it, but too close to the truth to be widely professed*). Democracy versus Evil is best, rooted as it is in Reagan's crusade against the Evil Empire, and in the savvy religiosity of the younger Bush. It speaks to the masses—who are not

---

* Except by William Bennett on CNN when he said we were in a "struggle between good and evil," and that Congress must declare war on "militant Islam," namely Lebanon, Libya, Syria, Iraq, Iran, and China. (Quoted by Patrick Buchanan in *The American Conservative*, March 24, 2003.)

the same masses they were in the Vietnam era—and it ignores the intelligentsia, who have changed too. It battens on fear.

In each administration in which they have nested, the neocons have pressed to demolish the legacies of the Cold War. But only under George W. Bush has the US shaken off the uncertainties attached to the end of the Cold War—to the unexpected collapse of a bipolar system which the US and the USSR had constructed over forty years of brinkmanship. And even the Bush administration wobbled until the September 11 attacks provided it with the political leverage it needed to launch a national security strategy of unprecedented reach and audacity; one that was capable of building over time—Wolfowitz calls the war on terrorism "a Hundred Years War"— a unipolar system promising greater security than anything dreamed of during the Cold War. Greater security for American interests, not for the Free World—a quaint concept that has gone the way of the USSR.

In the main, the Bush administration has succeeded in extricating Washington from a dense network of international agreements and treaties—the Kyoto Protocol, the International Criminal Court, the ABM Treaty, and nonproliferation treaties generally, all inherited from détente—which in its view impinge on America's ability to act unilaterally. In the place of nonproliferation it has substituted a more muscular approach called "counterproliferation," which includes everything from missile defense to forcibly dismantling weapons. Counterproliferation is an application of the first-strike doctrine—the doctrine of "prevention and preemption," which, according to Rumsfeld, permits US military forces "to find and destroy the enemy before they strike us."[7] As the world's sole surviving superpower, the United States can no longer be constrained by the defensive concerns of secondary powers, whose weakness leads them to retreat from the dangers—rather, the challenges—that America's superior military power now places before it.

Think of the bear prowling in the forest of which Robert Kagan speaks in "Power and Weakness," the essay that became the clarion call for the Bush doctrine. If a man is armed only with a knife, he might have to learn to live with the bear. But if he has a rifle, well then, he will look on the matter differently. He will see himself as potential bear meat and go after the beast—for "Why should he risk being mauled to death if he doesn't need to?" This is a most revealing story, for it shows how weapons—the defense industry and its appendages—have taken the lead in defining policy options. Thus has Halliburton built US bases in Afghanistan, Kuwait, Jordan, Uzbekistan, Djibouti, the Republic of Georgia, and Iraq. And Halliburton's 2002 annual report describes counterterrorism as offering "growth opportunities."[8]

The neocons are politically smarter than the men of Camelot, with the conspiratorial habits of underdogs. While few Americans understand it, they have secured a political base for a transformation of US foreign policy and military strategy that extends beyond the Bush administration. They alone have managed to articulate a post-Cold War strategy, focused on Iraq, which touches on major national interests. It is a military strategy, based on US military supremacy, with the extension of military bases at its core. The war in Iraq will be fought *for new bases in the Middle East to supplant the bases the US will have lost in Saudi Arabia; for direct access to the second largest oil reserves in the world; and, least understood because almost entirely undiscussed in the American media, to shore up the dollar in the hidden war between dollars and euros in the oil trade.*

Monetary shifts in the reserve funds of foreign governments away from the dollar, and toward the euro, began in January 2002, and stepped up in Asia in July 2002. The majority of reserve funds in Iran's central bank were shifted to euros in response to Bush's Axis of Evil speech. In January 2003, Canada sold gold, and commenced a gradual shift into euro reserves.[9] An article by Hazel Henderson outlines the dynamics and potential outcomes of these shifts. US overreach in the war on terrorism, already leading to vast deficits, combined with historically high trade deficits, leads to a further run on the dollar. If other developing countries follow Venezuela and

China in diversifying their currency reserves away from dollars, such a shift could bring the dollar and euro close to parity beyond sterling (where parity almost exists). And, most important, OPEC could act on internal discussions and decide to announce that its oil will soon be re-denominated in euros, or even a new oil-backed currency of its own.

Further, as public efforts to shift energy policy toward renewables, greater efficiency, higher gas taxes, etc., are blocked by fossil-fuel industry supporters, the US remains vulnerable to both energy supply and price shocks. The European Union recognizes its own economic and political power as the euro rises and becomes the world's other reserve currency. The G8 pegs the euro and dollar into a "trading band," removing them from the trading screens of speculators (a "win–win" for everyone). Tony Blair persuades the British of this larger reason for the UK to join the euro. Developing countries lacking hard currencies follow Venezuela's lead and start bartering their undervalued commodities directly with each other. (President Chavez has inked in thirteen such country barter deals for its oil, such as Cuba's exchange of Cuban health paramedics who are setting up clinics in rural Venezuelan villages in return for Venezuelan oil.[10]) If just one third of these potential developments is realized, the US dollar is in deep trouble.

The diversification of Venezuela's currency reserves and its barter plan explain why Bush approved the failed military-led coup against Hugo Chavez in April 2002. Moreover, there is evidence that the US is still active in attempts to overthrow the democratically elected Chavez administration—which has, in March 2004, threatened to cut off oil to the US if the *norteamericanos* do not desist in their efforts to dislodge Chavez. Venezuela is the fifth largest producer of oil in the world, and the corporate elites whose political power runs unfettered in the Bush/Cheney oligarchy appear interested in privatizing Venezuela's oil industry. Even the potential barter deals might effectively cut the dollar out of the vital oil transaction cycle; for if these special deals proliferate, they could create more devaluation pressure by removing the dollar from its crucial "petro-recycling" role.[11]

But the most significant change in the Middle East has already happened—when Saddam Hussein switched to the euro on November 6, 2000, and later converted his $10 billion oil-for-food reserve fund at the UN to euros. "Baghdad's switch from the dollar to the euro for oil trading is intended to rebuke Washington's hard-line on sanctions," said Charles Recknagel on Radio Free Europe,[12] in one of the few reports to appear in the US media. At the time, many analysts were surprised that Saddam was willing to give up about $270 million in oil revenues for what seemed a political statement, but the steady depreciation of the dollar since then shows that Iraq profited handsomely. The euro has gained almost 25 per cent against the dollar since late 2001; and in 2003 Iraq's UN reserve fund had moved from $10 billion to 26 billion euros.

According to a former government analyst, the following scenario would occur if OPEC made an unlikely but sudden collective switch:

> the oil consuming nations would have to flush dollars out of their [central bank] reserve funds and replace these with euros. The dollar would crash anywhere from 20–40% ... and the consequences would be those one could expect from any currency collapse and massive inflation ... You'd have foreign funds stream out of US stock markets and dollar denominated assets ... much like the 1930s ... the budget deficit would go in default ... Your basic 3rd world economic scenario. ... The ultimate result would probably be the US and the EU switching roles in the global economy.[13]

Unlikely but plausible.

There is little doubt that the Iraq war plan was designed for a quick victory, with the US military securing Iraq's vital oilfields at the very onset of hostilities. No wonder then that Kenneth Pollack, in an article entitled "Securing the Gulf" published in the *Foreign Affairs* of July/August 2003, referred to the "sweeping American and British military victory in

Operation Iraqi Freedom [that] has now cleared the way for the United States to try to establish a more durable framework for Persian Gulf security." Even writing in April, which is when he probably did, he would have to have been following Fox News or MSNBC to call the Iraqi campaign a "sweeping victory," and it took the boosters of this war (Pollack wrote *The Threatening Storm: The Case for Invading Iraq*) a long time to come to terms with the Iraqi resistance.

In any event, the need to gain access to Iraqi oil as well as to maintain the dollar's viability in the world's oil trade is where the dream of imposing a Pax Americana on the Arab world begins. Pollack maintains that America's primary interest in the Persian Gulf is to ensure the uninterrupted flow of inexpensive oil to a global economy that would collapse without it. Saudi Arabia, the world's largest oil producer—and, after September 11, an uncertain partner—is the flashpoint; not just because of the Saudi contribution to the bombing of the World Trade Center, but (unmentioned by Pollack) because the kingdom's production capacity is soon due to peak. In February 2004, Matthew Simmons, an investment banker and key adviser of the Bush administration, told CSIS that the extraction of oil in Saudi Arabia will become increasingly difficult. In an assessment disputed by Saudi oil executives, he claimed that, "the easy oil era is over," and cited Ghawar, the world's largest oil field, which has accounted for up to 60 percent of Saudi oil.[14]

Pollack points to internal unrest in other Gulf states: Bahrain, Kuwait, Oman, Qatar, and the United Arab Emirates. But their volatility is nothing alongside the fragility of the long-running Saudi franchise. He argues that the US must prevent any "hostile state from gaining control over the region and its resources and using such control to amass vast power or blackmail the world." But wait a minute. We're in a post-Cold War unipolar universe. Where is the state that is capable of keeping the US out of the Middle East, much less of blackmailing the world? Or the non-state power? This is a setup, a false threat to hide the real threat, which may be called "Peak Oil" in Saudi Arabia, a successful revolt of militant Wahabbi forces against the Saudi princes and their US supporters, or a hostile currency takeover—or all three. When we turn the argument around, as Pollack does, to say that the US must gain control over the region and its resources, it is so Washington can make sure that Middle Eastern oil, *vastly augmented by Iraq's stepped-up contribution*, continues to be traded in dollars.

Pollack makes no reference to the dollar war; but he doesn't have to, since it's understood. Washington's plan to use a US-controlled Iraq as a cockpit for keeping the oil trade, and not just the US oil trade, moving in dollars seems clear enough. For Pollack, the argument points to another rationale for invading Iraq: to position US forces in the heartland of the Persian Gulf, a geostrategically critical location, near the Middle East, Central Asia, Eastern Africa, and South Asia. From this vantage point, Washington will be able to influence events in the key regions of the world. But this is the Council on Foreign Relations speaking (the publisher of *Foreign Affairs*)—so far above the fray as to be without meaning.

A striking feature of President Bush's national security strategy is the web of suspicion it weaves around the intentions of all other nations, be they "conquering states" or "failing" ones. Little wonder then that in Europe only the former Soviet bloc countries, harmless vassals like Romania and Lithuania, are visited by the American president. The fear of the traditional Atlantic alliance seems an oddly paranoid vision for a great power that has "won" the Cold War, and now plans to step forth like a mighty Atlas to carry the burdens of world security on its shoulders. There is a hint of premonition in it, as there sometimes is in the fear of the victor for the left-behind, but this is different.

This is the fear of a military behemoth for the weaknesses that exist on other, non-military levels of power where the game of international relations is played. In *The Paradox of American Power*, Joseph Nye identifies two such levels as (i) economic power, and (ii) the multifarious and proliferating nongovernmental activities that shape the world: currency flows, migration, transnational corporations, NGOs, international agencies, cultural exchanges, the electronic media, the Internet, and terrorism. Non-state actors, including terrorists, communicate and operate across this terrain virtually unconstrained by government interference—although the Bush administration is doing its best to change that through the Patriot Act.

It is only on the military level that the United States appears supreme, and even here, supremacy has not passed the first test of practice. US military success in Afghanistan, for example, dealt with the easy part of the problem, toppling an oppressive and weak government in the poorest of nations. But all the precision bombing that was available to the US military destroyed only a fraction of al Qaeda's network, which still retains cells, according to Nye, in some sixty countries. The burst of fireworks which the Pentagon set off in Afghanistan in retaliation for the terrorist attacks was not, in the end, compelling.

Operation Anaconda in eastern Afghanistan's forbidding Shah-I-kot Valley was a case in point. The largest battle of the war, it took place in March 2002, and shared with earlier battles a recurrent problem. In the days preceding Anaconda's launch, according to *Army Times* writer Sean Naylor, "commanders assured their troops that 'every national asset'—satellites, spy planes, Predator drones—was focused on the valley. Yet despite these high-tech systems, the intelligence estimate failed to accurately portray the enemy's size, location, principal weapons and course of action." While hundreds of al Qaeda fighters were "probably" killed, it was impossible to say how many got away; only that they had included senior enemy leaders.[15] By July, after the Pentagon said it had shifted its strategy to rely more on ground forces, the results were worse. Whole villages were wiped out from the air on the say-so of a warlord settling scores in the province of Oruzgan; a convoy of elders headed for Kabul, who refused to speak up for the warlord's candidacy for governor, was also attacked. The Americans, who were still airborne, had not detained a single Taliban leader but had killed more than eighty civilians in a week's work. And this was "the most accurate war ever fought in the nation's history," according to General Tommy Franks, head of Central Command;[16] a war in which the US kept no records of the Afghan dead.

A report released by the Army War College in November 2002 attested to how quickly al Qaeda had adapted to the weaponry the US used in its attacks, especially the Predator drones. By March, during the Anaconda operation, "al Qaeda forces were practicing systematic communications security, dispersal, camouflage discipline, use of cover and concealment," the Army report said, "and exploitation of dummy fighting positions to draw fire and attention from their real positions." Al Qaeda, according to a senior officer in the special operations community, is "extremely adaptive and very cagey. These guys are not weekend terrorists."[17]

Indeed, the earliest cracks between doctrine and reality in post-Cold War warmaking appeared in the Afghan campaign, which was, one guessed at first, conceived in panic and planned in haste, in a moment best captured by the words of Robert Kagan, writing in the *Washington Post* on September 11: "Congress could immediately declare war. It does not have to name a country. Fortunately, with the Cold War over, there are no immediate threats to prevent us from concentrating our energies and resources on fighting this war on international terrorism as we have never fought it before." But weeks before the terrorist attacks, according to the *Independent*, the US ignored the warning of a Taliban emissary that Osama bin Laden was planning a devastating attack on American soil in the immediate future. It was just one of the reports from over eleven countries that gave advance warning to the US of September 11. This one came from an aide to Wakil Ahmed Muttawakil, the Taliban foreign minister, who was known to be deeply unhappy with the foreign militants in Afghanistan, including the Arabs. Muttawakil, now in Kabul, believed that the Taliban's protection of bin Laden and other al Qaeda militants would lead to the destruction of

Afghanistan by the US military. "The guests are going to destroy the guest-house," he told his aide. But in a peculiar failure of intelligence, the report of the attack was ignored because of what sources described as "warning fatigue." The emissary went first to meet the American consul general in the Pakistani border town of Peshawar, who failed to pass the message on. "We were hearing a lot of that kind of stuff," a diplomatic source said. "When people keep saying the sky's going to fall in and it doesn't, a kind of warning fatigue sets in." So there were other warnings, too. Meanwhile, the aide talked about launching a new Desert Storm—like the campaign to drive Iraq out of Kuwait, but this time called "Mountain Storm," and the foreigners would be driven out of Afghanistan.* The aide also warned that Pakistan should be stopped from supporting the Taliban[18]—which was impossible; for while Pakistan conceded the US right to chase the Taliban out of Afghanistan, the Pakistani president General Pervez Musharraf let them take refuge in Pakistan, in the adjacent Hindu Kush mountains, and in the town of Quetta.

We know that the Taliban was engaged in oil and gas pipeline discussions with Unocal in Houston and Washington in 1997; and that shortly after that, on February 12, 1998, Unocal executive Jack Maresca addressed the House Subcommittee on Asia and the Pacific and urged support for an investor-friendly climate in Afghanistan. "[W]e have made it clear that construction of our proposed pipeline cannot begin until a recognized government is in place that has the confidence of governments, lenders and our company," he said—which suggested reservations about the Taliban. When, later in 1998, the Clinton administration fired cruise missiles at targets in Afghanistan, after terrorists under the Afghan-based Osama bin Laden had bombed US embassies in Kenya and Tanzania, Unocal pulled back from the trans-Afghanistan pipeline, and began to look towards a

---

* The US would wait two and a half years before launching "Mountain Storm" in a US–Pakistani assault in the Hindu Kush mountains in the spring of 2004.

post-Taliban Afghanistan, as did members of the US national security establishment. With the arrival of President Bush and Vice President Dick Cheney, it's likely that discussions with the Taliban were revived and continued until August 2001 (a contention of Jean-Charles Briscard and Guillaume Dasquie in *Bin Laden: The Forbidden Truth*), when they were halted once again because of Taliban demands for "rent": for roads, water supplies, telephone lines, and power lines, as well as a "tap" to provide oil and gas for Afghanistan.

In retrospect, it's easy to see how the terrorist attacks of September 11 gave the United States a passport to invade Afghanistan, oust the Taliban, and install a regime of former Unocal employees—President Hamid Karzai, also a Pashtun royalist, and US envoy Zalmay Khalilzad*—who would have eased the way for the new pipeline system if they had the power. But they did not; and the isolation of the Karzai regime in Kabul became so severe, and attacks by rebels (which now included the Taliban's old enemy, the *mujahedeen* Gulbuddin Hekmatyar) increased to such an extent, that in June 2003 US and Pakistani intelligence officials met with Taliban leaders at the Pakistani Air Force base of Samungli, near Quetta, to explore the basis for a Taliban return to Kabul.[19] Hamid Karzai had already spoken of the willingness of his interim administration to reach out to the Taliban—who might throw their weight behind Karzai and against Defense Minister General Qasim Famin, and his Northern Alliance allies, who were said to be pro-Russian and pro-Iranian. For there was another deal going on in Afghanistan, between the Russian oil company, Rosneft, and Russia's giant gas trader, Itera.

In August 2002, the two companies pledged to rebuild Afghanistan's virtually destroyed petroleum industry, and signed a protocol to that effect with the Afghan Ministry of Mining and Industry. The agreement included

---

* As an adviser for Unocal, the Afghan-born Khalilzad drew up a risk analysis of the proposed gas pipeline from Turkmenistan across Afghanistan and Pakistan to the Indian Ocean.

exploration, development, and production (Soviet geoscientists had discovered the first oil and gas in the country during the 1980s), as well as the domestic and international transport of gas and oil via the proposed pipeline. In short, the Russian companies had revived the trans-Afghanistan pipeline from Turkmenistan's giant Daulatabaud gasfields to Pakistan and India that Unocal had proposed. Feasibility studies were said to be underway, to be completed in March 2003, with the Asian Development Bank (ADB) providing funding.[20]

But on October 27 *Oil and Gas International* reported that the project was "postponed indefinitely." Turkmenistan's president, Saparmurat Niyazov, was responsible for the indefinite delay. The same story stated that a new, unidentified pipeline agreement would be signed by Afghanistan and Pakistan with Niyazov. It was produced by the ministries of energy in each country, in consultation with the ADB, but the sponsors remained unnamed. At the same time, a $2.8 billion US pipeline was mentioned as one of three major international lines planned between either Turkmenistan or Kazakhstan and the Asian markets. And feasibility studies, currently underway, were also due in March 2003.

The most important American media outlets, television networks and major national daily newspapers, had maintained a silence about Central Asian oil projects that amounted to deliberate self-censorship. A rare exception came on September 26, 2001, when Frank Viviano observed in the *San Francisco Chronicle* that "the map of terrorist sanctuaries and targets in the Middle East and Central Asia is also, to an extraordinary degree, a map of the world's principal emerging [energy] sources in the 21st century"; and added that "it was inevitable that the war against terrorism"—starting with Afghanistan—"will be seen ... as a war on behalf of America's Chevron, Exxon, and Arco; France's TotalFinalElf; British Petroleum; Royal Dutch Shell ... which have hundreds of billions of dollars investment in the region." On December 15, 2001, the *New York Times* reported on "post-Taliban energy projects in the region, which has more than 6% of the world's proven oil reserves and almost 40% of its gas reserves." On a visit to Kazakhstan, Secretary of State Colin Powell said he was "particularly impressed" by the money that American oil companies were investing there, and he estimated that $200 billion could flow into Kazakhstan over the next five to ten years.

Cabinet members had flocked to the area accompanied by oil company CEOs, such as David O'Reilly of ChevronTexaco who escorted Secretary of Energy Spencer Abraham in November 2001. During a December 14 visit to Baku, capital of Azerbaijan, Defense Secretary Rumsfeld assured officials of the oil-rich Caspian state that the administration would lift the sanctions imposed in 1992 over a conflict with Armenia. Both Azerbaijan and Armenia had offered the Pentagon transit rights and the use of air-fields, and Rumsfeld's visit was the reward. On November 28, 2001, the White House hailed the opening of the first new pipeline by the Caspian Pipeline Consortium (CPC), a joint venture of Russia, Kazakhstan, Oman, ChevronTexaco, ExxonMobil, and several other oil companies. This pipeline linked the huge Tengiz oilfields in northwestern Kazakhstan to the Russian Black Sea port of Novorossiysk, where tankers were loaded for world markets. The president's press release stated that the "CPC project also advances my Administration's National Energy Policy by developing a network of multiple Caspian pipelines that also includes Baku–Tbilisi–Ceyhan, Baku–Subsa, and Baku–Novorossiysk oil pipelines and the Baku–Tbilisi–Erzurum gas pipeline."[21] But none of them traversed Afghanistan.

These four pipelines preceded the three international lines planned in 2002 to connect Turkmenistan and Kazakhstan with the Asian markets. But there was no press coverage of the announcement, or of the previous story about the "post-Taliban energy projects." Nor did the American media take note that the pipeline consortium involved in the Baku–Tbilisi–Ceylan plan, led by BP, was represented by the law firm of Baker & Potts, and that the principal partner of Baker Potts was James A. Baker III, the Bush family confidante and secretary of state under George H. W. Bush.[22] Just as American military action in Afghanistan was unraveling, and the chance for a trans-Afghanistan pipeline was on hold, investments in the larger region mushroomed.

The United States had gone for the oil and the transit rights, and gotten them, and built its military bases. But it had shortchanged the war; and by June 2003 the resistance network composed of Heckmatyar's forces, the Taliban, and the fighters of Osama bin Laden's International Islamic Front had turned from escalating attacks on foreign soldiers to hit and run raids on the towns of Zabul, Helmand, Kandahar, and Urgan in the south. It was essentially the same resistance that had been mustered against the Soviet Union in its misadventures in the 1980s, only stronger. The Islamic Front was recruiting more fighters from Pakistan and the Central Asian Republics; but the killing fields had expanded too, and now they included Iraq.

I remember reading Michael Klare's "Oil Moves the War," and agreeing with the picture he drew of how President Bush's "two great foreign policy initiatives"—the global war against terrorism, and the global campaign to expand US access to foreign oil—had come together. He cited the national energy policy paper of May 17, 2001, known as the Cheney Report, with its call that "the President make energy security a priority of our trade and foreign policy." The focus on Central Asia was there; in addition to Georgia and Kazakhstan, I learned that permanent bases were going up in Tajikistan, Uzbekistan, and Kyrgyzstan.[23] But something was missing. And that was the recognition that the war on terrorism was largely a farce. The 7000 American troops looking for al Qaeda and the Taliban, and NATO's 4800-strong International Security Assistance Force (later boosted to 12,000 and 6000 respectively), were still stuck in Kabul.

Bush was an oilman who craved military power, and enjoyed using it even more. Yet he had misunderstood the relationship between the selective application of force and real power. Overwhelming military force tends to be degraded when actually used because its flaws and limits become immediately apparent, and the resistance it provokes is unexpected and often effective. The US was a much more intimidating power before the Afghan campaign, contrary to the widespread support that action received, even on the Left, because of the unpopularity of the Taliban and the unquestioned goal of catching Osama bin Laden. But after the raids on Tora Bora late in 2001, the US drew back from any serious effort to capture bin Laden. Whatever the reason—a secret agreement with General Musharraf not to provoke the inevitable retaliation of his own militant Islamists? The coming war with Iraq?—in any event, efforts to capture the world's leading terrorist were put on hold. "The goal has never been to get bin Laden," declared General Richard Meyers, head of the Joint Chiefs of Staff, in an interview on CNN in the spring of 2002.[24] (Only in February 2004 was the hunt resumed, in honor of Bush's reelection campaign, with Task Force 121 fresh from the capture of Saddam Hussein dispatched to the Afghan side of the mountains, while Pakistan's army was assigned to Pakistan's side; but this too soon fell apart.)

Meanwhile, Afghanistan has slipped back into the hands of provincial governors and warlords, a number of them supported by Iran and Russia. Many are growing rich again on the opium trade, after the lean times imposed by the Taliban, who are also back. There is another world out there, an oil world, and it's only partly national, which is to say American or British or French or Russian or Chinese. The companies work in huge consortia out in front of national foreign policies, and by and large eschew military conflict. Like Unocal, most oil companies would prefer a UN-led peace process over a unilateral military intervention. I recall speaking at a conference on the Pacific Rim in Washington in 1968 or 1969, and afterwards being surrounded by young men in suits who asked me intelligent questions about postwar North Vietnam; I said, "You're CIA, aren't you?" and they said, "No, we're from Exxon." They were from the international relations desk, or whatever it was called then. I was impressed.

Now America has its oil services company Halliburton to attend to the military logistics of the business. "I can't think of a time when we've had a region emerge as suddenly to become as strategically significant as the Caspian," said Dick Cheney in 1998, when he was Halliburton's CEO. "Occasionally we have to operate in places where, all things considered, one would not normally choose to go. But we go where the business is."[25] And Halliburton had Kellogg Brown & Root (KBR), whose Government Operations Division was awarded an "open-ended" Pentagon contract in December 2001, which covered everything from running dining facilities to handling fuel and generating power at the giant Khanabad Air Base in Uzbekistan. The Dallas-based company was contracted to build forward operating bases to support troop deployments for the next nine years wherever the president chose to make war on terror—or to protect the pipelines. The British Ministry of Defence awarded KBR $418 million to supply tank transporters, able to carry tanks to the front lines at speeds of up to fifty miles an hour.[26]

Halliburton has close connections with the Bush family. Aside from Cheney, there is Lawrence Eagleburger, a Halliburton director and former deputy secretary of defense under Bush Sr. during the Gulf War; and James Baker, whose law firm represents Halliburton. When Halliburton was Brown & Root Services, it sponsored the stolen election of future president Lyndon B. Johnson to the US Senate in 1948, and thereby helped build the state's spectacular political–industrial machine. Now it is the number one oilfield services company in the world. Its chief competitor, Houston-based Baker Hughes (James Baker again, and Edward P. Djerejian, assistant secretary of state for Near Eastern affairs under both Bush Sr. and Clinton) had a head start in exploiting the immense wealth of natural gas in Uzbekistan, entering into partnership with the state-holding company that controls the oil and gas sector. Uzbekistan is opening up eighty oilfields to drilling by multinational oil companies. And all this after large parts of Afghanistan were reduced to rubble by US bombs.

Actually, the latest chapter in the Great Game, as mastery of the east–west trade routes in Central Asia has long been called, commenced with a forgotten ultimatum. *Give up Osama or face the consequences,*

President Bush ordered the Taliban in October 2001. After a few days of hemming and hawing, Mullah Omar and his crew, in a last-ditch effort to save their jobs, and maybe their country, did just that, or tried to. But Bush slapped the offer away like a pesky fly. He didn't want Osama bin Laden— he wanted Afghanistan, an Afghanistan cleansed of the Taliban. And a few weeks later the bombs began to fall.

Is it ironic, or forward-looking, that the oil industry has protested both the severity of the damage caused by the US bombardment of Afghanistan, and the swiftness with which American authorities have quit the scene? It began on October 29, 2001 when *Oil and Gas International* noted that

> despite how much this terrorist [bin Laden] and his henchmen and the Taliban themselves are despised by most of the civilized world and the majority of Afghans themselves, can that be a justification for the present bombing of the country and soaring number of innocent casualties?… If bin Laden were still in Saudi Arabia, would the same punishment be given that country?

And later: "Now that the 'war on terrorism' is looking elsewhere to find Osama bin Laden or fix upon another target … it is time to think about what can be done to repair the badly damaged proving grounds of phase one of that 'war'—Afghanistan." Forward-looking, no doubt, as oil people usually are. The magazine continued:

> There is a place for the international petroleum industry in this undertaking— a role that might be led by the likes of Unocal, which once thought to pipe a million b/d of Caspian oil and a comparable amount of gas across Afghanistan to market in Pakistan and perhaps India—a profitable project that would not only bring sorely needed revenue to the impoverished nation, but jobs and industry as well.[27]

But no reparations were forthcoming, not from Unocal, and not from any other company.

There was a time when reconstruction was discussed, when the decades of destruction that had made Afghanistan so vulnerable to the fanaticism of the Taliban and the whims of its warlords was considered reversible, but that time was brief, and the discussion superficial. What the US accomplished in Afghanistan was a feat of destruction. It has built a highway to connect Kabul and Kandahar, but the country which was the site of a multibillion dollar war has remained among the poorest in the world.

Bottom Lines

Oil Shares

In 1999, planet Earth had about six billion human dependents. Fewer than one-fifth of us (18.6 percent or 1.1 billion) lived in the twenty-four industrial countries of the OECD. The US population accounted for about one-quarter of this "rich country" total, or 4.6 percent of humanity.

In that year, more than one-quarter of all world oil use occurred in the US, at a rate of 1096 gallons per person. The other 23 OECD countries averaged 427 gallons per person. The other four-fifths of the people on the planet used just 101 gallons per person, less than one-tenth of the per capita consumption in the US.

Lifetime Consumption Burdens

The world's richest countries, with 20 percent of the global population, account for 86 percent of private consumption; the poorest 20 percent account for just 1.3 percent. A child born today in an industrialized country will add more to consumption and pollution over his or her lifetime than thirty to fifty children born in developing countries.

THE END OF DETERRENCE

September 22, 2002, *Los Angeles Times*

On Friday, in a national security document prepared for Congress, President Bush described more completely than ever before the cornerstone of his administration's overhaul of US military strategy: that is, the strategic doctrine of preemptive action which underlies his drive to topple the regime in Baghdad.

Most Americans learned of this radical departure from traditional bipartisan policies of deterrence and containment (where you don't shoot people unless they threaten you directly) when President Bush told the graduating class at West Point in June 2002 that US security requires "a military … ready to strike at a moment's notice in any dark corner of the world," one that will "be ready for preemptive action when necessary to defend our liberty and … our lives."

This new first-strike doctrine, however, far from being a response to September 11, as many suppose, has been around for at least a decade, ever since defense planners began to toil and trouble over a post-Cold War strategy where opposing forces could no longer be held in check by mutually assured destruction and backroom deals between Moscow and Washington.

The strategy was spelled out for the first time in the "National Security Guidance" prepared for the Pentagon in 1992 by Paul Wolfowitz and Lewis "Scooter" Libby—today, respectively, Defense Secretary Donald Rumsfeld's No. 2 man and Vice President Dick Cheney's chief of staff. It was an oddly paranoid document, considering that the US had just emerged triumphant from a forty-year contest with the "evil empire." The brand new "unipolar" world, it seemed, had become infinitely more perilous.

Our allies ("regional hegemons" in the document's lingo) were seen as "potential competitors" who had to be prevented from "aspiring to a larger regional or global role" than we assigned them. US military intervention would become "a constant feature" of world affairs.

The US would "retain preeminent responsibility for addressing selectively those wrongs which threaten not only our interests, but those of our allies or friends." A first-strike option, "preemption," was designed for potentially hostile states engaged in the development of weapons of mass destruction—a strategy the president embraced this year.

One thinks of Secretary of State Dean Rusk's nightmare during the Vietnam years when he said: "The world is round. Only one-third of its people are asleep at any one time. The other two-thirds are awake and causing mischief somewhere." With North Vietnam's diplomatic and military victories over the United States, Rusk's world really had slipped its traces. In 1991, however, the US was top banana.

So what explains the projection of force as the solution to every conflict, even potential conflicts? And what is the source of the overweening contempt for dialogue—for "laws and rules and transnational negotiation and cooperation," which the conservative writer Robert Kagan, in an essay in *Policy Review*, calls the "tactics of the weak"? "[N]ow that the United States is powerful, it behaves as powerful nations do. ... The 'unipolar moment,' he asserts, "[has] made the United States more willing to use force abroad."

But surely Kagan, whose United States inhabits a "world where power is the ultimate determinant of national security and success," confuses force with power. As do Wolfowitz and the irrepressible Richard Perle, assistant secretary of defense under Reagan who now helps orchestrate the attack-Iraq campaign from his chairs at the Defense Policy Board and the American Enterprise Institute. These first-strike spokesmen include William Kristol, co-editor with Kagan of *Present Dangers*, which argues for the missile defense shield and a massive military buildup, and *New York Times* columnist William Safire, who has leaped into the ring against Brent Scowcroft "and his leave-Saddam-alone acolytes."

True power, as Machiavelli and Confucius knew, asserts itself through countless channels, mostly pacific. On this score, Vietnam taught the US a hard lesson, or tried to. "The amount of violence at the disposal of any given country," political philosopher Hannah Arendt noted in 1969, "may soon not be a reliable indication of the country's strength or a reliable guarantee against destruction by a substantially smaller and weaker power." She foresaw a "complete reversal in the relationship between power and violence, foreshadowing another reversal in the future relationship between small and great powers."

This reversal is very likely the nightmare that haunts today's defense ideo-logues—and the inspiration for the administration's assertion in its new policy statement that the US must never again allow its military supremacy to be challenged as it was during the Cold War.

Bush's advisers are not stupid, after all, and must contend with the legacy of the Vietnam War. The hawks' widespread aversion to Secretary of State Colin Powell (with whom Wolfowitz, then No. 3 man in the Pentagon, quarreled during the Gulf War) is probably partly because he reminds them of Vietnam.

In any event, try substituting "Ho Chi Minh" for the "aggressive despot" in Safire's case for preemptive action against Iraq: "The need to strike at an aggressive despot before he gains the power to blackmail us with the horrific weapons he is building … is apparent to most Americans."

In Vietnam, the "horrific" weapon was a hard-fought war of national liberation, materially supported by Moscow and (less so) Beijing but not controlled by either, and therefore not subject to Cold War arm-twisting. Once we decided to invade, the US had to fight essentially on Vietnamese terms, as well as from our chosen position in the sky.

"If only we had taken Ho out in 1965, think of the losses we would have avoided, including the blow to US military prestige." Such, one imagines, is the intelligent war planner's version of General Curtis E. LeMay's take on Vietnam: "They have got to draw in their horns and stop their aggression, or we are going to bomb them back to the Stone Age!"

Arendt's "complete reversal," meanwhile, is the true portent of the September 11 attacks, whose perpetrators operated out of a half-dozen countries, including our own, without being accountable to any government. This statelessness, together with the ability to turn the might of US technology itself into terrible weapons against the US, sets Osama bin Laden's network outside the parameters of conventional international security systems. It's hard to imagine a "force posture" capable of trapping such chameleons, but if you want a big bang to divert attention from your failure to cope with the paradoxical nature of power in the real world, then bomb Iraq.

THE BIG PICTURE

October 24, 2002, *Lincoln County Weekly*

President Bush's victory in Congress came despite the heroic efforts of Senator Robert A. Byrd, so reminiscent of another Southern gentleman, Senator Sam Ervin, who presided over the Watergate Hearings with the same old-fashioned rectitude. Like Ervin, Byrd is still capable of outraged common sense, and of flights of oratory grounded in history and the classics, together with a reverence for the Constitution that summons the Enlightenment world of the "Framers" as few others have.

Byrd saw through the attack-Iraq campaign so assiduously crafted over the preceding weeks. It began with Bush's "emotional" September 11 speech, and the "tougher" UN address of September 12, followed by the presentation of the lengthy national security statement on preemptive war to Congress on September 20, the Iraq resolution of October 1, and the modified resolution and "softer" speeches the next week. All served to reinforce the demonization of Saddam Hussein.

Twenty-three senators opposed the resolution, more than one expected listening to the debate (but less proportionately than the 133 who stood up to Bush in the House). The battle was probably lost from the start, if only because of the president's success in harnessing the genuine fear in the land since September 11 to the case for a war that nobody really wants.

"Weapons of Mass Distraction," cartoonist Mike Peters calls Saddam Hussein's symbols of terror in Iraq, which, like the butcher of Baghdad himself, help keep the US populace from brooding over a foundering economy—or seeking accountability from Republican leaders. Or, more important, from confronting the big picture; one that snapped into focus with punishing clarity the day after Bush's victory.

When the White House presented its plan to install a US-led military government in Baghdad when Saddam was driven from power, one modeled (complete with war crimes trials) on the post-World War II occupation of Japan, Iraq finally took its place in the Larger Scheme of Things. As long as the US and Britain (the "coalition") administer Iraq, they will control the second largest reserves of oil in the world, nearly 11 percent of the earth's proven resources. From such a pivot, anything is possible, including, for the oil cabal in Washington, a long-desired reorganization of OPEC.

Iraq hasn't posed a danger to the US for years. From Israel comes the observation that if "you had told Israeli leaders and analysts two years ago that the US would be on the verge of attacking Iraq today, they would have been astonished. ... The dominant perception across the political spectrum," writes the *Jerusalem Post*'s Barry Rubin, "was that Iraq was not a serious threat." Why? Because "international sanctions had ... weakened the Iraqi regime's power ... [Saddam's] armed forces were in bad shape, he was short of money, had great trouble importing new weapons or spare parts, and did not have a single ally." Conditions have worsened immeasurably since Britain and the US have stepped up the bombing, not only in the no-fly zones but beyond them.

This is not to suggest that Israel doesn't expect to gain from a US takeover of Iraq—it does, though it would prefer to see the campaign move on to incorporate regime change in Tehran and Damascus. Another story.

In any event, when the White House rolled out the attack-Iraq carpet in September (because, as chief-of-staff Andrew Card remarked, "You don't introduce new products in August"), it was faced with the formidable task of creating a threat worthy of the military might it had already thrown into the Middle East. This includes more than a dozen new bases throughout the Gulf and Central Asia, with the number-one oilfield services company, Dick Cheney's Halliburton, overseeing the construction of every one.

On October 6, *Newsweek* reported that a division's worth of Abrams main battle tanks had disappeared from Europe and may have been spotted atop transport trucks in Kuwait. Meanwhile, US Special Forces teams, along with Mossad agents from Israel, have been quietly hunting Scud missiles and probing defenses *inside* Iraq for months. In forward operating bases throughout the Gulf region, more than 60,000 American troops are waiting.

The attack-Iraq campaign was alternately aimed at the American public, lawmakers, the UN Security Council, even Iraq—whose soldiers were enjoined in a mass leaflet drop on October 9 from firing back at "coalition" bombers. OpEd pages, talk shows, the floors of Congress, the international media, the Internet—all entered into a grand debate over issues largely hand-picked by the White House to obscure the facts in the Middle East. Now that this cynical leadership has nailed its coonskin to the wall in Congress, victory in the UN seems inevitable.

It doesn't matter whether Iraq agrees to weapons inspections or not, for President Bush it's a no-lose situation either way. Under the proposed UN resolution, decisions about which sites should be "inspected" are to be made not by the UN alone but also by "any permanent member of the Security Council," such as us. The inspectors can also be chosen by Washington, and they will enjoy "unrestricted rights of entry into and out of Iraq," along with "the right to free, unrestricted and immediate movement" within Iraq, "including unrestricted access to presidential sites." They will be allowed to establish "regional bases and operating bases," where they will be "accompanied … by sufficient US security forces to protect them." They can declare additional no-fly zones and "ground and air transit corridors," fly and land as many planes, helicopters and surveillance drones in Iraq as they wish, and seize "any equipment" they choose to lay their hands on.

The resolution the United States has placed before the Security Council—the one in which so many worried members of Congress placed their faith—is an invasion plan, unopposed.

4

MAKING WAVES

On Wednesday, August 28, 2002, about fifty people turned up at Senator Susan Collins's office in Augusta to meet with her rep, Bill Card, and register their grievances about the oncoming war. It was an early MoveOn.org action, a clever blend of local and national organizing, with small groups presenting their views, along with a petition representing a larger set of views, to two senators in every state, at the same time, all across the country. I was a "local leader," along with Emanuel Pariser, who was Eli Pariser's Dad. Eli, MoveOn's National Coordinator, was in the group too, as "Elijah Pariser," along with at least one more member of MoveOn's tiny collective, Noah Winer, and Eli's Mom. A couple of days before we met, somebody who knew him said Eli was twenty-one, and I had a chuckle over that. It was one thing to discover that the fellow whose name was on all that Internet mail, lived (at the time) just thirty-five miles up the coast in Camden, Maine, and quite another to learn he was a year younger than my son Simon.

It was odd to go back into action after thirty years by lobbying a Republican Senator, even a "moderate" Republican, but times have changed. Most US senators are Republican, and most Republicans are conservatives. Most lobbyists are well-paid professionals. The US Congress is a well-oiled machine for delivering votes in preordained directions; not that money talks. But money talks. That's the way it goes. With its command of the Internet, which is to say of all those unknown people who sit silently at their stations, chatting, shuttling information back and forth, "googling" for new stuff, MoveOn.org is in the van of a revolution against Big Money. And Eli knows how to do it:

> Dear Local Leader: A few notes for you as we enter the final stretch. ... If you wish, you can download the petition for your state at [site]. ... If you wish to print it out, be prepared with plenty of paper—it averages a little under 10 comments per page. ... You may want to ask a copy shop to do this—we can reimburse you for the printing costs. ... If you haven't cut off registration for your meeting, it's quite likely that folks will be registering through Tuesday. If the time or location of your meeting has changed ... we advise emailing the list on Tuesday night to make sure everyone's up to date.

MoveOn had heard that security procedures at many Senate offices were "pretty rigorous," so Photo ID was urged. As for numbers, "any group bigger than zero will make an impact. Especially if the weather isn't good ... remember the thousands of people who signed MoveOn's petition." The problem might come if *more* showed up, and a few solutions were suggested; but ultimately it was up to us, though we were advised to discuss the possibilities (online) with other local leaders. The idea was clearly to bring all those strangers together. The "worksheet" had indicated that on Monday, MoveOn would be inviting members of its lists (which had already reached 500,000) to "drop in" on the meetings in their state, but given that most meetings were now full and some had hundreds of participants, this wouldn't be done. List members instead were encouraged to sign the petitions, and invite "their friends and family" to sign, thereby increasing by "hundreds or thousands" the people represented at each meeting.

A local leader in Atlanta suggested asking for a written response from the Senator. It was "a great way of underlining our message," Eli agreed. If we didn't have time to come up with our own queries, we could use the other person's. And there followed "Our Questions for Senator Max Cleland [the paraplegic Vietnam veteran who was defeated in November 2002]. 1. Will You Assert The Constitutional Authority Of Congress In Any Decision To Declare War On Iraq? 2. Will You Ask The Bush Administration Tough Questions Regarding War With Iraq?" Among them,

Why don't our allies support a preemptive strike against Iraq? What are the long-term consequences of a US "go-it-alone" approach in a war with Iraq? How would a US war with Iraq affect the stability of the Middle East?... What impact will American action have on governments such as Jordan, Egypt, Saudi Arabia, Pakistan and Turkey?... How would the Administration keep a post-Saddam Iraq together and avoid a balkanized outcome?

On September 12, the president delivered his much ballyhooed UN speech. Eli was on top of that too, praising it as great marketing, noting that it was a day after September 11, which was, according to administration sources, "a centerpiece of the strategy," helping to "move Americans toward support of action against Iraq." But the speech had nothing to say. The case wasn't made. All the old grievances were "entirely unsubstantiated" or "based on the testimony of sworn enemies of Saddam Hussein." (And the reader was linked to articles in the *New York Times* and CNN.) "We need to let Congress know that we see through this promotional campaign," Eli said. "Please call your Senators today at [their names and numbers]. Ask the questions that concern you. Here are some ... that we've heard: Where's the beef? Where's the evidence of clear and present danger? What happened to bin Laden and al Qaeda? If our allies don't support this, are we going ahead or not?... " We were asked to let MoveOn know if we called, because, Eli said, "we'd like to keep a count. Your call will build on the momentum started September 9 and 10 by Peace Action's national call-in days."

MoveOn often built on the momentum of other organizations, but nobody could raise money as plentifully and quickly as it could. Overnight in October 2002 it took in the $200,000 that Walter Mondale needed to run in deceased Wisconsin Senator Paul Wellstone's place. (He lost.) MoveOn came up with the names of its favorite four candidates running against the war, and invited its lists (now over 650,000) to support them. One million dollars were raised, but none of the candidates won.

Eli ploughed on. He never spoke of the losses but focused only on the gains: the growing membership list, the speed with which money could be raised, the *amounts* of money. His delight was palpable, I knew, because I saw it on August 28, when he loped around the edges of the crowd, and spoke excitedly about how many people were turning out in North Dakota, Texas, Arkansas, Alabama, as if by magic. He was all business, though he worked with a gentle touch, not forgetting anything, picking up suggestions from the field, laying it all out so that even a neophyte could understand the process.

MoveOn, which was started in 1998 to stop the Clinton impeachment campaign by two former software entrepreneurs, Wes Boyd and Joan Blades, had become the mouthpiece—or rather the organizer—of the great washed middle class. In the 1960s, it had taken years to mobilize this kind of crowd. Or so it was said when it seemed as if nearly everybody was against the war. Former national security chief Brent Scowcroft, Republican Senator Dick Armey, former head of Central Command for the Middle East, Anthony Zinni, even Henry Kissinger spoke up against the go-it-alone war. But no one put it better than the voices from Maine, who wondered about American "fascination with ... the collusion among corporations, the legislature and the military [which] continues as we watch George W. Bush strutting to the podium in a kind of buffed, buffoon-like caricature of Mussolini ..." Perhaps the "practice of democracy [is] too burdensome, too taxing ... too complex ...?" (Dick Bernard).

Or is the US "taking us to war at a time when its global economic system is exposing itself as a failure and a fraud ...? Is this mere coincidence?" (Stephen F. Kelley) Back then, it seemed as if the power was all on the American side, and that what was coming wasn't "a war" at all, but "a massacre" (Mark duBay).[1]

When the big antiwar demos were organized on October 26, January 15, February 15, and March 22, 2003, Eli was much in demand as a speaker. He was uneasy with the old left groups that ran A.N.S.W.E.R. (Act Now to Stop War and End Racism) and NION (Not In Our Name), and uncomfortable with the pro-Palestinian brigades, though he kept his public mouth shut about them. "I've always been a real believer that the best ideas win out if you let them happen," he said.[2] He saw his job as bringing in new "folks" who hadn't participated in an action before. And by and large this was who came out to meet Susan Collins and Olympia Snow, Maine's other Republican senator: School teachers and nurses, college students, fishermen, retired people, filmmakers.

A fisherman, blond, fortyish, accompanied by his wife, said he saw something on TV that morning he couldn't believe: Ashcroft saying "it's not necessary to have a majority to do what's right," and how "lonely it gets" doing right. "We don't need a majority to go to war?" the man asked. "A thing we've never done unprovoked? And who says what's right!" He knew a lot of fishermen who would have come if they thought it would make a difference. They were there for their boy who had just turned eighteen, and they were scared for him and for the country. "How many kids will have to go and die," he said, "because a couple of guys in the White House say it's *right?*"

Everyone had prepared a brief statement to present to the staff person; and the contrast between the seriousness and care with which they spoke, and the presentations made by the White House, was profound. A female filmmaker talked of traveling through the world, and how the US was no longer looked at as a good guy, but with fear. "You get to know someone, and it's not long before they say, 'What's happening to your country?'"

A silver-haired man wearing a pink dress shirt protested "the lack of transparency in the Bush administration. Their real activities," he said, "are not what we've been told." He was sure this applied to Iraq, and that the duplicity "was related to oil."

Bill Card had started writing rapidly; exhibiting "writing behavior," I believe it's called. The larger group had broken up into six-person teams to meet in Card's office for about eighteen minutes each. He had never seen anything like it; had obviously expected a protest crowd, large and unruly; not this quiet, well-spoken stream of voices, lobbying against a war which was already in preparation, though neither Card nor most us knew it at the time. A few days before, he had asked for a copy of the press release we had written—the word "press" terrified him—and I had sent it, though it occurred to me that I should have consulted Eli first, and this led to another fax. "He saw nothing wrong with my sending it to you as a gesture of goodwill," I wrote, and "reminds me that we are addressing our Senators nationwide as constituents, and that it's not up to their offices to review or judge our public positions." The wording of this message was just right; I never would have thought of it. After the fourth or fifth team emerged, Emanuel Pariser said that Bill Card would like to come out and talk to everyone; but most of us had left for the press conference, and never heard what he had to say.

The press conference was scheduled for 4 pm on the open roof of the state employees' parking garage; an excellent choice, since many of us would be collecting our vehicles there, and because it was both public and private, and almost deserted. Emanuel, who had proposed it, reminded me that Deep Throat met the press in the basement of a federal parking garage in Washington. When we arrived, there was the TV van from Channel 5 and Charlotte Renner from NPR and somebody from AP; Charlotte had already defied the prohibition on press participation, and simply walked into one of Olympia Snow's meetings. Now she was wrapping up her story, and needed a few more statements. The local Channel 5 reporter looked like a high-school girl, and was busy interviewing a volunteer from the Collins' group. The AP man was a dud. "What arrangements have you made so that Iraq doesn't use weapons of mass destruction?" he asked. *Huh?* That was the national media speaking, tired and bored with this provincial protest—which was also happening at a hundred other places at the same time.

On January 22, 2003 MoveOn.org wrote to thank its membership. "We exceeded our wildest dreams," said the MoveOn Team: Carrie, Eli, Joan, Peter, Randall, Wes, and Zack. "Our plan was to launch an antiwar television ad campaign, hold 12 local press conferences, grow our 'Let the Inspections Work' petition, and have meetings in Congressional offices around the country," they said. "We knew it would be big. But we never thought it would be this big." One hundred thousand new members had joined in a week; 310,000 people signed the petition. The "Let the Inspections Work" message was aired on most major TV news shows, and George Stephanopoulus showed the petition to Defense Secretary Donald Rumsfeld, and grilled him on the dangers of war. News programs in Australia, Pakistan, Russia, and Japan had broadcast the petition and discussed it.

A new national poll showed public support for the war was dropping, while front-page stories discussed the breadth and tactics of the burgeoning antiwar movement. In October, Congress had voted to support Bush's war resolution. But MoveOn was unperturbed. Now it was the Congressional meetings over the inspections that engaged its attention, and the results were thrilling. "It was fantastic! Probably the best meeting I've ever been at—ever," one member wrote. "Eighteen regular people who came together as strangers were in agreement with one another, speaking eloquently, passionately, respectfully and from the heart." Over thirty members of Congress signed onto a Dear Colleague letter to the president, asking him to let the inspectors do their jobs and abide by the UN process. *Congress was taking up their petition!* "In one of our most exciting moments," MoveOn continued, "a pro-war-resolution Representative took a look at the letter, listened to our members, and then signed on the spot. Now that's democracy in action!"

What was going on? Together with Win Without War, the American Friends Service Committee, Business Leaders for Sensible Priorities, Global Exchange, Greenpeace, Leadership Conference of Women Religious, NAACP, National Council of Churches, National Organization for Women, New England Health Care Employees Union, Peace Action, Physicians for Social Responsibility, Sierra Club, Sojourners, Tikkun Community, TrueMajority, United Methodist Church, Us Foundation, Veterans for Common Sense, Women's Action for New Directions, and Working Assets, MoveOn had produced a series of events that gave the media, some of it anyway, something to talk about. The attention MoveOn gave the mass media was unseemly but inevitable. The media was all-powerful, and shimmered like a bright, shining lie over the heads of millions and millions of people; and was no more "free" than a media without a message, one that said simply *Shop*. But there was nothing else, no other way to show how the people felt; and MoveOn focused on the programs that focused on them.

The media was so important that the Pentagon had procured the bureau chiefs to embed 300 reporters with the outgoing troops—if, that is, there was a war. This *if*, spoken with marmoreal sweetness by the heads of the embed program as late as February, was a clue that the whole period of dissent was a farce, as far as President Bush was concerned. The protesters were like a marketing "focus group," he said, and who in their right mind would use a "focus group" to decide matters of peace and war. But the street demos were building, and the times really did seem to be changing. The handmade signs, for instance. "Can you beat these?" I e-mailed friends in New York: "BODY BAGS AND TAXES ARE FOR THE LITTLE PEOPLE. ... AXES OF ASSES. ... LET'S BOMB TEXAS, THEY HAVE OIL TOO. ... WATCH OUT FOR MAD COWBOY DISEASE, and on a dog, I BARK FOR PEACE, and another, I DO NOT

LIKE BONES OF CONTENTION." Signs like these were unheard of in the '60s. They were from a February 15 march I went to in Portland, which wound around a part of the city I didn't know, and produced many familiar faces I hadn't seen since Simon had graduated from high school.

February 15 was an international success, with the BBC reporting 750,000 people converging on Hyde Park, 100,000 in Dublin, and 25,000 rallying in Glasgow. The largest rallies were in London, where Tariq Ali reported 1,200,000, along with 2,000,000 in Rome and 250,000 in Berlin, "the biggest since the wall came down." But there were also protests in Canberra and Oslo and Cape Town and Damascus. "It was truly amazing … a day when history kisses you on the mouth," said Tariq, and he found "a real feeling of internationalism that was like the old days." March 22, after the war began, was another big turnout, larger in Europe than in the US, where a mere 200,000 gathered in New York; more in countries where the government supported the US, like Italy and the UK.

Tom Englehardt wrote on his online blog: "It was increasingly clear that the people of the world do not want this war. … And several hundred years of 'the people' in all their complicated reality tells us that this is something governments ignore at their long-term peril." He quoted Alexander Cockburn: "In short, protests count, just as they did in the very earliest days of organizing against the war in Vietnam"; and Cockburn quoted antiwar veteran Lawrence Reichard, today a union organizer in Stockton, California. "To the absolute fury of the right wing, the antiwar movement of yesterday … shackles this country's ability to wage unfettered war," Reichard said, not without foresight. "Right off the bat, they have to forget about any war that might last more than six months or cost more than a few hundred US lives. For this, you can thank the peace movement and the Vietnamese, who, at tremendous cost, beat us militarily."[3]

Not all the old antiwar voices were in accord. At a New York University event in December 2002, former SDS president Todd Gitlin spoke out against the "various flavors of old left nostalgia," the "left-wing groupuscules" who considered "the no-fly zones that afford some protection to the

Kurds and Shi'ites illegitimate; who ... think the military action in Afghanistan illegitimate ..." Gitlin, who wrote *The Sixties: Years of Hope, Days of Rage* in 1989, and *Letters to a Young Activist* in 2003, had latched on to the Iraqi exile, Kanan Makiya, and trundled out the latter's belief that by deposing Saddam Hussein and occupying Iraq, "the US would install the first democratic regime in the Arab world; a regime that ... would undermine the autocratic consensus that governs the region, reverse the Islamist movement," and so on. That, of course, became the US government line, though Gitlin was smart enough to know that an American war in Iraq was unlikely to bring such a regime about. On the contrary, war was more likely to bring about raw carnage, including the use of weapons of mass destruction and more recruits for al Qaeda. So he called for containment: "smart sanctions," no-fly zones, and "inspections with teeth under multilateral, UN auspices. ..." You had to call for something. "The negative knee-jerk is not a policy. ... The Bush doctrine," said Gitlin, "requires of a saner, more sober America something more intelligent"—like the embrace of UN-imposed inspections, "proportionate to the threat, and therefore just." Smartness and sanity and sobriety were important grown-up values, with a future. "An antiwar movement that simply reflexively opposes Bush has none."[4]

Meanwhile, Donald Rumsfeld was raising hackles in "Old Europe" and making it more difficult for France, Germany and other countries to make behind-the-scenes compromises with the US, if that was their plan. "Sometimes the stalking horse gets a little far out in front of the parade," a White House official said nervously.[5] But Bush stood behind him. Rumsfeld was in fact talking to Americans. He was working doubletime to build a following for a war that would, in fact, look no more like the one he planned than the one some antiwarriors conjured up.

"In our name, a half million human beings are being threatened with death in the next few weeks—dreadful deaths not unlike those of the victims of 9/11, except far greater numbers will be burned and crushed and suffocated ..." This was Peter Matthiessen, writing *in extremis* in *Orion* in February. The planned "shock and awe" armadas of bombs and rockets "hit" Americans especially hard, convincing Matthiessen that they will "effectively remove any impulse to resist, especially in those that were killed." Iraqis were an "essentially defenseless people ..."; and "the precedent set by a preemptive attack upon Iraq may one day be seen as the single most catastrophic blunder in American history." A Buzzflash commentary concluded that "It doesn't matter if five million people march in New York City on February 15. ... Once the guns begin to roar, the Bush Cartel, as it's been called, will write the dark history."[6]

Eli Pariser never made any predictions but labored on, keeping his growing membership busy, soliciting ideas for TV and newspaper ads, running the "10 best" ads and tallying up the votes. In the fall of 2003, he asked MoveOn's 1,500,000 members to vote for their favorite Democratic presidential candidate, and while most votes went to Howard Dean, the choices were surprisingly eclectic. The vote was for the membership; by and large Eli stayed away from the primaries. When it became clear that John Kerry was the Democrat's choice, he went into action. "We'll work via the Internet, the telephone, and face to face conversations with voters. And we'll take back our democracy," he said, "city by city, block by block, and voter by voter."

The war, when it came, was a surprise. On March 23, three days after it began, Susan Sontag recalled the "violent light and sound show ... displayed on maybe a billion TVs worldwide, while scores of embedded reporters checked in from their square inch of sand as an American advance swept through the deserts. ..." Already it reminded her of Vietnam, though "in fast-forward time." The first "fragging" (the killing of a US officer) had taken place in a Kuwaiti camp. The equivalent of the "Christmas bombings" of Hanoi in 1972—when Nixon and Kissinger tried to shock and awe North Vietnam's leaders into better peace terms—happened at the start of this war. The first American POWs had appeared on Iraqi television, also a later phenomenon of Vietnam. And an unexpected word appeared in a news briefing about the fighting in the port city of Umm Qasir: *guerrilla*.[7]

The parallels between Iraq and Vietnam were obvious, but Iraq is not the problem, said Bobby Muller, president of the Vietnam Veterans of America Foundation. "Iraq will be over in a few days. The problem [is] an ideology that is controlling this administration [which] has to do with how you look at ... America's role in the world. It's called the Bush doctrine." And Muller laid out the history, starting in 1992 when then secretary of defense Cheney and Paul Wolfowitz leaked the draft of a plan for the aggressive establishment of American dominance in the post-Cold War era. It sparked a firestorm, and Bush I repudiated it; but it resurfaced in 1997 with the Project for the New American Century, and was taken up by William Kristol, Cheney, Wolfowitz, and Rumsfeld, among others. In September 2002 it found a home in the National Security Strategy. The NSS was the subject of Muller's talk, and he wanted his audience to know that "we are more than a decade behind in understanding the magnitude of what we are up against. ..."[8]

Muller got Iraq all wrong, and he was only partly right about the ideology—which we heard about endlessly as the war wound on. Missing was the payola: the mad rush to substitute America's military superiority for its growing economic inferiority; to win by force what it was losing over the cash barrel, as the region's oil producers flirted with the euro, and US petrodollars stood on the brink. But nobody knew about that; everybody was talking about weapons of mass destruction, or yellowcake uranium, or the Butcher of Baghdad, or our evangelical president, or Israel, or the Project for the New American Century, or all the other false cues the Bush administration threw out to the American public in the months leading up to the war, not all of which were false. Everybody but MoveOn, that is, who just kept moving on.

You never knew how Eli Pariser read the war, not from his online presence. You suspect he would agree with Senator Robert Byrd of West

Virginia, who said on February 12, 2003: "This war is not necessary at this time. ... Our mistake was to put ourselves in a corner so quickly. Our challenge is to now find a graceful way out of a box of our own making. Perhaps there is still a way if we allow more time." But for Eli, who had raised a vast new constituency against the war, each "way" was a step on the ladder of change.

THE DANCE OF THE WARRIOR BEES

January 12, 2003, *Boston Globe*

Here comes North Korea, a runaway starveling from the fallen Communist bloc, rattling its keys to the Bomb in Uncle Sam's face. And wouldn't you know it, the world's supercop has turned the other cheek.

Why? Because of Iraq, where there are no plutonium reprocessing plants such as the one Kim Jong Il has unlocked in Yongbyon. Nor is there evidence in Iraq of a single nuclear weapon, or of missiles with the delivery capability of Pyongyang's, much less high-tech weaponry for sale to dubious customers, like the Scud missiles North Korea recently sold to Yemen.

In Iraq there is oil. And by now many people have concluded that if the United States gains access to the world's second largest oil reserves, it will dominate global oil markets, thereby lowering energy prices and reviving the American economy, while undercutting OPEC and patrolling Saudi Arabia (an al Qaeda safehouse).

Such outcomes may ornament civilian defense planning. But the prospect of an invasion of Iraq has sent oil and gas prices higher and disrupted economic recovery everywhere. Energy experts who met in Washington on November 12 predicted the Iraqi war could push the cost of crude up to $80 a barrel (it's $33 a barrel now), in which case "the global economy would be destroyed."

There is a growing gap between the image and reality of American promises, and perhaps of American power itself, which is brought to the fore with Washington's response to North Korea's defiance. Not that anything's wrong with President Bush's resort to diplomacy, even if it is other people's diplomacy. The drama of negotiations is full of surprises—as when South Korea emerged as North Korea's advocate (viz. the *Korea Times* headline: "Seoul will ask US to guarantee survival of N. Korea").

Unilateralists squirm at this violation of the new national security strategy, which scorns international agreements, including nonproliferation treaties that have failed to prevent many countries from obtaining weapons of mass destruction. In their place, the United States has substituted a doctrine of "counterproliferation" that asserts America's right to forcibly dismantle the offending weapons. Theoretically, that is. In practice, "counterproliferation" is reserved for Iraq.

The gap between doctrine and reality in US policy began with the retaliatory campaign in Afghanistan, which was planned in response to the overwhelming call for military action against al Qaeda and the Taliban that followed September 11. Conceived as a blitz, Afghanistan has emerged as a sinkhole for the United States, as it was for the Soviet Union. It has failed to capture Osama bin Laden or to destroy the Taliban, but it has destabilized Pakistan, a tinderbox of radical Islam.

Pakistan, which first sold fissionable materials to North Korea, is the only country in the larger Middle East, other than Israel, that possesses nuclear weapons. Alongside Iraq's negligible threat to regional security, Pakistan's potential for trouble is terrifying. Yet while the United States is moving on to Iraq, its real foes have dug in for a long fight in both Afghanistan and Pakistan.

By virtue of its matchless military strength, the US stands alone in the world and, in the words of the national security statement, would "not hesitate to act alone to exercise our right to self-defense by acting preemptively." But the first-strike doctrine is not actionable by a nation that deploys carrier battle groups in every ocean, and projects on to the ravaged face of Iraq an impossible dream, one of reordering the entire Middle East. It's not actionable except by unmanned Predator attacks on roving terrorists, as in Yemen; and North Korea knows it.

Contrary to what Donald Rumsfeld says, the United States is not prepared to open a second front in Korea, and Pyongyang knows that, too; as does China and a worried Japan. Washington is more likely to bow to Seoul's wishes that the US troops in South Korea go home.

"America," says the strategy document, "is now threatened less by conquering states than … by failing ones." That is true, but the Bush team has missed the full import of the threat. The boldness of rogue nations such as North Korea, and of terrorist groups whose proliferation is underreported in the United States, is traceable, in part, to the strategic confusion that has become the hallmark of the war on terrorism.

Robert Kagan was only half right about the post-Cold War vacuum in which the United States marches. The Red Queen is gone, true, but the warrior bees are swarming.

US MILITARY PLANS THE WAR OF WORDS

February 19, 2003, *Los Angeles Times*

It's time to take a close look at the Defense Department's plan for managing the press during the impending invasion of Iraq. Called "embedding," it will position chosen reporters and photographers inside military units—not for a week but for the duration of the war. "Embedding for life" is how deputy Assistant Secretary of Defense for Public Affairs Bryan Whitman sees the program—which appears to be viewed somewhat differently by the military than it is by the media.

At a recent orientation meeting with Washington bureau chiefs, Whitman described the ideal "embed" as one who follows a unit (ground, air or sea) from load-out to deployment through combat (subject to field approval) to the "march on whatever capital we happen to march on" to the return trip home and the "victory parade." This could take "two weeks, two months, two years." If reporters leave a unit there is no guarantee they can return or even join another unit. Probably they will be "pooled" in mobile media clusters that form and dissolve as the action dictates. "Itinerants" (reporters working independently) are not encouraged.

Nearly 300 reporters have already been inducted into the program at a half-dozen media boot camps along the East Coast, and more one-week sessions are foreseen. Participants are prepped on US military policy and weapons capabilities, and taught rudimentary survival skills, including how to suit up in the event of chemical or biological weapons exposure. Lieutenant Colonel Gary Keck, who wrote the training program, stresses that enrollment doesn't guarantee an "embed opportunity." Nor must embeds take the course, although commanders are reassured when they have.

The media boot camps are overtures to a larger strategy in which the Pentagon, for the first time, has actively integrated reporters and photographers into its war machine. The significance of this audacious decision, whose sponsors are Defense Secretary Donald Rumsfeld, General Tommy Franks, and Joint Chiefs chairman Richard Myers, becomes clearer when it's set beside the media policy that governed Gulf War I.

Under then Secretary of Defense Dick Cheney and Army chief General Colin Powell, the press was confined to the National Media Pool, and ordered to submit all copy, photographs, and film to military censors. Most TV footage, usually bombers streaking across desert skies, was supplied by military crews. High-level briefings were orchestrated by Cheney and Powell themselves because, as Cheney later told an interviewer from Freedom Forum, "the information function was extraordinarily important. I did not have a lot of confidence I could leave that to the press."

As a result, according to Patrick J. Sloyan, who won a Pulitzer for his coverage of Desert Storm in *Newsday*, not a single pool reporter produced an eyewitness account of the clash between allied and Iraqi troops. Nor did a single image of dead bodies find its way into the American media. By the time the press was taken to the scene of a battle, the Iraqi bodies were gone; buried, on one occasion, by giant plows mounted on Abrams battle tanks, followed by Armored Combat Earth movers that leveled the ground.

"The best covered war ever," Cheney told the Forum interviewer. "The American people saw up close with their own eyes through the magic of television what the US military was capable of doing." But in the months to come, writes John R. MacArthur in *Second Front*, "it was difficult to find anyone [in the media] who didn't … count Desert Storm as a devastating and immoral victory for military censorship and a crushing defeat for the press and the First Amendment."

In Afghanistan, the reliance on special operations units and air power tipped the balance even further toward military control, until even the pools were abandoned. In one instance, journalists stationed at a Marine base were locked in a warehouse after US forces were hit by "friendly" fire a hundred yards away. Later, briefing officers distributed press releases from Central Command in Tampa.

But in Afghanistan the controls sprang leaks. Public Affairs Officers (PAOs), who didn't know a mullah from a Pashtun bandit, didn't know how to manage the information flow either. When Special Forces raided Taliban leader Mullah Omar's compound, cutting reporters out of the action, the official version of the botched operation invited a scathing account in the *New Yorker* by Seymour Hersh. Exposés like this led the Pentagon to think that perhaps it could use the media in a more creative way. Instead of shutting it out of the battle for public opinion, why not enlist its vast resources?

When Bryan Whitman lays out the "very aggressive embed plan"—with reporters transmitting "products" from the Pentagon, foreign capitals, and "in theater," via embedding, mobile pools, CPICs (combined press information centers) and sub-CPICs—he sounds like a general massing his troops. PAOs scan *all* the media, he says: print and electronic, domestic and international; calculating markets, circulations; blending twenty-four-hour news channels, nightly news shows, and news-magazine formats with entertainment divisions who also want "to do some embedding."

Does the planning, one wonders, include the thirteen-episode "reality" series on ABC that Maureen Dowd wrote about last February, the one that hopes to profile "our troops abroad?" What about the VH1 show called the "Military Diaries Project," in which soldiers are to star in their own war movies? "Moonwalking in the endzone," ABC News executive Dan Rather called this stuff; and he found it "ridiculous" and "very awkward," he told Dowd, that while the news side was pounding the Pentagon for "bare-bones access" to the war, the military had rolled out the carpet for ABC Entertainment.

Embedding, it seems, had not yet been extended to the news media. Now that it has, the question is whether journalists will be brought any closer to the facts of war.

The Pentagon's goal is clear: embedding is designed to focus public attention on the troops. As field commanders told CNN chief executive Walter Isaacson during his recent tour of the Gulf, "the best representatives to convey America's intentions and capabilities are the soldiers and sailors in the field." American intentions and capabilities, of course, are in hot dispute, and no doubt will be as long as the US pursues its Middle East interests by military means. So it's not hard to follow Pentagon thinking.

Embedded reporters will develop the relationships, trust, and understanding of unit customs which are likely to produce savvy human interest stories. Embeds are more likely to play up acts of heroism than embarrass their units with negative stories, and risk losing access. This is not to suggest they won't try to be objective; or that their minders don't respect journalistic "objectivity."

"It's the reporter's job to report objectively," insists Lieutenant Colonel Keck. "If we took some casualties, he'd report it. ... But an embed is more sensitive to things that can't be said," Keck adds, recalling a reporter from "a previous war" who decided to quote an officer "when it was the worse thing he could have done, and hurt his career."

Whitman's boss, Victoria Clarke, offers the official answer. "The fundamental principles on which we will say no, you can't transmit ... [are] operational security, success of the mission, and safety of the people involved." Like Keck, she notes that "somebody who is embedded with a unit ... has a full appreciation for that."

These are the principles that were invoked to silence the press during the first Gulf War, and are nearly always summoned in times of stress between public and military interests. It's when and by whom and *how* they're applied that makes a difference.

Some reporters were based in forward units during that war, too, but their dispatches and film often took so long to get back to the hotel in Dhahran that they were too dated to use. "Censorship by delay," the problem came to be called. Today's press will be loaded down with its own transmission devices, and this alone marks a significant departure from the pool system. But how often will reporters be asked to "turn off their electronic devices," as they say on commercial aircraft?

When that question was asked by Cissy Baker, bureau chief for Tribune Broadcasting, at the Pentagon meeting, Rear Admiral Steve Pietropaoli described the occasions and circumstances when sat phones or cells going live from the decks of a carrier would be silenced. "You guys would like to be able to go live 24×7," he said, "and we would like to be able to control your timing."

The cautious optimism toward embedding that is currently expressed by the media may be misplaced. "There's a kind of strange naivete on the part of journalists, especially in a war situation when it comes to accepting official explanations," says Richard Rubenstein, professor of Conflict Resolution at George Mason University. "One gets the feeling that the press is being played."

Indeed, it's a sure bet that the military is not simply trying to rectify past wrongs. It sees missed opportunities for publicizing its successes in the last war. As CNN's military analyst, General Wesley Clark, told Isaacson: "We made a huge mistake trying to restrict press coverage in the first Gulf War because of our Vietnam mentality. We had a First Armored Division tank battle that was just incredible, perhaps the biggest armored battle ever, but not a single image was reported or documented for history by the press."

It's the better part of wisdom to recognize that the last thing the government wants is to let a free press cover war. In Vietnam, many journalists understood that; and disdained the "5 o'clock follies" (the official briefings) and the military escorts, and found their own units to ride with. Or like David Halberstam, no enemy of the army, they attached themselves to their own officers, as Halberstam famously did with John Paul Vann. The access may have been good for journalists, but for the military it meant little control of the news streaming home. And the news was bad. Images of body bags and napalmed children were beamed back nightly to suburban television sets, and over time public opinion turned against the war.

Nothing like this is likely to happen again, but just to make sure the Pentagon has insisted that the media centralize the process of selection so that a single point of contact (POC) for each news organization, preferably a bureau chief, works with a POC at the Pentagon. This is to avoid "people cutting deals," which reporters have already attempted, Clarke complains; and adds: "The only deals that will be made on the embeds ... will be the deals that are made here."

TRASH TALK FROM MR. PERLE

March 20, 2003

It's hard to know whether Richard Perle simply lost it on CNN's Late Edition or whether he meant business when he called Pulitzer Prize-winning writer Seymour Hersh "the closest thing American journalism has to a terrorist." Either way, at this charged moment in time, with Washington engaged in a controversial war, an inflammatory remark like this could spell trouble.

On Late Edition March 9, he was paired with Win Without War leader Tom Andrews in a debate over whether inspections, given time, could bring disarmament. Andrews, a former Maine Senator, took the lead and held it, much to Perle's evident surprise. Afterwards, CNN host Wolf Blitzer asked Perle his opinion of an article Seymour Hersh had written about him in the current *New Yorker.* "There is no question that Perle believes that removing Saddam from power is the right thing to do," he read from the text. "At the same time, he has set up a company that may gain from a war."

It was like the moment in therapy when the shrink finishes with a patient, escorts him to the door, and then it comes out. Perle started to defend himself, halted mid-sentence, and said: "Look, Sy Hersh is the closest thing American journalism has to a terrorist, frankly."

Blitzer, taken aback: "Why do you say that? A terrorist?"

Perle: "Because he's wildly irresponsible. If you read this article, it's first of all impossible to find any consistent theme in it ..."

Blitzer: "But I don't understand. Why do you accuse him of being a terrorist?"

Perle: "Because he sets out to do damage and he will do it by whatever innuendo, whatever distortion he can—look, he hasn't written a serious piece since Maylie [sic]."

Maylie, of course, is My Lai, the 1969 massacre of Vietnamese civilians, which was uncovered by Seymour Hersh—though he first had to set up his own news service to do it, because most newspapers refused to print it.

But Hersh is also respected for a half-dozen books on national security issues.

In the *New Yorker* article "Lunch with the Chairman" Perle is presented in his capacity as businessman; specifically, as managing partner of a venture-capital company named Trireme. Trireme, Hersh reports, was registered in November 2001 in Delaware to invest in companies dealing with technology and services of value to defense and homeland security.

The article focuses on a lunch Perle and an associate set up in Marseilles to solicit investments in Trireme from two prominent Saudi businessmen. This was particularly noteworthy in that Perle is an outspoken critic of the Saudi regime, and last year brought a Rand analyst to the Pentagon who shocked his audience by calling Saudi Arabia "the kernel of evil, the prime mover, the most dangerous opponent [in the Mideast]."

Nor were the two investors ordinary Saudi businessman. The more prominent, Adnan Khashoggi, once brokered billions of dollars in weapons and aircraft sales for the House of Saud. During the Reagan administration he was a middleman between Oliver North and the Iranian mullahs in the Iran–Contra scandal. To Hersh, Khashoggi commented, apropos Perle and his partner, "You Americans blind yourself with your high integrity and your democratic morality against peddling influence, but they *were* peddling influence."

Perle's entanglements are nothing beside the massive profits to be reaped by Vice President Dick Cheney's former company Halliburton and its giant subsidiary, KBR, as new orders roll in for well-heads and military bases in Central Asia, Kuwait, and Iraq. Indeed, in the Bush administration, if a defense planner is not poised to make money from the policies he oversees, then he has probably lost his way and will soon depart.

Perle is also a director of Hollinger International, which owns the *Jerusalem Post* and is part owner of the *New York Sun*. Last week the *Sun*, which uncritically backs Ariel Sharon, and calls antiwar marchers traitors, reported that Perle plans to sue Seymour Hersh and the *New Yorker*— "in Britain because it is easier to win such cases there, where the burden on plaintiffs is much less." The *New Yorker* and its writers are famously well defended, both by their lawyers and the magazine's bulldog fact-checkers.

The problem is that T-word, which could be lobbed at anyone who succeeds in rattling a notoriously thin-skinned administration. It's ordinary journalists who may be frightened by incendiary charges such as Perle hurled at Hersh on CNN. We're in a war on terrorism, right? If you're called a terrorist for writing out of line, what then? Do you go to Jail without passing Go? Get a oneway trip to Guantanamo?

At Harvard, meanwhile, where Hersh accepted a journalism award on March 11, he spoke of the frustration of Washington reporters with the aggressive style of the Bush team. "It's scary," he said. "I have never seen my peers as frightened as they are now."

5

MOUNTING WAR

On TV, at the start, it was all weaponry. US warships and submarines in the Persian Gulf launched forty-two Tomahawk cruise missiles at selected targets where the CIA had determined Saddam Hussein was hiding. This was the "decapitation strike." And the next day, there he was, slightly disheveled, talking on the streets of Mansour in Baghdad to a collection of followers. President Bush repeated his goals: Destroy the weapons of mass destruction, Change the regime, Eliminate the source of aid and weapons for the terrorist camps, Liberate the Iraqi people from tyranny, Turn Iraq into a model for democracy in the Middle East. Only the second one counted. Loren Thompson of the Lexington Institute said of the larger strategy: "It's really a replacement of containment theory from the Cold War years, with a new, more activist global strategy, and a new adversary."[1] Thompson was one of countless security experts from right-wing Washington think-tanks who joined the former generals and ex-intelligence agents who flooded the mass media to explain the war to Americans.

A Reuters report caught the unequal nature of the conflict: "Burned-out vehicles and incinerated bodies littered a plain in central Iraq on Sunday after US forces overwhelmed Iraqi militia fighters in a battle south of the holy city of Najaf. ... 'I don't know why they don't just surrender,'" said Colonel Mark Hildenbrand. "'When you're playing soccer at home, 3–2 is a fair score, but here it's more like 119–0,' he said"; adding that, "'You can't put an SUV with a machine gun up against an MI tank—it's heinous for the SUV.'"[2] But almost before it started, the mood changed. Traveling unescorted into Safwan, ABC News reporter Jon Donovan heard somebody call him a "Satan." "Why are you here in this country?" he was asked. "Are you trying to take over? ... Are the Israelis coming next? Are you here to steal our oil? When are you going to get out?"

A reporter asked Defense Secretary Rumsfeld if "shock and awe" might actually cause Iraqis to hunker down and resist like the Japanese and Germans did in World War II. Momentarily thrown off by the question, Rumsfeld said the reporter had to keep in mind that the Iraqi regime wasn't a benign one (and so, presumably, wasn't supported by its people). "A slip obviously, given the German and Japanese comparison, but the point was worth considering," said Tom Englehardt. "After all, the Russians at Stalingrad were not fighting for a benign regime either. The real question is, will Iraqi nationalism kick in among many thousands of well-armed men embedded in a major city?" If so, he believed, "the endpoint will be the same, but far more horrific for both the Iraqis and the Bush administration."[3]

The *Toronto Sun*'s Eric Margolis compared the war with the first major Islamic resistance against European colonial occupation: the revolt of the Mahdi and his Dervish army, who had taken Khartoum by storm and killed Charles "Chinese" Gordon, the British proconsul in Sudan. The British Empire had sent a "coalition" army of white troops and Egyptian native units up the Nile under Lord Kitchener with orders to crush the Mahdi before his calls for freedom from imperial rule infected all of Africa. Despite the fanatical bravery of the Dervish cavalry, their spears and broadswords were useless against Britain's field artillery and Maxim guns. The Dervishes suffered 10,000 dead and 16,000 wounded, while British losses were 41 dead and 382 wounded. Whence the lines of the poet Hilaire Belloc: "Whatever happens we have got / the Maxim gun and they have not."

Now the US-British imperial forces were racing up the Tigris and Euphrates valleys to lay fire and sword upon Baghdad. "If Iraq's three divisions in the southern region fail to stoutly defend their positions, it will be shown as a collapse of military morale by the regular army," said Margolis, and "the road to Baghdad is wide open." Margolis found it impossible to determine whether the Iraqis would fight, or succumb to a long, intensive US psychological warfare campaign which had been carried out to shake the loyalty of the regime's troops and provoke a coup or mass defections. If the Iraqi forces did fail to resist with vigor, the US wouldn't be able to use many of its new high-tech weapons. The Pentagon will be sorry, Margolis said, but there's always Iran or Syria, both of which are being named as the next priority targets by Bush administration hard-liners linked with Israel's right-wing Likud party. Margolis concluded that Saddam's days were numbered.

The Imperial forces may have no more trouble reaching Baghdad than Lord Kitchener did … Khartoum. The war between 286 million Americans and 22 million Iraqis, half of whom are in revolt against their own government, is a war between a mastodon and a mouse, with but one conclusion. … the US has the Maxim gun, and the Iraqis have not. And that … is the might that makes right.[4]

Yet five days into the war, the optimistic assumptions of the Pentagon's civilian war planners were not panning out. The outcome was not yet in doubt, but getting there was going to take longer and cost more. If the weather or Iraqi resistance turned sour—as if the resistance was but a passing thing—three American divisions were strung out over 300 miles, with the back-up force, the Army's 4th Infantry Division, still in Texas. Neither Saddam nor his lieutenants appeared either shocked or awed, and instead of surrendering, some Iraqi army units were actually harassing

American supply lines. Weeks later, before Iraqi forces melted away, and the US entered Baghdad apparently unopposed, American forces seemed surprised that the Iraqis had fought at all.

Meanwhile, sparked by word of significant American casualties, the tenor of the coverage on television, in newspapers, and on the Internet reflected sudden anxiety about the conduct of the war. A Patriot missile had shot down a British plane. Two missiles had hit Turkey. One blasted a bus in Syria. And another landed in Iran.[5] The Pentagon's chief spokeswoman, Victoria Clarke, refused to share the number of American casualties. The word *quagmire* began appearing in news reports; and a newspaper referred to "bloodied American bodies." The image of awesome American firepower was replaced by images of vulnerability. "Because of the way in which it is being fought, this is shaping up as a savage little war that may or may not end quickly," said Ed Offley, editor of the online *Defense Watch Magazine*. "And that's a different story than what was first reported." Before the first battle, an ABC correspondent embedded with troops in Kuwait described how they "tuned up their weapons like an orchestra on opening night." But now images of the *son et lumière* over Baghdad, of tanks speeding at 40 mph through southern Iraq, of American soldiers ripping down posters of Saddam Hussein with the help of villagers, were followed by a more ambiguous story. Of the tanks racing through the desert, a CNN anchor said, "this is not the war; this is getting to the war." There were risks inherent in the fast-moving Pentagon war strategy, the most obvious being the long supply lines, which had been exploited by Iraqi troops using "ruses, ambushes and other guerrilla tactics."[6]

From Casablanca to Qatar, many Arabs expected Iraq's defenses to fold when faced with the overwhelming US attack, just as they had in the 1991 Gulf War. So the lethal resistance that US troops encountered in Umm Qasr and Nasariya, which was supposed to be a six-hour fight and turned into eight grueling days, left Arab citizens amazed. To many, the hard fighting had pierced a post-Cold War myth of American invincibility, which was already dented by the September 11 attacks. Of course, the

Arab world saw a different war than the Americans did, with newspapers and TV stations in Abu Dhabi, Lebanon, Dubai, and Qatar showing civilian casualties while the US embeds—"inbreds" or "sweaties" to the journalists based at As Saliyah in Qatar—focused on US soldiers, but still the degree of Iraqi resistance was clear.

"If there is no quick American victory, I don't know what will happen, but we are in deep trouble," said Mohammed al Sager, head of the foreign affairs committee in the parliament of Kuwait, which had cordoned off half the country for use by the US and British military. Already the Arab League had hardened its stance by condemning the "aggression" in Iraq, and demanded (for what it was worth) an immediate pullout of American and British forces. The "resistance of the Iraqi people [had] changed the course of the war," said the League's secretary general Amr Moussa—whose home country, Egypt, sent a massive contingent to fight against Iraq in 1991, but in 2003 permitted the US military merely to use its airspace and the Suez Canal.

On March 27, Lieutenant General William S. Wallace, the Army's top ground commander in Iraq, told the *Washington Post* and the *New York Times* that unexpected tactics by Iraqi fighters and stretched supply lines were slowing down the campaign. "The enemy we're fighting is a bit different than the one we war-gamed against because of these paramilitary forces. We knew they were here," said Wallace, "but we did not know how they would fight." Changing in and out of uniform, merging with civilians, just the way paramilitary forces usually fight; were the American troops unprepared? Were there enough of them? There were close to 90,000 US troops in Iraq, with 100,000 to 120,000 on the way. The 4th Division would be deployed in northern Iraq, joining 1000 airborne troops who had parachuted in to secure the airfield, but with Turkey's refusal to allow US forces to use its base at Ircirlik, it would take more than a month for the tank-heavy division to prepare in Kuwait. (Wolfowitz, who had been in Ankara twisting arms, must have been stunned by the decision. But then the US couldn't *pay* the third-ranking governments on the Security Council to fight.) Now other forces heading to the region, including the 3rd Armored Cavalry Regiment, based at Fort Carson, Colorado, and the 1st Cavalry Division, from Fort Hood, Texas, were also counting on months to move their heavy armor from bases to combat.

At the same time, the 3rd Division was alarmingly low on water and in danger of running out of food, while the chaos was made worse by constant sniping from the enemy and the immense traffic backlogs from the Kuwaiti border. Sometimes, an officer said, the whole system resembles "just a bunch of guys out there driving around." Much of the Army's killing power was grounded when 100 Apache attack helicopters were put out of commission because of persistently foul weather and by battle damage from an "unsuccessful" pre-dawn raid on March 26. And the ground troops were nowhere near Baghdad—where Rumsfeld predicted a Shi'ite welcome in the city when US forces arrived.[7]

The war wasn't going anything like John Warden's *The Air Campaign* said it would. Warden's was the last word on air force warfighting doctrine since Desert Storm, and a bible for armchair strategists. The US hadn't gotten through the first stage, the suppression of enemy air defenses. On March 28, the Pentagon said the coalition lacked command of the air over Saddam's hometown of Tikrit or over Baghdad. The entire purpose of the air campaign was the maximum destruction of Iraqi ground forces, of tanks and divisions and companies. But the Iraqis had learned from Desert Storm, and from the airwar in Yugoslavia, and the victors hadn't. The battle analysts were busy calculating the time it would take for tactical and strategic bombers to eliminate six Republican Guard divisions, and the Special Republican Guard, as well as the regular army, when most of these were preparing to melt away or already had. The 51st Iraqi division had surrendered twice, and popped up to fight again at least three more times—something that could be glimpsed at Camp As Saliyah, the US Central Command HQ in Qatar, and never imagined by the embeds on the road.

The Pentagon began to release its casualties: thirty-seven US soldiers and Marines had been killed, with about 100 wounded. No Iraqi casualties were reported at all. This was one lesson that had been learned from Vietnam, where the enemy "body count" meaning nothing, meant everything. But the problems in Iraq were deeper and different than in Vietnam, where the military was in command. In Iraq, the war was in the hands of the nonmilitary: of Rumsfeld, Paul Wolfowitz, and Douglas Feith, for whom the Iraqis were the least of their problems, or so they thought. The initial plan, or what they were willing to share of it, was to get to Baghdad as rapidly as possible, change the regime, bring in humanitarian aid, and declare victory. Even the Pentagon embed chief, Bryan Whitman, spoke before the war of taking reporters home for the victory parade. There was more to it than that, of course, which had to do with permanent American basing, with oil and petrodollars and infrastructure, but that was enough for the media.

Out of this fundamental misreading grew a number of errors: the fascination with "shock and awe"; the indifference to the weather, which was always clear; the enemy was always exposed; and precision bombing always worked. But Rumsfeld had General Tommy Franks, head of Central Command in the Middle East, on his side, along with General Richard Myers, head of the Joint Chiefs of Staff. Most of his military critics were retired generals, like Anthony Zinni, former chief of CentCom in the Middle East, or the Army chief of staff, General Eric K. Shinseki, whose congressional testimony that "several hundred thousand" troops were needed for Iraq was contradicted by Wolfowitz on the spot as "much too high." There was Colin Powell in the State Department, and the Powell Doctrine from the first Gulf War, with its emphasis on adequate preparation, overwhelming force, and multilateral support; but with critics like that, you went about your business. Until the end of March, when a quiet change rippled through the uniformed command, and top Army officers in Iraq said they believed they needed to restart the war. Before launching a major ground attack on Iraq's Republican Guard, they planned to secure the supply lines and build up combat power.

No longer would Rumsfeld's office be allowed to meddle in the deployment process, vetoing the priority and sequencing of joint forces into the region, de-synchronizing the timing of arrival of people and their equipment. Rumsfeld, retired General Barry R. McCaffrey said, "sat on each element for weeks and wanted an explanation for every unit called up out of the National Guard and Reserve and argued about every 42-man maintenance detachment. Why would a businessman want to deal with the micromanaging of the force?"[8] A good question. As a result of Rumsfeld's interference—and not because of the bad weather or Iraq's surprising resistance—the timelines for the duration of the war now stretched into the summer.

A war that lasts months, some strategists worried, would encourage trouble elsewhere. If the Pentagon deployed into Iraq all the troops currently scheduled to come (which it did), about half the combat power of both the Army and the Marine Corps would be there. North Korea, for one, would be free to pursue its nuclear program unhindered—which was how retired Army Colonel Andrew Bacevich, now a professor of international relations at Boston University, saw it. The US could not fight two wars at the same time, he said, in spite of the Pentagon's assurances to the contrary. But North Korea, it turned out, wasn't interested in a showdown with the United States, and was tilting for desperately needed oil and food in exchange for a halt in the nuclear experiment at Yongbyon.

When the clouds lifted, it was as if none of this had happened; or as if the officers had indeed restarted the war. "So much for Donald Rumsfeld's flawed war plan," editorialized the *Wall Street Journal* on April 5. In just over two weeks, US forces were moving with impunity into Baghdad, and the "coalition," the paper said, controlled the rest of Iraq. Ahmed Chalabi and a 1000-man Iraqi National Congress force were flying in that weekend to join the troops. "Partly this is about giving coalition troops more local knowledge and language skills," the editorial maintained, incredibly; but mostly it would "send a signal about US intentions" vis-à-vis the UN administration of the country. It is hard to imagine that UN supervision was still an issue. More likely, the *Journal* was carrying out a mopping-up operation. Washington didn't yet have Britain in line, not for domestic policy. The British were said to have presented Colin Powell with their ideas for postwar Iraq, which included a major role for the UN. Mr. Blair wanted to patch up relations with "Old Europe," which included "continued UN involvement in Iraqi oil production. ... Mr. Bush," the *Journal* said, "should be prepared to tell him no."

What was going on? The oil-for-food program was being administered by Kofi Annan under a forty-five-day arrangement that expired May 12. But the French and Russians wanted to keep it going indefinitely. The *Journal* called this "game as transparent as it was cynical," because French and Russian companies participating in the program—oil companies, mainly—would benefit. Nothing was said about the sanctions—nothing was ever said about the sanctions—or about the ten-year US and British bombing campaign against Iraq that would surely have eliminated them from benefitting.

If Paris and Moscow got the US to concede the program's continued legality, the *Journal* went on, they could use their UN veto to blackmail Washington and a new Iraqi government into "honoring the dirty oil contracts and loans they arranged with Saddam Hussein's regime." This was a "rhetorical battle the US can win," said the *Journal*, and it laid out the issues: the oil belongs to the Iraqi people, what do Iraqis owe the creditors who helped an "illegitimate regime" oppress them? And (closer to the facts) the continuation of oil-for-food would give France and Russia a tremendous influence in post-Saddam Iraq.

But the real reason why the oil-for-food program had to end, and why the US had to take it over, was not explained. It had to do with currency reserves, with the hidden war between the dollar and the euro for global hegemony, and the fact that in November 2000 the French had convinced Saddam Hussein to defy the United States by selling Iraq's oil in euros.

This was done when the euro was worth 83 cents, thereby netting Saddam a short-term loss, but Iraq soon made off like a bandit when the value of the dollar started to sink. The euros were on deposit in a special UN account of the leading French bank, Paribas. Radio Liberty of the State Department ran a short wire on this news, but the story was quickly hushed.

And Russia? Why was Russia a villain? Because it was a principal consumer of Iraqi oil, and was engaged in oil exploration projects itself before the war. Russia was Iraq's great power partner. As for the euro war, it is interesting to note that in a Russian meeting in mid-October 2003 with German Chancellor Gerhard Schroeder, President Vladimir Putin suggested that Russian oil sales could be re-denominated from dollars to euros. "We do not rule out that it is possible. That would be interesting for our European partners," Putin said at the joint news conference that followed two days of talks.

Catherine Belten of the *Moscow Times* spelled out the implications of this proposal. "A move by Russia, as the world's second largest oil exporter, to trade oil in euros," she said, "could provoke a chain reaction among other oil producers currently mulling a switch and would further boost the euro's gradually growing share of global currency reserves." Such a move would be "a huge boon to the euro zone economy and potentially catastrophic for the United States. Dollar-based global oil trade now gives the United States carte blanche to print dollars without sparking inflation—to fund huge expenses on wars, military build-ups, and consumer spending, as well as cut taxes and run up huge trade deficits."[9] But Russia did not make the move.

For the *Wall Street Journal*, the urgency of a provisional Iraqi government was now obvious. It noted the conference in February 2003 in northern Iraq, before the war, which selected a "leadership council" composed of, among others, Chalabi, Kurdish leaders Jalal Talabini and Masoud Barzani, and Shi'ite Abdel Aziz al-Hakim, the four leaders of today's Governing Council. This group, rather than "the kinder, gentler elements of the brutal status quo," promoted by the British, the UN Security Council, and to a lesser degree the US State Department, should be the choice. "The policy should be in the hands of those most devoted to seeing it succeed."[10] The *policy*—securing the petrodollar against the onslaught of the euro—was as close as the *Journal* came to identifying an underlying reason for the invasion.

The use of embedded journalists who were given a front seat on the war had turned nearly all of them into weapons of information. They were all *at war*; shown what the military wished them to see, and, wittingly or not, they spread the message the Pentagon wanted the world's media, as well as the Iraqi regime, to believe. "Itinerants," or independently operating journalists, were obviously unwelcome, and indeed there were a number of deaths, and at least one so-called friendly fire incident, among them. Operation Iraqi Freedom was underway.

AFI Research Intelligence Briefing, which was run by Richard Bennett, compared April 5's "extraordinary armored incursion into the southwestern suburbs of [Baghdad] by combat teams from the 3rd Infantry Division" to the "Union cavalry raids made famous during the US Civil War when their special blend of reconnaissance, destruction, and psychological intimidation played a major role in undermining the rebel confederacy." But no serious attempts seemed to be made to defend the city. A few days later, Bennett concluded that many of the surviving units of the Republican Guard and Special Republican Guard had retreated through the northern outskirts of Baghdad, thus leaving behind a few spokesmen and the militias to delay the "Allied forces" with token resistance. The CIA and Special Forces were understood to have negotiated the defection of most of the 4th Corps, according to Bennett, and these troops may in due course form the nucleus of a new National Army. Little did he know that the upcoming US administrator, L. Paul Bremer III, would disband the entire army, without pay, thereby making them all eligible for the resistance. Anyway, the remaining Iraqi forces certainly presented no long-term military threat, Bennett decided, but the US would want to defeat them. And he predicted a "spectacular display of airpower" to prepare the battlefield for ground operations to "bring closure to at least the conventional stages of this war."[11]

The newspapers were full of this kind of reporting. Months later, long after the opposition to the American presence had taken on the character of a guerrilla campaign, the war would still be called a "victory." "Despite the apparent swift US military success in Iraq, the US dollar has yet to benefit as safe haven currency," former Republican state Senator Tim Ferguson posted on his website on January 19, 2004. "This is an unexpected development, as many currency traders had expected the dollar to strengthen on the news of a US win. Capital is flowing out of dollar, largely into the euro."

There were flaws to the victory scenario, like the pillaging of the National Museum in Baghdad of its priceless artifacts. "A country's identity, its value and civilization resides in its history," said Iraqi archaeologist Raid Abdul Ridhar Muhammad. "If a country's civilization is looted, as ours has been here, its history ends. ... [T]his is not a liberation; this is a humiliation." Many Iraqis watched with horror as the looting that began with attacks on museums and libraries, and the palaces and villas of Saddam Hussein and his inner circle, broadened into a tidal wave that struck all government institutions, "even ministries dealing with issues like higher education, trade and agriculture, and hospitals."[12] American troops intervened sporadically or not at all. Rumsfeld maintained it was an Iraqi affair, a way of seeking revenge on Saddam; but looking back, it seems like something else was involved. If the US was planning to take over Iraq, and it was—within five months, on September 19, the Coalition Provisional Authority would formally throw open the country to foreign business—what better way to clear the deck than to stand aside while the national institutions were dismantled.

Meanwhile, pockets of resistance continued, and the White House turned its propaganda arm, the Office of Global Communications, to the job of knocking the pockets down to size. Iraqi fighters in urban guerrilla battles that continued against US forces were to be called "terrorists," "death squads," or "thugs." "Fedayeen," to describe the Iraqi militias loyal to President Saddam Hussein, was dropped as having "almost heroic implications" in Arabic that would undercut propaganda efforts. Soon Rumsfeld and Bremer came up with "dead-enders" and "bitter-enders"; and later, with the resistance growing by leaps and bounds, they began calling more and more of the fighters "foreigners," or members of al Qaeda.

Whatever they were called, they were increasing; no longer pockets of resistance, but cells that had been organized from the Iraqi army before the war. This theory was set forth by an American officer a few weeks later, and made sense, though fresh grounds for hating the occupying force were born every day. The cells, if that's what they were, were soon embedded in a subculture of opposition, a sea in which the guerrillas could swim. "He has beaten Saddam … not the Iraqi people," said a tribal leader from Mosul, after hearing an American colonel read the riot act to thirty religious, tribal and community leaders.[13] And in the south, thousands of Shi'ites marched through a Basra slum waving a green flag and a banner reading, "We want an honest man." That was all. The Shi'ites lived in an area where the Saadoun tribe held near absolute power under Saddam's regime. "No Muzahim, no Saadoun," they cried.[14] And now they were occupied by the British. Once again.

"It's like we won the Super Bowl but we have to keep on playing," said Sergeant Richard Edwards from Brooklyn; which was an American way of seeing it.[15] But the killing was harder when it was close-up and constant. And Marine infantrymen occupying the eastern half of Baghdad were trying to talk about it. It was another lesson from Vietnam, that troops may come home more intact if they talk to each other about what's happened, so platoons were holding informal group-therapy sessions—"critical incident debriefings," in military lingo—in which they shared their feelings about "eye-thumping," for example, when soldiers poke a man's eye with a rifle muzzle on the theory that no man alive can avoid scrunching up his face in response to such a provocation.

"The touchy-feely stuff—that's no joke," said Second Lieutenant Isaac Moore, whose platoon had just encountered an escalating series of firefights with pro-regime militants armed with rifles and rocket-propelled grenades. Lieutenant Moore started them off by relating his experience as a hunter, growing up in Wasila, Alaska; and talked about how he shot his first caribou at the age of seven, and how thrilling it was to see the animal fall, until he got close and saw it was still alive, and convulsed in pain, and how he wasn't sure whether he was supposed to feel good or bad. Over the years of hunting caribou and bear, he grew accustomed to eye-thumping and to death. "That queasy feeling—I don't get that at all," he said, describing how when he looked down the staircase of a building in Baghdad and saw three Iraqis, he didn't hesitate. The Iraqis had been wounded by a burst of machine-gun fire, but were still moving. The lieutenant shot one man point-blank in the head and watched the results; the next man was twitching, and he shot him too. "This is not somebody you need to worry about killing," he said. "When you stand outside the Pearly Gates … you're not going to be looked at any differently for what you did here."

But one of the men was worried that for the rest of his life he would be haunted by the image of a clean-shaven, twenty-something Iraqi in a white shirt, lying wounded in an alleyway and reaching for his rifle—just as Corporal James Lis pumped two shots into his head. "Every time I close my eyes I see that guy's brains pop out of that guy's head," he told his platoon mates, as they sat in the ruins of the Iraqi Oil Ministry's employee cafeteria. The first shot was fired by Sergeant Timothy Wolkow; the man started moving again, and this time both Marines shot him in the head. Then Corporal Lis performed the eye-thump ritual. "It's the sickest feeling I've ever had in my life," he said, but Sergeant Wolkow had a different reaction. "As much as I love the Marine Corps and want to kill people, for a few seconds there was a kind of eerie feeling. ... It went away," he said, "and I shot the guy some more."[16]

Another platoon was luckier, and had taken over Saddam's palace, a complex of five houses overlooking the Tigris, each house grander than the next. A satellite-guided bomb destroyed a portion of the compound, but most was left intact for the future use of the Coalition Provisional Authority, though nobody knew that yet. The lawns were freshly trimmed, the flowers in bloom. One house contained a vast sitting room of blue velvet couches and chairs, a marble staircase, and a two-story mural of Saddam and his family. Another held a dental office, an optician's studio, a beauty salon with three chairs and magazine covers of Britney Spears pasted to a mirror. The Marines had found children's scooters in the garage, and loaded down with their weapons and ammo, they rode them blithely around and around.[17]

A few days later the war was declared over. The US had won. The American media were jubilant—flags waving, soldiers "yahooing" as they ridiculed the antiwar camp, lambasting Germany and France and other "naysayers." The media touted it as the most effective military campaign in history; the most humanitarian, with the least civilian deaths and damage to "infrastructure." But the facts were as follows. Since 1991, Iraq was transformed by the sanctions. Nothing could enter or leave the state without the approval of the US-led committee overseeing the sanctions regime. Iraq's mechanized brigades, artillery pieces, mortars, and heavy rifles already needed repair. Imagine their condition in 2003. By March 20 Iraq had no heavy weaponry worth mentioning; not only no weapons of mass destruction, the last of which was destroyed in 1998, as the United States knew well, but hardly any conventional weapons—except, stocked away, hundreds of thousands of Kalashnikovs, rocket-propelled grenades, and handmade explosives.

While the United States polished its military might to unbelievable heights, Iraq's army dropped from one million commissioned men to barely 300,000. Development virtually ground to a halt, while the telecommunications sector crumbled. Not surprisingly, disease and malnutrition spread, and the World Health Organization released data showing the return of cholera and typhoid. Water mixed with sewage was common due to the lack of spare parts to fix the crumbling water filtration plants. The UN reported more than 500,000 children had died because of acute shortages in the health-care system, a figure that was acknowledged by former Secretary of State Madeleine Albright as worth the necessity of bringing Saddam Hussein to heel.

Iraq, now a Third World country, some $383 billion in debt, sank lower into poverty, misery, and backwardness.[18] And yet when American companies arrived later in 2003 to undertake repairs, they were shocked by the debilitation they discovered in hospitals, schools, sewage systems, and telephone networks. "In almost every case," a project director said, "the jobs were studded with difficulties no one had anticipated." Kellogg Brown & Root CEO Randy Harl said that KBR operated in forty to fifty countries, "and every reconstruction project presents certain challenges. ... But Iraq is unique because you face all of the challenges at the same time. All of them." George A. Laudato, a vice president of Abt Associates, which has a contract for repairing the health-care system, found that some hospitals in southern Iraq "were as bad as anything I have seen in sub-Saharan Africa. Pools of blood on the floor ... needles reused"; a ward of heart attack victims in Basra had no equipment to do anything for them, "not even an IV." Surprisingly, the sanctions were not mentioned. Perhaps they were not considered. Laudato said Iraqi patience with American involvement was wearing thin. "Almost to a person, they told us: 'We're happy you're here. We need your help. But we hope you can do it quickly and then get out.'"[19]

The Iraqi army, once the vanguard of the Middle East, had been reduced to a skeleton of hungry and desolate men. The only force equipped and trained to sustain military conflict was the Republican Guard, whose gear was antiquated. Why did the US call this war a victory? Even a *safqa*, "a deal made fast and in secrecy," which was what the Arab media called the sudden collapse of the Iraqi regime, doesn't explain why the US went to such lengths to turn the event into something it was not. Who was fooled by President Bush's descent in his phoney flight suit to the decks of the aircraft carrier *Abraham Lincoln* on May 1— when the carrier had to be turned around so the skyline of San Diego couldn't be seen? Who, that is, but most Americans watching the scene on television. For a while.

WHITE HOUSE PRESS CONFERENCE

April 14, 2003

Q: Can victory be declared in this war without accounting for not just Saddam Hussein, but those leading figures of the regime?

Mr. Fleischer: Let me deal with the speculation about victory and whether the president will declare victory, what victory would look like, what criteria he's looking for, because the answer from the president's point of view is it is much too soon to be discussing it. We remain in the middle of a conflict. Yes, indeed, the regime has ended, as General Franks said this morning. But, yes, indeed, fighting remains. It is still a battlefield. While the central command and control elements of the regime have been collapsed, there remain pockets of loyalists who continue to fight and present harm for our armed forces.

So from the president's point of view, it is a matter that he is not yet speculating about. He continues to work—in the middle of a war—to make certain that we win the war.

Q: Sorry. So he hasn't thought about what would constitute victory?

Mr. Fleischer: The president is not yet ready to publicly speculate about what it is he would say or when he would say it.

Q: That's not the question. You're turning the question around. The question is, what has to happen for victory to be achieved?

Mr. Fleischer: Just what I told you this morning. The president has always said the mission is the disarmament of Iraq and liberation for the Iraqi people.

Q: And, therefore it is securing those weapons of mass destruction, and until that's done—

Mr. Fleischer: The president has always said that is the mission. I am not going to be able to shed any more light on when the president will say the mission is accomplished.

Q: But you just laid it out there that disarmament of Iraq, "disarmament" meaning weapons of mass destruction, correct?

Mr. Fleischer: The president has always said that is the mission, but I'm not going to define for you what the president will later define as victory.

Comment: "Bush's press secretary, Ari Fleischer, just reported that after sending scores of American soldiers to their deaths, killing thousands of Iraqi soldiers, conscripts, and civilians, spending $75 billion borrowed tax dollars, dividing NATO, the UN, and the entire world, it turns out that Bush hasn't figured out how to tell when we've won the war ..."

—The Angry Liberal, BuzzFlash.com

Dallas, Texas
October 11, 2003

... You should make a trip to Midland sometime. Just going there will explain a hell of a whole lot about GWB. It is a town totally created by oil money, and now that the fields are drying up, deserted by more and more people. But Bush grew up in an environment where oil was the only business, everyone he ever associated with during his formative years was in oil, and everyone including the ministers at church believed that oil was the answer to everything in life. It is a whole culture. Most of the downtown today is boarded up. There isn't much traffic there, and every year there are less and less people of wealth and position in that town. Also it is incredibly isolated, far from the next town, far from any sort of change in geography or topography. GWB has been cited as the least intellectually curious person to have ever become president. If that is so, then what propels him are values he gained from the people around him during his formative years and they were basically in Midland, Texas. Andover and Yale and perhaps Harvard Business School (which didn't seem to rub off much as he took under every business he ever really ran) were just places he visited, and every vacation he went back home to Midland.

Midland is quite alone out there on the Texas flat. There's Odessa. Midland is ... where the lawyers and the banks were, and the country club. Odessa is the city where the roughnecks lived, the oil field workers, and they are, by and large, the wildest sons-of-bitches that this state has. I think people in Odessa are now so poor that they can't leave. One of the great rivalries in state football, and football is king here still (I write this when it is dangerous to drive on Dallas streets because of the partying going on around tomorrow's Texas/Oklahoma game at the Cotton Bowl) were the games between the high schools of Midland and Odessa. It wasn't football. It was class warfare. And perhaps still is.

One of the bizarre stories coming out of Bush's term as governor here was that when he stopped being governor and ran for president, he had his papers collected [and] ... shipped to his father's presidential library where they were duly stored under the same secrecy provisions as the presidential papers, which is twenty-five years unless extended by the president himself or a member of his family who was living at the time he was president—something like that. One of the newspapers, the liberal *Austin Statesman*, I think, requested information from GWB's governmental documents under the state's freedom of information act, was rebuffed by the presidential library and actually had to sue for access on the grounds that these were state papers, not federal ones. A court, and I don't know if the decision was fought to an appellate level, ruled that the papers didn't belong to George and had to be shipped back to the state's archives. Which in time they were. My point is that Bush didn't understand this relatively simple point in governmental law, and actually fought it.

Anthony (Hume)

Dallas, Texas
October 14, 2003

... Actually I don't think there was anything much in there.

The problem was that he didn't turn them over, as had every other governor, to the state archives for its possession for posterity. He didn't see the need to. Didn't comprehend his duties as governor, that what he did in office wasn't private, but public and open to scrutiny ...

Anthony (Hume)

6

VIETNAM REDUX

I wonder why I keep sliding back to Vietnam at the start of the war. As if Vietnam was a real war, and this one isn't. "There were certainly plenty of bombs dropped, guns fired and Iraqis killed by the American and British forces," an armchair reporter said yesterday online; "but there has not been one single clash with Iraqi forces that could remotely be described as a battle. Compared to the major wars of the past, the entire campaign adds up to little more than an extended skirmish. The Big Battle to Come was always the one just around the corner—in Basra, or Baghdad, or Tikrit—that never quite came."[1] This was April 10, too soon to say "was." But the fellow has a point.

Vietnam was the only war with two sides that the US has fought since Korea—or four sides: the US, North Vietnam, the Saigon regime, and the National Liberation Front (NLF). Most of the others were either preemptive strikes (before preemption became national security doctrine) against largely defenseless foes—like the new Marxist regime in tiny Grenada (1983) and "Let's get Shorty" Noriega in Panama (1989). (Noriega escaped and later turned himself in, so Panama, aka Operation Just Cause, doesn't really count.) Or else the conflicts were essentially hit and run operations fought from America's favorite perch in the sky, against enemies without air power or significant air-defense capabilities—as in the first Gulf War (1991–92), Bosnia (1995), Kosovo (1999), and Afghanistan (2001–). When US soldiers climb down to earth to fight mano a mano, against enemies so out-gunned as to seem refugees from another century—Somalia comes to mind (1993)—they invariably get bogged down only to withdraw in a fog of ambiguity which has in one form or another trailed every US military engagement since Vietnam.

Even America's war games are fixed so that only the good guys win. Vietnam historian Marilyn Young tells the story of Millennium Challenge '02, the biggest war game ever. Two years in the making, it cost over $250 million and involved 13,500 participants in a three-week exercise designed to test Secretary of Defense Donald Rumsfeld's strategic concepts. In the game, which took place in the summer of 2002, General Paul Van Riper (right out of *Dr. Strangelove*), commanding the forces of "an unnamed Middle Eastern state," managed to sink most of the US naval fleet through the use of unconventional tactics—whereupon the game was halted, the fleet was re-floated, and Van Riper quit. "Instead of a free-play, two-sided game," he told *Army Times*, "it simply became a scripted exercise. They had a predetermined end. ..."[2] The game began again and the unnamed Middle Eastern enemy duly lost the war.[3]

So I return to that other war, which is after all *my* war, as the geezers say. The occasion now is an interesting document I've just received that has brought me up close to a time and place when my own history overlapped "World-History," which is what Hannah Arendt and her husband, Heinrich Bleucher, used to call the truly significant events that pitch the world forward in unexpected directions. Wars do that, but not all wars. Vietnam did it, and the consequences are still playing themselves out. (September 11 is still doing it.)

The document before me is the unpublished journal of a trip to Hanoi, written by a twenty-four-year-old community organizer from Cleveland named Carol McEldowny who traveled to North Vietnam in October 1967 with nine other Americans. She died in a car crash during a cross-country trek in 1973. Old friends have retrieved the manuscript which is to be published by the University of Massachusetts Press. Carol's group included two leaders from the antiwar movement, Tom Hayden and Rennie Davis; also Norm Fruchter, who helped found the radical film collective Newsreel; Ron Young from the American Friends Service Committee; several black journalists and community activists: Bob Allen, Stoney Cookes, John Wilson; and Jock Brown, an Episcopal minister with Clergy and Laity Concerned. The other woman, Vivian Rothstein, like Carol, Norm, and Tom, was attached to Students for a Democratic Society (SDS).

All of them had just attended a week-long peace conference in Bratislava, Czechoslovakia with some twenty-odd other young Americans who met with delegations from North Vietnam and the Vietcong. Such a face-to-face encounter with the other side hadn't happened before; and the meeting was an American debut of sorts for the Vietcong—more properly, the NLF—who had just formed the Provisional Revolutionary Government of South Vietnam. None of the Americans represented anybody but themselves, and were a diverse group, which included myself, editor of *Viet-Report*; Sol Stern, a journalist from *Ramparts*; Carol King, a black welfare organizer from Detroit; *New York Review of Books* writer Andy Kopkind; and the editor of an alternative newspaper at Boston University, Ray Mungo, who wore an immense rucksack throughout the sessions—which were accompanied by semi-simultaneous translations and headphones, like a mini-UN. We were recruited by Dave Dellinger from *Liberation*, and Nick Egleson, then president of SDS.

This is the cast of a curious story which has not to my knowledge been told, or not in any depth. Someday I'll find my way back to it, but Bratislava had little to do with Carol McEldowny's journal other than to introduce her to her future hosts. Titled "Trip to Hanoi," the manuscript is 275 pages long and is a detailed and cogent account of living under the American bombing campaign—as told to American "friends" of no great military or diplomatic sophistication. Carol, for instance, had queried herself sharply about her qualifications for going on what was a coveted journey for movement people, journalists, and writers alike; a kind of reward for hard work, in the case of the politicos. An adventure for everybody—though never the same adventure, as the highly personal memoirs published the following year by Mary McCarthy (*Hanoi*) and Susan Sontag (*Trip to Hanoi*) suggest.

Embedding oneself behind enemy lines in the 1960s could have unexpected effects, as happened to Mary, who discovered a lost ideal America in this "pioneer country, where streams have to be forded," and where the ethnic minorities reminded her of American Indians. Two-seater toilets, with a water buffalo ruminating outside, brought back "buried fragments" of her Western origins. McCarthy arrived with "the confidence of the American who knows himself to be fair-minded, able to see both sides, disinterested, objective, etc. as compared to the single-minded people he is about to visit." But these qualities, she discovers, are the "fossil remains of the old America, detached by an ocean from the quarrels of Europe, having no colonial interests compared to the Great Powers, a permanent outsider and hence fitted to judge or bear witness. ..."[4] Not by any measure the America then blistering the face of Vietnam; and soon she finds her claim to being a "disinterested party starting ... to shrink"; and more, that her "detachment and novelistic powers of observation were not only inappropriate but also a sort of alibi."[5]

Susan Sontag wonders how the Northerners she meets "appear so singularly and straightforwardly involved with the virtue of courage, and with the ideal of a noble, brave life," when "we live in an age marked by the discrediting of the heroic effort."[6] It was as if the embattled Vietnamese these writers observed were fulfilling an *American* dream, long gone; their virtues are repossessed, as it were, and handed back to the American reader as object lessons in self-improvement. Observing her hosts, Sontag reflects: "It is *not* simple to be able to love calmly, to trust without ambivalence, to hope without self-mockery, to act courageously, to perform arduous tasks with unlimited resources of energy." In

American society, she thinks, "a few people are able just faintly to imagine all these as achievable goals—though only in their private life."[7] Even in *The Other Side* (1965), a book with a straightforward political agenda, historian Staughton Lynd and activist Tom Hayden evoke another mythic ideal from the American past: "When we say that our highest loyalty is not to America but to mankind," they write, "we affirm a lost part of the American tradition."[8] Such statements reflect the depth of estrangement that engulfed American intellectuals in those years, not just to the US intervention in Vietnam but to an entire culture. And yet they're full of longing, as of a child for a parent who has died.

"Should a non-writer, non-speaker, non-peace movement activist go?" Carol wondered in Prague, where her group had repaired for pre-trip planning. And throughout the two-week visit she asked herself whether she was ready to leave inner-city organizing to work with an antiwar movement that was growing by leaps and bounds, but that "lack[ed] a political perspective and [did] not lead to building permanent organized bases." She was "turned-on" but didn't want to "lose [her] head and go off on some cockeyed peacenik scheme." Nor did she "want to be swept away by the intrigue of underground organization or whatever without a great deal of careful thought," which is interesting to hear as early as 1967. Two and a half years later some of McEldowney's SDS friends formed Weatherman, an armed underground organization that carried out non-lethal bombings of government buildings (usually from ladies' rooms), which were pegged to Nixon's escalations in Indochina and to the incarceration of black radicals. Yet Carol proved to be a shrewd reporter, mulling over Hanoi's claim that the widespread destruction of schools, churches, hospitals, and market towns was *deliberate*, with the same careful sifting of argument and observation practiced by the *New York Times* correspondent Harrison Salisbury, who visited North Vietnam in late December 1966.

Carol noted that Vietnamese officials from the War Crimes Commission (which was taken more seriously in Hanoi than at the Bertrand Russell War

Crimes Tribunal headquarters in Paris) argued that the attacks were deliberate for three reasons:

1. US has many reconnaissance planes and know what they are hitting. (Not very convincing, since the Vietnamese also tend to discount reliability of US reconnaissance and we know it is not that accurate…)
2. US planes dove in and fly low enough to aim. (This is reasonable, although given the effectiveness of self-defense rifle units, it would seem that many more planes flying low would be hit.)
3. Certain targets have been hit repeatedly. (This is the most convincing argument to me. Regardless of what explanation the US gives about these targets, they have been hit over and over again and quite systematically in some areas.)

The district capital of Thanh Hoa, for instance, had been nearly pulverized after repeated bombings, as I saw myself during an earlier visit with an investigating team from the Bertrand Russell War Crimes Tribunal. The same was true of the textile city of Nam Dinh, leading Harrison Salisbury to wonder (apropos "a city so obscure that we would have to hunt for it on the map of a country whose name most of us could not pronounce"): "What earthly meaning could be extracted from this destruction? What military purpose was it serving?"[9]

Carol McEldowny's report is an enumeration of civilian casualties and the destruction of civilian targets that in most cases were far from the roads, bridges, factories, and petroleum dumps listed among the Pentagon's official targets. The journal is also an introduction to what might have been called civil society had all branches of Vietnamese society not been mobilized for self-defense, mutual aid, and stepped-up production. And self-reliance, I might add, from my observation of a machine shop relocated inside a hollowed-out mountain in Hong Gai, which possessed its own administrative committee, cultural troupe, first aid team, and rifle militia, drawn from the workers. The militia shot at low-flying planes that flew in from the Seventh Fleet and were occasionally, though rarely, downed. US bombers were more vulnerable to teenage rifle militias in the interior when planes would swoop in low to try to take out the same battered bridge day after day—scattering nearby hamlets like haycocks in a cyclone.

Collateral damage, this would be called now. But having studied air force manuals before I left for the North in January 1967, I knew the military rationale for such destruction extended far beyond that.* It was meant to create panic and chaos among the civilian population, sowing seeds of distrust for government war aims. The idea was that a totalitarian regime couldn't survive the strain of decentralization, so that when you forced administrative headquarters, factories, schools, and hospitals to break up and relocate throughout the countryside, you could more easily make the central government collapse. How profoundly the Americans failed to take the measure of their opponents! Decentralization only appeared to unleash the historic fighting capability of this ancient agricultural society. With many men of military age engaged in the South, peasant women whose teeth were lacquered black in the traditional fashion ran local administrative committees, while teenage boys and girls operated mobile anti-aircraft batteries. Urbane officials from Hanoi bowed courteously to rural elders. "I have told you that we must absolutely win this war because we are fighting for the most elemental things," Prime Minister Pham Van Dong told the Russell team. And we believed him, for we had seen the same steely determination in the eyes of nearly everyone we met, including many of the wounded—though of course in me they saw an American, the only American in my group.

In a people's war the bombing of civilian targets was also intended to tie up human resources in rescue and reclamation efforts that might otherwise

---

* "A military target is any person, thing, idea, entity or location selected for destruction, inaction or rendering nonusable with weapons which will reduce or destroy the will of the enemy to resist." USAF manual, Fundamentals of Aerospace Weapons Systems, 1967.

be engaged in offensive operations—moving men and matériel down the Ho Chi Minh trail, for example, to support Vietcong operations in the South. "They are intelligent. They know that people are the resource for all *matériel*," Pham Van Dong said; and added, referring to the Pentagon's recent introduction of B-52s to both North and South: "Massive bombing is not designed to kill guerrillas."[10]

But it was Hanoi's analysis of American aims in Southeast Asia, as presented to McEldowny's group by Colonel Ha Van Lau, that has caught my attention today. I heard something like it myself, and from the same source, for I saw a great deal of the handsome Colonel Lau during the month I traveled with the investigating team from the War Crimes Tribunal. But the analysis didn't carry the same significance for me then that it does now. I would have taken the larger purpose ascribed to American intervention in Vietnam as political hyperbole, with which I agreed but incompletely understood.

"The nature of US imperialism," the subject of the discourse, was something I first associated with the banana republics my father railed against in the 1950s, when he cornered his midwestern business friends at cocktail parties. A trace of late-nineteenth-century anti-imperialism, the anti-imperialism of Mark Twain, lingered in our house; along with a wisp of socialism that emanated from my mother's younger brother, Uncle Jack, who became a Trotskyist in his youth. Some study had taught me to see imperialism in classical Marxist terms, if not as the last stage of capitalism, then as its most advanced. But I had no fix on how the link between capital accumulation and expansion was forged on the anvil of anti-communism. And I don't think I grasped the larger imperial goal the US pursued even then.

In New York, in the late '60s, I was a student of the "new imperialism," with a special interest in the ways that Washington used foreign aid and economic development in the Third World to break down the resistance of indigenous cultures to modernization, or to buy off a budding insurgency. I was intrigued by the early, liberal years of the Vietnam War, the Kennedy years when all the trouble began. I'm not one who believes that, had Kennedy lived, he would have pulled us out. I recall the warlike speeches: "Let every nation know, whether it wishes us well or ill, that we shall pay any price, bear any burden, meet any hardship, support any friend, oppose any foe to assure the survival and success of liberty," which quiver with a martial fervor not unlike President Bush's. More eloquent, true, and delivered by a president who asserted in the same inaugural address: "If a free society cannot help the many who are poor, it cannot save the few who are rich," but it was nonetheless a global vision with which Paul Wolfowitz could live quite nicely.

John F. Kennedy, in fact, was the first president to knock the starch out of the Cold War structure of détente, not Ronald Reagan or George W. Bush. By jettisoning the military doctrine of Mutual Assured Destruction (MAD), which was based on nuclear parity, and substituting a provocative program of "graduated military response" whose starting point was fighting guerrillas in Indochina, Kennedy might have set the stage for the permanent war that we face today had it not been for the American defeat in Vietnam. Eisenhower, of course, introduced covert action as a way around the problem of massive retaliation in the coups the US carried out in Guatemala and Iran. And Eisenhower set the Bay of Pigs in motion.

Indochina was Kennedy's new frontier in Asia whose lure, of course, was not new; for behind the obsession with Vietnam lay the vast hooded phantom of China, a loose fish, running wild in the Cold War sea. China was America's Moby Dick, Mao told the American journalist Edgar Snow in late 1964. In Vietnam Mao saw America as Captain Ahab fighting to strike through the mask at the demon leviathan that taunted him—which was not so different from how Secretary of State Dean Rusk saw the ever-escalating US mission. Nobody in that administration, or the next, understood that Vietnam, with as much help from its quarreling allies as it could muster, was fighting for national independence, and had fought against one powerful invader after another for a millennium. To testify to Washington's astonishing ignorance we have Robert McNamara's post mortem, *In Retrospect: The Tragedy and Lessons of Vietnam*. But it wasn't just the history of Vietnam or of Indochina that the American government overlooked, it was history itself: the weight and portent of past events as they bear on the present and future, particularly events that happen far from home.

In Indochina, meanwhile, first in Laos and then in South Vietnam, Kennedy planned for American power to break free of the rigor mortis that had set in under Eisenhower's nuclear umbrella. He wished to test America's mettle in a new kind of war with new weaponry and a more flexible military doctrine capable of inserting US forces into distant battle-fields. If this sounds familiar, it should. Here is Mr. Bush campaigning on December 2, 1999: "Our forces in the next century must be agile, lethal, readily deployable, and require a minimum of logistical support. We must be able to project our power over long distances, in days or weeks rather than months. On land, our heavy forces must be lighter. Our light forces must be more lethal. ..." *Lethal* is the operative word in 2003; and in Afghanistan and Iraq the signature of Rumsfeld's vision has been the Pentagon hit squad, the man-hunting teams, fusing intelligence, communications, and precision weapons in a brew not yet concocted in McNamara's time.

In his Harvard dissertation *Why England Slept*, Kennedy provided himself with the worldview that dominated his administration's foreign policy. With its focus on the need for "shocks" to wake up a sleeping democracy to the dangers lurking outside, it anticipated a popular screed in neoconservative circles: *While America Sleeps: Self-Delusion, Military Weakness, and the Threat to Peace Today* (2000), by Donald and Frederick Kagan, father and brother respectively of Robert ("Power and Weakness") Kagan. "America is in danger," write the Kagans, striking the embattled note. "Unless its leaders change their national security policy, the peace and safety its power and influence have ensured since the end of the Cold War will disappear."

And elsewhere: "The absence of 'global peer competitors' does not make the world safe for the foreseeable future—it only makes it uncertain and difficult to understand."[11] Both books descend from Winston Churchill's *While England Slept*, which pointed out the dark implications of Britain's failure to play the role of peacekeeper in the 1920s and '30s, and explored the predilection of democracies for isolationism and stability—old-fashioned American traits that Mary McCarthy celebrates in *Hanoi*.

In his first major defense statement, President Kennedy harnessed the warning to a new foreign policy that fairly crackled with paranoia, the kind that goes hand-in-hand with an aggressive military posture and stepped-up defense spending. "The free world's security can be endangered not only by a nuclear attack but also by being slowly nibbled away at the periphery, regardless of our strategic power," he said, "by forces of subversion, infiltration, intimidation, indirect or nonovert aggression, internal revolution ... or a series of limited wars." I have already quoted that, but it bears repeating.

By 1966–67, the Vietnam conflict had reached an altogether different level from the one Kennedy's men had promoted in the early 1960s. Still "limited," the war had left the heady promises of counterinsurgency and rural pacification far behind, and now looked more like a nasty conventional ground war in the South; consuming more and more troops and arms, racking up ever increasing American casualties and enemy "body counts," and propping up one clayfooted Saigon regime after another.

In Hanoi, early in January 1967, speaking of US military planners, Pham Van Dong told Harrison Salisbury: "The situation is very bad. Worse than ever before. And they are now facing an impasse. What are they bound to do? Increase their strength in South Vietnam? How much? Where will they fight? And how to win victories?" When Salisbury pointed to America's seemingly inexhaustible material resources, Pham Van Dong (for whom, McCarthy thought, "bombs were a low-grade intrusion into the political scene which he conceived, like the ancients, as a vast proscenium"[12]) had responded by noting that escalation was not a strategy.

The US had escalated once, twice, three times, four times. Why should victory come after the fifth escalation?

The two had discussed the airwar in the North, which the prime minister characterized as a defeat for the Americans, both in the propaganda sense—world opinion had turned against the bombing—and in a military one: the continual bombardment had not materially affected the situation in the South. There is much to say about this now that we know something of the delicate relations that existed between Hanoi and the National Liberation Front. We could start with the irreversible changes brought about by the Tet Offensive of 1968 ("World-History" again), not only in the US, with President Johnson's exit from politics, and the sudden draining of popular support for further escalation, but inside Vietnam, where the unexpected attacks on US and South Vietnamese army outposts throughout the country, including guerrilla uprisings in Saigon itself, thoroughly demoralized the Southern regime and shocked the Pentagon. It also marked a changing of the guard in the South; for the Tet Offensive was a last hurrah for the Vietcong, who suffered tremendous casualties from which it never fully recovered. From then on, strategic leadership shifted to the PLAF (People's Liberation Armed Forces), and Hanoi sent more troops and supplies, including anti-aircraft and tank units, down the dense network of trails winding through Laos, Cambodia, and into the Central Highlands of South Vietnam.

From then on, too, the US government began to plot its tortuous one step forward, two steps backward retreat from Vietnam. Thus, in 1972, the same year that a stroke of clever diplomacy on Henry Kissinger's part brought him and Nixon face to face with Mao Zedong and Zhou Enlai in Beijing, and Vietnam's peace negotiations entered their third year in Paris, Nixon unleashed B-52s on Hanoi's central city (the "Christmas bombing") principally to appease a nervous President Thieu in Saigon. It was well known that such attacks had no effect on Hanoi's and the NLF's negotiating terms. Instead, the massive raids marked the beginning of a now familiar pattern whereby the world's greatest superpower resorted to the sheer destructive impact of its weaponry to cover over the faults in its strategic doctrine and the poverty of its diplomatic efforts. If Johnson, McNamara, Rusk, General Westmoreland, and the rest had learned anything, it was what American commanders from the Korean theater had already told them, which was to not fight a land war in Asia. After Vietnam, that was updated to avoid land wars, period.

Pham Van Dong, in the meantime, reminded Salisbury that this was a people's war, and people's wars were of necessity long. "How many years would you say?"—Dong asked, smiling—"Ten, twenty—what do you think about twenty?" Salisbury, who like many visitors hoped to bring home evidence of a softening in Hanoi's terms for a settlement—whose core premise was that the US recognize Vietnamese sovereignty and independence, as set forth in the Geneva Accords—replied wanly that he "thought this would be a good year to stop the war." But the prime minister spoke of how the younger generation was already preparing itself. "Our history is one of a very proud nation," he reminded his guest, referring to the Mongol invasions, thrice defeated, as well as to the Chinese. "Now, how many times does the Pentagon want to fight?" he asked. "So—how many years the war goes on depends on you. Not on me."

Salisbury's reflection on this conversation is noteworthy, especially when one considers that it was eight years before Saigon fell—sooner than Hanoi expected, for it well understood the tyranny which the credibility factor exercised over policy changes in Washington. When push came to shove as it did in April 1975, on the roof of the US embassy and the decks of its warships, no one was more astonished than the advancing troops from the North to discover how abruptly all resistance collapsed. At the same time, there were seven years and 20,000 *more* US soldiers killed *after* Lyndon Johnson and Robert McNamara threw in the towel (in 1968), and passed the mopping-up and cover-up operations on to the Nixon administration.

"Was the effort worth it?" *Newsweek* editor, Evan Thomas, asks in a recent review of Henry Kissinger's apologia, *Ending the Vietnam War*:

Why didn't the Nixon administration withdraw from Vietnam right away and spare the United States, not to mention the peoples of Vietnam, Cambodia and Laos, further agonies of war?

Kissinger argues, persuasively to me, that just walking away from Vietnam was a poor option. The "domino effect" was real. Not the domino effect predicted in the 1950s—the fall of all Southeast Asia to the Communists—but rather, Kissinger writes, the encouragement given by America's pullout from Vietnam to Soviet and Cuban adventuring in Africa, to the Soviet invasion of Afghanistan and to the aggression of Islamic radicals in the Middle East.

Kissinger tried, with faltering success, especially after Watergate, to preserve American credibility.[13]

Salisbury, meanwhile, was certain Pham Van Dong exaggerated North Vietnam's strength. He didn't think the balance in the South was as strong as Hanoi maintained, and he knew the economic consequences of the bombing in the North were more severe than the prime minister acknowledged. "Yet, over all, I did not believe he had badly overstated his case. It was a piece of close-grained reasoning," he thought, and "thus far, based on actual results, the balance between this small, backward, underdeveloped country and the world's foremost military power had been remarkably even."[14]

In the end, the bitter pill Washington had to swallow was that it was the US which had overreached itself in Vietnam, not its "small, backward" enemy. Nor had Kissinger's efforts prevented the effects of the other domino factor that Evan Thomas raises, the ripple effect of *losing face, losing control*. Kissinger, by the way, was already busy in 1975 establishing an Iraqi pipeline to Israel, thereby launching the Haifa Project whereby the US would guarantee Israel's oil resources and energy supply in times of crisis.[15] "Oil is much too important a commodity to be left in the hands of the Arabs," he said. As for the defeat in Vietnam, if one is deeply identified with American military preeminence—as are Kissinger and Thomas, together with many Americans—this event was a terrible affront. The loss of Vietnam was a crisis of a different order than September 11, not just because the US invested so many years, so much blood and treasure, *and international credibility,* to prevent it, but because at every fork in the road Washington chose to escalate, often increasing enemy casualties but in the end falling all the harder on the ruins of its objectives. Which brings us to Ha Van Lau's discussion of the nature of American imperialism.

Carol McEldowney's group had prepared some questions for the meeting with Lau, which was also attended by two cabinet ministers: the head of the Supreme Court, Pham Van Bach, and the Minister of Health, Pham Ngoc Thach. This trio, all originally from south of the Demilitarized Zone, interestingly enough, headed up the War Crimes Commission, and was occasionally sighted *en plein air* by visitors like Mary McCarthy, who met them in 1968 outside the Thong Nhat Hotel with the Minister of Health's pretty Vietnamese–French daughter. I came across the diminutive Pham Van Bach early in 1967, sitting alone at the diplomat's café in Hanoi, dressed in a navy blue Mao jacket and loose pants, reading a newspaper over a cup of tea. The entire room was full of tea drinkers sitting out an air raid. Encounters like this led Mary to think of Renaissance Florence, "where the notables take the air in the evening on the main street,"[16] and me of running into Mircea Eliade one stormy afternoon at Jimmy's, a popular tavern in Chicago's Hyde Park.

McEldowney's questions were as follows: How did the North interpret American war aims? What was the purpose of the airwar? What did the North think would be the next stage of escalation? They were odd ones to ask the other side, but Americans were always asking them, as if in Hanoi they would find answers that were concealed at home. Not like today, when court advisers such as Richard Perle and Michael Ledeen repeatedly remind people who don't want to listen that invading Iraq is a precondition for reordering the balance of power in the Middle East in America's favor. As Ledeen said the other day, addressing the Jewish Institute for National

Security Affairs (JINSA), "the time for diplomacy is at an end; it is time for a free Iran, free Syria, and free Lebanon."[17] Alleged possession of weapons of mass destruction and ties to al Qaeda are trundled out to mobilize mass fears and engage the cognoscenti in fruitless debate—just as "we're-fighting-Communism-in-Southeast-Asia" kept the fires burning in Vietnam long after it was obvious to Washington that this war of national liberation was not replicable anywhere else on earth.

Americans who gave the war any serious thought found it hard to understand exactly what the US was doing in Vietnam. North Vietnam hadn't committed acts of aggression against the US or its allies. There were no significant natural resources for American business to lust after— not like the oil in Iraq whose allocation under US auspices is supposed to give Washington a potent tool for dominating other nations. Vietnam's cheap labor and market potential wouldn't beckon until much later, in 1993, when US multinationals felt squeezed out of the race to invest in the latest Asian Tiger (prematurely, as it turned out), and President Clinton finally lifted the postwar economic embargo. So what was it then? *Imperialism*, radicals said, but how did imperialism work in a bipolar world?

Colonel Lau had begun by disposing of Washington's official arguments for bombing North Vietnam: to protect the South against aggression from the North, etc.; and then moved quickly to the "actual *long-range purpose.*" In McEldowney's notes: "US wants to dominate the world under banner of anti-communism, and to do this must interfere in the affairs of other nations. Much attention has been given to SE Asia, especially since the founding of the PRC [People's Republic of China] after WWII. US plan was to first dominate Indochina and then the world."

No mention of the balance of power with the Soviet Union, which President Kennedy had, in any event, openly scorned. When Khrushchev established a missile base in Cuba in 1962, then offered to withdraw it if the US removed its missile bases from Turkey, Kennedy refused, set up a naval blockade, and Khrushchev withdrew his missiles. Moscow had been restless, too, but Washington gave no quarter—publicly, that is. Privately,

Kennedy had agreed to a partial quid pro quo in Turkey. But McEldowney's notes mention neither the Soviet Union nor Communism. Only that "under the banner of anti-communism," Washington nursed a larger strategic goal. With China's arrival as a full-fledged power now standing outside both American and Russian spheres of influence, the US sought to reorder the balance of power in the Pacific by seizing control of Indochina.

According to Lau, this would take three steps: first, to enter Indochina, America had backed up the French in the First Indochina War ("aiding French colonialists in their repression"). The next step, then underway, was the "occupation of South Vietnam, to use it as springboard and *neo-colonialist military base*"; the third was "to occupy North Vietnam, then Laos and Cambodia." The object was to encircle China from the south— not unlike the current plan in Iraq, where the Pentagon wishes to maintain several military bases as springboards for use against neighboring Arab states that are seen as harboring threats to Israeli security and to US economic hegemony in the region.

The first step, according to Lau, had been defeated on three fronts: at the battle of Dien Bien Phu in 1954, where the Vietminh routed the US-backed French Expeditionary Corps; at Geneva later that year, where international recognition was given to Vietnam's right to independence and eventual reunification; and with the creation of the socialist DRV (Democratic Republic of Vietnam) in 1945. Before moving to the next step in the takeover attempt, Colonel Lau (who had been chief of diplomatic liaison in Geneva) underlined the primary circumstances that fed the American drive to world dominance: the fact that the US had emerged from World War II with the least destruction—indeed, as the true victor— and the formation of the socialist camp.

The second step, starting in 1954, began with a five-year effort to create a separate "neocolonial" state in South Vietnam, in violation of the Geneva Accords. The old form of colonialism was impossible because postwar public opinion condemned it. Thus began the stage of the "stooge puppet administration and army," first under the unpopular Catholic

president, Ngo Dinh Diem (until 1963, when the CIA abandoned him to
his assassins). Diem's regime was punctuated by periodic intervals of
"denouncing Communists" in which all those who favored peace and
reunification—according to Geneva, reunification was to have been
decided in 1956 by country-wide elections—were subject to extreme
repression. Victims included sympathizers and families of the Vietminh
(Ho Chi Minh's forces) who had remained in their villages after regroup-
ment in 1954. The years 1959–60 marked the onset of the "General
Uprising" when the NLF and Hanoi began to coordinate the political
struggle and the armed struggle.

"Not a family was untouched by the terrorism," I read in my own report
of a similar presentation. "Jails everywhere, people in SVN living in very
dark times. HVL stands at map, pointer in hand, runs it down to the
[Mekong] Delta. 'Someday we will march all the way to Saigon without
opposition,' he says." I remember how remote Lau's prediction seemed at
the time. South Vietnam had become one big American military base.
Agent Orange and scorched earth operations had destroyed so much paddy
that the South was *importing* rice from Texas. Yet I knew he was right.

Suspected Vietcong villages were razed and recalcitrant peasants roped
into Strategic Hamlets, *aka* New Life hamlets. This was when Vietnam had
first caught my attention, when I was teaching Orwell's "Politics and the
English Language" in Chicago in 1963, and using the *Chicago Tribune*'s war
reporting as a laboratory. "Strategic Hamlets" reminded me of concentration camps, while my students, mostly the offspring of Black Muslims,
were reminded of Chicago's new "Model Cities" program which tore up
black neighborhoods and forced inhabitants into tightly patrolled housing
projects. Either way, you knew something nasty was going on behind those
voodoo words. In Democratic circles, however—and remember, this was
a Democratic war, though old-school anti-imperialists like Democratic
Senators Wayne Morse and Ernest Greuning were the first Congressmen
to oppose it—New Life hamlets evoked visions of spanking new Asian
villages, where Communism and poverty had been swept away and simple

peasants got a boost up the ladder of progress by way of new latrines and imported seeds.

Nation-building was more than a cover for the counterinsurgency (CI) program. The "Special War," Lau called the CI operations, which ran like armed protection squads alongside rural development projects. For Cold War liberals, nation-building was an attempt to resolve the standoff between the Vietcong's policy of "land to the tillers" and the monopolization of privilege and wealth by a Saigon regime that had only contempt for the countryside and its exotic religious sects, including the majority practice of Buddhism. Nation-building was a piece of the Third Force solution, to which a good many spooks were also drawn (viz. Alden Pyle in *The Quiet American*). Kennedy had a watchword for it: "Those who make peaceful revolution impossible, make violent revolution inevitable." But the government's peaceful revolutions carried within their wide bellies helicopters, Gatling guns, and M-16s, ready to be disgorged when organized resistance spread too far.

By 1963, nation-building had given way to something darker. It hadn't worked in Vietnam essentially for the same reason reconstruction won't work in Iraq. The interests of the builders collided with the interests of the nation, whose population for the most part favored Ho's watchword: "Nothing is more precious than independence and freedom." In South Vietnam, nation-building had succeeded in creating the infrastructure for military escalation. The important two-lane north–south highway was turned into an "autobahn," Colonel Lau reported; deepwater ports were enlarged; Saigon's Tan Son Nhut airport was transformed into a giant air base, with similar bases built at Bien Hoa and Danang, all under the pretext of "development." The US had learned early on that it was in for a long war, but neither Kennedy nor Johnson had taken the measure of the other side—just as the Pentagon has failed to grasp the level of political organization among the Iraqi insurgents, or to recognize the historical memory that appears to be pulling a disparate society together around a hatred of empire.

The year 1963 was a turning point, said Lau, referring to the defeat of 3000 puppet troops with modern weapons by 200 guerrillas at the village of Ap Bac just thirty miles south of Saigon. Ap Bac, which preceded the first of a series of coups in Saigon, caught the attention of Neil Sheehan:

> SAIGON, Jan. 6 (UPI) Angry United States military advisers charged today that Vietnamese infantrymen refused direct orders to advance during Wednesday's battle at Ap Bac and that an American Army captain was killed while out front pleading with them to attack. ... One US adviser said bitterly, "These people (the Vietnamese) won't listen—they make the same mistakes over and over again in the same way." (*The Washington Post*, January 7, 1963)

"The problem was not the men," Colonel Lau said of the Saigon regimes, "but the American policy which gave birth to henchmen." The same policy presumably explained the lack of aggressiveness of the government's infantrymen.

At Ap Bac, the Vietnamese had taken a lesson from People's War 101, wherein the guerrilla draws the enemy deep into the countryside he controls, then surrounds its bases and attacks them one by one, cutting them off like the fingers of a hand from supply camps near the central cities and ports. By 1967, the US was defending nearly sixty military outposts throughout the South, with less and less success as the year wore on. Defending an isolated airstrip and valley at Khe Sanh in May 1967, nearly half the American combat troops there were killed (160) or wounded (746) in a twelve-day campaign reported by Jonathan Randal for the *New York Times*.

Ten months later the bare red hills of Khe Sanh were still under siege. John Wheeler sent these paragraphs out by AP wire on February 8, 1968:

> Outside the random explosions sent thousands of pounds of shrapnel tearing into sandbags and battering already damaged mess halls and tent areas long ago destroyed and abandoned for a life of fear and filth underground.

This is the life in the V Ring, a sharpshooter's term for the inner part of the bull's eye. At Khe Sanh the V Ring for the North Vietnamese gunners neatly covers the bunkers of Bravo Company, 3rd Reconnaissance Battalion. In three weeks, more than half the company had been killed or wounded. ...

A blank stare in the eyes of some is not uncommon at Khe Sanh where the Communists have fired up to 1500 rounds of rockets, artillery and mortar shells in a single day. ...

At night the men in [nineteen-year-old Lance Corporal Richard] Noyes' bunker sit and talk, sing, play cards, almost anything to keep from being alone with their thoughts. During a night when more than 1000 rounds hit Khe Sanh, Noyes turned to a buddy and said:

"Man, it'll be really decent to go home and never hear words like incoming shells, mortars, rifles, and all that stuff. And the first guy who asks me how it feels to kill, I'll ..." A pause. Then: "You know, my brother wants me to go duck hunting when I get home. Man, I don't want to even see a slingshot when I get out of here."...

Lance Corporal Richard Morris, 24, of North Hollywood, Calif., began playing a guitar. Two favorites that night were "Five Hundred Miles" and "Where Have All the Flowers Gone?"

A hard emphasis accompanied the verse that went: "Where have all the soldiers gone? To the graveyard every one. When will they ever learn? When will they ever learn?"

This was American war reporting without handlers.

Hanoi's Communists tended to think in "step-by-step plans" (and often in threes) whereby strategic goals were plotted over extended periods of time, and on a variety of fronts. It's hard to imagine such a practice in the United States where the tilt of foreign policy aims (rarely the substance) are interrupted every four to eight years by a new administration. An interest group bent on enacting a long-term strategic goal that departs from established practice, as unilateralism departs from multilateralism, would have to exercise a kind of deep leadership capable of withstanding the shifting winds of domestic politics. One looks in vain for precedents in American history of the cabal that rules today, which began swarming as early as 1975 inside the Ford administration, when Rumsfeld was first secretary of defense, then flowered under Reagan, and nursed its vision of a unipolar world based on absolute US military supremacy through four administrations.

Such leadership, with its underground component, its resort to front organizations (think-tanks, OpEd pages, talk shows), harkens back to the American Communist Party, which is not surprising when you consider that one branch of the neocon family tree is rooted in the sectarian battles of New York in the 1930s. This is the grandparents' generation: Irving Kristol, Norman Podhoretz, Midge Decter, Jeanne Kirkpatrick, and Sidney Hook. (Hook, now deceased, helped relieve me of my post as teaching assistant at New York University in 1964 after I asked him to review the proposal I was circulating for *Viet-Report*. Politicking on professional time was the charge, not to mention being on the wrong side of the political tracks.)

Scratch a hardline anti-communist, the freethinking Dwight Macdonald used to say, and you'll find a former hardline Stalinist. It was the hardness of the line, and the love of intrigue and power, that marked the breed. Hannah Arendt found the perfect type in Whittaker Chambers, the ex-Communist turned FBI informer who sent Alger Hiss to prison. Reviewing Chambers' memoir *Witness* for *Commonweal* in 1953, she noted that like many former Communists, he had little interest in the political life of the Party. "He looked down on it and escaped it into the inner apparatus where commands were given and obeyed … behind the scenes of official Communist politics."[18]

It's fascinating how the *éclat* of belonging to the Communist Party could be cashed in at the dock of McCarthyism in the 1950s, and how quickly it yielded a cadre of second-generation careerists eager to serve the imperial state. "There was an enormous prestige ... for people who belonged to the Party," the critic Malcolm Cowley recalled in 1966. "They were listened to as if they had been at meetings where the word was passed down from Mount Sinai."[19] Mount Sinai was Moscow, the administrative capital of another country, whose great land mass and untold resources have long haunted the imaginations of American intellectuals and diplomats alike. Think of Secretary of State William Seward's effort to acquire Russian America after the Civil War. Seward saw Russia as a kind of reverse mold of the United States, or a vast extension—troubling, mysterious, tantalizing in its Byzantine obscurity, whose Siberian land bridge lay submerged in the icy waters off Alaska.

At the turn of the last century, the economic theorist Charles Conant, editor of the influential *Banker's Magazine*, predicted that in another generation Russia would emerge as England and America's chief competitor for the commercial and military domination of the world. It was Czarist Russia's highly centralized, absolutist form of government, he believed, that offered it distinct advantages over a democracy in the struggle to control underdeveloped countries. Conant actually wanted the United States to study Russia's techniques of centralization, just as Russia, he thought, should learn a greater internal liberalization from America. In 1900, he envisioned the two countries moving closer together as each assimilated the best of the other's system.

Perhaps it's not surprising that a good many Americans who embraced the Communist Party in the 1930s, and repudiated it later, reentered the mainstream of American politics without an ideological hair out of place. To the degree that they attached their loyalty to the Soviet Union, where party and state were one, and not to American radical traditions (although other Communists did), it took not much more than a leap of faith to shift their allegiance to Franklin Roosevelt or Henry Luce, or even to Albert Wohlstatter, grand master of strategic analysis at the Rand Corporation, and mentor to Richard Perle, when visions of a more powerful world order hove into view.

Anti-communism became the through-line for decades of American policymakers, not just because Communism threatened to unleash the pent-up energies of the poor but also because it perpetuated the belief in the essentially aggressive nature of the Soviet Union. Fear of the "Evil Empire" fueled the Reagan administration's promotion of SDI, or Star Wars, and the maintenance of ever increasing levels of military spending. It didn't matter that as early as 1975 Soviet military spending had begun to taper off, as CIA analysts discovered in 1983. Even in 1984, when Gorbachev started the round of drastic cuts in the military budget that helped bring down the regime, apparatchiks in the Reagan administration: Paul Wolfowitz, Scooter Libby, Douglas Feith, Richard Perle, and Michael Ledeen, who oversaw annual increases in the defense budget of up to 8 percent (*six times the USSR's*), convinced themselves, and others, that the Soviets were poised, not for territorial aggression, but for new bursts of military spending. Anti-communism would not falter, Reagan's defense secretary Caspar Weinberger reiterated in his memoirs, so long as "there were two superpowers, one of which had the governmental structure and military might of the Soviet Union."[20]

And when that superpower collapsed—what dark empire would take its place? Of Caspar Weinberger's two superpowers, the US had long possessed the superior military might, a fact that few historians dispute today. Nothing in the Soviet arsenal or governing "structure" could match the dynamic influence that America's arms industry exercised over national defense planning and spending in the United States. But after Nixon's overture to China, and after Vietnam, political Washington had returned to Moscow-bashing to fuel the race that drove the military–industrial estate: no longer the race to secure the world's runaway colonies, or the race to the moon, but principally the arms race, and the push to launch a unilateral space-based missile defense system.

A friend of mine remembers watching an ashen-faced George Bush Sr. announce the fall of the Berlin Wall, and therefore the end of the Evil Empire, on television. What's wrong with this picture? he wondered, staring at the stricken president who looked as if the earth had cracked open and swallowed a million people, or as if a major ally had fallen— which in a sense it had. How would the US pursue its hegemonic interests without the whipping boy of Communism? For thirty years the Free World had been schooled to think in political terms of democracy versus totalitarianism, the US versus the USSR. Every tinpot dictator from Guatemala to Cambodia was drilled (usually at the School of the Americas in Georgia) in the principles of the Cold War's National Security Doctrine, which taught them to view local and regional conflicts within the context of the global struggle against the Soviet bloc. Political opposition to ruling juntas were "threats to the state," liberation movements were "arms of Communist subversion."

The problem of the missing scapegoat was real—for some, an almost theological crisis—and it persisted for Bush Jr., who confessed during his presidential campaign that he wasn't sure who the enemy was. "When I was coming up, with what was a dangerous world," he said, "we knew exactly who they were. It was us versus them. ... Today we're not so sure who the they are but we know they're there." Addressing the Council on Foreign Relations in February 2002, Dick Cheney admitted that before September 11 he too had puzzled over this question. "When America's great enemy suddenly disappeared, many wondered what new direction our foreign policy would take. We spoke, as always, of long-term problems and regional crises throughout the world," he said, "but there was no single, immediate, global threat that any roomful of experts could agree upon. All of that changed five months ago. The threat is known and our role is clear now." Commenting on these admissions, Frances FitzGerald points out that what both men were saying was "that the main purpose of American foreign policy was to confront an enemy—and that a worthy successor to the Soviet Union had finally emerged, in the form of international terrorism."[21]

Terrorism was the natural successor to Communism for a foreign policy steeped in the tradition of confronting enemies; it too could be presented as a conspiracy whose tentacles lay hidden under any rock that obstructed the pursuit of a ruling interest which was otherwise difficult to defend. Thus the Bush administration seized upon the huge domestic support the president reaped after September 11 to pursue its original objectives, some of them, such as the seizure of Iraq, originally justified as part of the war on terrorism. Under cover of fighting terrorism in Afghanistan and Iraq, the US could likewise openly pursue its geostrategic interests in dominating Central Asia, the Caspian, the Caucasus, and the Middle East, because of their vast oil and gas deposits, mostly untapped in the case of the former Soviet territories. But there was another, more distant strategic interest, which is that like Indochina these regions have been orphaned by the breakup of former empires, and are therefore potential prey— especially the seven republics in the Asian heartland—to the world's sole remaining great power, which is China.

To encircle China from the west may be the longer run purpose behind the proliferation of military bases the Pentagon has built in Uzbekistan, Kazakhstan, Kyrgyzstan, and Georgia. A look at the map is instructive. It's not just China but Russia too that is presently hemmed in from the south, and now that the bloc countries have sworn fealty to the Bush administration, from the west, as well. "Washington cannot know today whether Russia, or for that matter China, will be neutral, friend, foe or part of a hostile alliance in the future," state the authors of a right-wing think-tank report on US nuclear planning issued just as President Bush took office. For that reason they advocate watching both countries closely.[22]

What is noteworthy about Ha Van Lau's reading of America's long-range purpose in Vietnam is that as early as 1967 he saw anti-communism as cover for a drive toward empire that would manifest itself through a pattern of implanting military bases in the countries surrounding rival powers. The US preoccupation with China was actually something Vietnam clearly shared. American visitors were often struck by the emphasis their hosts placed on the long domination of Vietnam by the Chinese. "You have to understand that for most of our history we never thought about the Americans," Norm Fruchter remembers hearing. "The Chinese are the colossus that we worried about."[23] Popular literature was, and remains, filled with accounts of uprisings led by Vietnamese heroes and heroines against Chinese invaders—like the epic battle of Bach Dang that I heard from a young interpreter who narrated it with such feeling while we "spent the night on the wheel" (Vietnamese for driving all night in a blacked-out car) that by the end of the account we were both crying. In the story, Chinese invaders are poised for victory; their great warships massed at the mouth of the Bach Dang River, which our rickety Soviet sedan had just crossed on a pontoon bridge. The Vietnamese lure the vessels upstream where they have planted spikes in the riverbed. When the tide falls and the enemy ships are forced to retreat, they are impaled and sink. When did this happen? I ask, thinking of the bamboo spikes the Vietcong set underneath hollowed out spots in jungle trails to trap unwary GIs. Tenth century, he said.

Nine hundred years later, a reunified Vietnam, led by Ho Chi Minh's Communist Party, pursued a trade relationship with the US in no small part to offset the strategic influence of China. Indeed, twenty years after the end of the war, Vietnam's policy makers seemed to worry more about America's ability to maintain its own strategic interests in the Pacific than about the subversive influence of the materialist culture creeping in on the heels of Western trade. Imagine my surprise when on a third trip to Vietnam, in October 1995 (the second was with my family in 1994), I was asked by a young scholar at Hanoi's Center for North American Studies if it was true, as she had heard, "that America's role is decreasing in Asia after the Cold War?" If so, she worried, "how does the United States plan to rebuild its stature in Asia in the future?" Following a foreign policy line that China herself pursued a century before—that of "balancing the barbarians"—Vietnam needed a genuine American presence in the Pacific to check Chinese ambitions.[24]

Now that Donald Rumsfeld has announced his intention to pull a few thousand US troops out of both South Korea and Japan, and has attempted to deputize Beijing to rein in North Korea, this ancient fear of the colossus to the north—joined today by the uncertainties unleashed by the rogue empire under George Bush's command—must terrify Southeast Asia.[25] Which, one suspects, is pretty much what Washington desires.

THIS AMERICAN WAR

January 29, 1967

Thanh Hoa City was bombed at 12:05 today. While we were eating lunch about 6 km away we heard the planes. I ran to get the tape recorder and moved inside the shelter. I recorded the sound of the planes, the "whompf" of anti-aircraft shells, and the concussions of the bombs. Also recorded was our chatter inside the shelter, the sound of birds outside, and a little boy running with his friends to a shelter, crying *My by my! My by my!* [American planes! American planes!] and *John-son, John-son,* by which the bombs are known. Later at 2 we were scheduled to drive to Thanh Hoa City. We were to meet in the First Aid Station where victims from previous attacks who had been evacuated from Thanh Hoa Hospital the day before were lodged. We did not leave at 2:00 but waited while some men from the local [War Crimes] commission went ahead to see if the way was clear after the bombing. Tu Van [the photographer] went with them. At about three we had to take to the shelter again. I recorded the same sounds.

We did not set out until nearly six. The road was filled with people coming from the city. Peasants came bearing stretchers. Whole families with rolled mats and their belongings on their backs. Ox carts piled with children and pots and food. A local militia unit bearing more stretchers. We had to stop the jeeps and get out to walk at one point, for the road had been hit and trucks were piled up for about half a mile. As we walked, Thanh Hoa City came into view. First the smell of burnt things, then the smoke itself, then the ruins. First the provincial hospital, bombed many times before, today completely leveled. Here general purpose bombs appear to have been used—not napalm—for the rubble was dry.

For some way down the road, houses had been leveled. The road itself was pocked but passable. We climbed back in the jeeps and crept slowly through crowds of people streaming out of the city. We had been told that Thanh Hoa had been evacuated months ago—since the direct bombings began April 18, 1966. Obviously many remained—many of them children.

We stopped again and moved on by foot. The rubble turned to live ash. Suddenly as far as I could see the ground was on fire. Where houses had been, now black ash smoldered. Red coals were heaped everywhere. We walked to the First Aid station where we were supposed to have met a few hours before. In its place was a field of burning ash. It was struck by general purpose bombs first at three, immediately followed by napalm (incendiary) bombs. Nothing was left standing. A charred bed was upturned, a bent corner of a sign, "X-Ray—" Most of the patients (victims of previous bomb-ings) had been evacuated just in time. Some were caught. Tu Van tells us she photographed one body, a charred corpse without arms or legs.

We moved on. On one side of the road we could see burning plots where houses once stood. Out of the darkness an old man and woman suddenly appeared. Each had occupied a house and had sought shelter in time to save their lives. Each had seen his family evacuated months ago. They would take what few bricks remained, we were told, and begin building anew far away, but still in Thanh Hoa province.

We walked through 200 or 300 yards of burning rubble. I had not taken Dong's advice, and had not worn socks, and the cinders burned my ankles.

Around a corner we came to a leveled area which was not burning. It was filled with craters. In the middle of the road a smallish pit, about 2 ft. wide, 4 ft. deep. It had been a missile, we were told. About 20 feet away was a shelter, ripped open with bits of cloth stuck to the mud walls. Two children had been incinerated inside from the heat of the missile.

About 50 yards behind that was an enormous crater, at least 70 feet in diameter, 60 feet deep. It was created by a 2000 lb. bomb. 9 houses had been blasted from their foundations and only broken teacups and vases, over which we stepped, remained. About 30 feet away two thatched roofs hung from high treetops. No one was killed or wounded here. The houses had been evacuated.

We walked through a stone building of some size. Here the smell of burnt flesh was overwhelming. But it was not human. This had been the general store, where meat had been displayed a few hours ago. One wing was a first aid station, and instruments lay blackened around the floor.

By this time our entourage had swelled to at least 30. Most of the people left, however, hardly watched us, but kept piling bricks quietly, digging, stacking broken dishes, bits of furniture, etc.

I asked the Chairman of the District Administration how far this part of Thanh Hoa City lay from the bridge of Ham Romg, a rather large one. He said 8 km. The place where we first saw the acres of burning rubble was 12 km away [from the bridge].

In the jeep driving back Phan [our guide] told me how much Pat and Diane [unknown] had wanted to come out to places like this. They had not been able to ensure their safety sufficiently, he told me. "Our friends are too precious," he said, "to risk their being threatened by the bombs. We do not have many real friends in the world. We are grateful for those who understand us. Some have thought we are a bellicose people—we must *like* war to have been fighting foreign aggressors so many years. But that is not true. We are a peaceloving people. We know that there is nothing more precious than independence and peace. That is why we must fight for it, until we have it." He told Tariq [Ali, another member of the investigating team] he liked what he said in his toast in Hanoi—that Tariq felt ashamed that he had not fought, that he and many others sympathetic to the VN people had made no sacrifices. "That was a correct feeling," Phan said. "It makes us feel very warm."

—unpublished Vietnam notebook, January 23–February 12, 1967

When I wrote this, I "forgot" that the patients who were killed at the First Aid Station had been brought there to meet us.

"NATION-BUILDING" IN IRAQ:
A PREDICTION

May 18, 2003

Even in Iraq, where there is no centuries-long history of repelling invaders, no unifying leader or leaders, no party to unite and mobilize the masses, no jungle to hide in, no sympathetic great powers to lend support, the American reconstruction program is likely to provoke fresh resistance to US occupation, followed by an enlarged American military presence, more resistance, and on and on. The attempt to raise "Our New Baby" from the war wreckage by way of "one of the biggest nation-building projects the US has ever undertaken," about which Tom Friedman enthuses, is likely to end with the mega-concessions doled out to Halliburton and its subsidiaries, along with Bechtel and the well-connected Fluor Corporation. Together they will build and service military bases and construction camps, and repair and expand damaged pumping stations and pipelines. Oil takes first place in the Iraqi war, surpassing civil security, and surpassing the fulfillment of promises made to the Kurds. The US has already rebuffed a bid by ethnic Kurds for a formal share in the state oil giants of northern Iraq. Instead, the Ba'ath structure is to remain intact, with major oil divisions staffed by Saddam's old team. This focus on production *uber alles*, in part because the US plans to finance its war and postwar debts out of Iraqi oil deals, has greatly upset Kurdish leaders, who had hoped for entrée into the oil industry.

Inadequate security, meanwhile, has scared away the smaller companies which were a short while ago swarming for "nation-building contracts" in postwar Iraq. A US telecommunications firm poised to install a cellular transmission system in Baghdad, where three weeks after "liberation" there are still no phones and no police force, waits in Kuwait for assurances of protection. Not everybody waits, however. Journalist Peter Maass visited the Oil Ministry on May 8 when the convoy of a Bradley fighting vehicle and several armored Humvees bristling with .50-caliber machine guns lumbered by. They were escorting a single SUV with two civilians inside who worked for KBR. The oldest and largest of Halliburton's subsidiaries, Brown & Root built America's air bases and deepwater ports in South Vietnam (and did it without military escorts).

Should Washington proceed to impose its hand-picked interim government on a country whose long-suffering Shi'ite majority is busy mobilizing around several leaders—among them, Ayatollah Muhammed Bakr al-Hakim, who opposes the US occupation and favors an elected government that will represent all ethnic and religious groups [killed one month later]—it may well find itself facing a situation not unlike the one that confronted Kennedy in 1960. Genuine opposition movements will be driven underground and encouraged to cross borders in search of allies and support, while US peacekeeping actions will slide deeper into open warfare against the Iraqi people. Already the Q-word has slipped into the vernacular of American and British news reporting. Even Iraqi exiles are using it. Speaking of the sudden collapse of the first American reconstruction team led by General Jay Garner on May 10, Kurdish leader Massoud Barzani, a member of the Pentagon's government-in-waiting, warns "that if we continue in this confusion, the wonderful victory we have achieved will turn into a quagmire."

At the same time, many Iraqis question the credibility of the returning exiles whose clout lies with their Pentagon patronage, though some are more disturbed by the patronage extended to the hated Ba'ath party, many of whose second-tier government loyalists, not only at the Oil Ministry, are being summoned back to work. The "wonderful victory" over Saddam Hussein appears not so wonderful to increasing numbers of people in the major cities, where bandits rule the streets, and the infrastructure of daily survival—water, garbage pick-up, food distribution, emergency health care, police protection, not to mention schools, jobs, pension checks—has been all but wiped out by a combination of war damage and systematic looting that extends to fixtures, plumbing, building materials, and government records. If Iraqi protests over the breakdown of law and order continue to be met by forced dispersal on the part of US troops, while pleas to secure mass grave sites and to protect hospitals, laboratories, and universities from further demolition are ignored, the current jockeying for political advantage among Shi'ites and Sunnis already underway in the volatile terrain of post-Saddam Iraq will give way to desperate measures.

The descent into chaos and violence that has followed the "end" of this war—a war that simply ran out of enemy like a car runs out of gas, and stopped—is truly shocking. "Unless we do something in the near future, it is likely to blow up in our faces," an American official says of Baghdad, which is erupting almost hourly in gunfire. The speed with which events are rocketing out of control—or reaching another *niveau*, Ha Van Lau might say—reminds one of those calendars in old movies where the pages curl up in smoke and fly away to mark the passage of time. Transitions that took years to develop in the aftermath of earlier invasions now ripen and break down in a matter of days. Thus two and a half weeks after General Garner arrived in Baghdad to restore services "as soon as possible"—promising that the Americans "will not overstay their welcome"—he is replaced by a Kissinger protégé and so-called counterterrorism specialist, L. Paul Bremer III. "We intend to have a very effective, efficient and well-organized handover," says Mr. Bremer (whether speaking of the handover from Garner's staff to his own much larger one, or from the Americans to the interim Iraqi administration, isn't clear). Two days later, "Lord Bremer of Mesopotamia," as the *Wall Street Journal* fondly calls him, announces that looters will be shot on sight, and two days later corrects himself, and says they will be "neutralized."

Barbara K. Bodine, a former ambassador to Yemen who actually spoke Arabic and was in charge of reconstruction for the Baghdad region, was also given notice; as was Margaret Tutmiler, a communications officer under General Garner, who came out of the public relations industry and worked with former secretary of state James A. Baker III under the first President Bush. In the "slam bang, thank you, ma'am" tradition of corporate firings, Bodine's dismissal arrived in a late-night call on a phone that had been installed in her office only hours before. She and Tutmiler were gone two days later.

Pentagon estimates of how long US troops will remain in Iraq shift from "longer than a year" (Rumsfeld) to "what the future will hold a year, two, three ... ahead of us is not exactly knowable" (Tommy Franks). General Franks made the last remark the day after Army Lieutenant General David D.

McKiernan, commander of allied ground forces, said his troops couldn't guarantee total security in a country the size of California with only 25 million people (a comparison that did not go over well in that state). With the 1st Armored Division based in Germany presently entering Iraq, and the departure of the 3rd Infantry Division, the main force that invaded Baghdad, now delayed, the total number of US troops, currently 140,000, will increase—just as Colin Powell recommended from the start. These are heavy combat units, not peacekeepers, ill-suited to the constabulary duties of patrolling civilian institutions or shooting looters (who, it has been said, are mostly very young and very poor).

And sure enough, the beefed-up military presence has triggered the largest political protest against the American presence yet, a protest that also opposed Washington's plans for the future Iraqi government. On May 18, 10,000 Shi'ite and Sunni Muslims marched peacefully through Baghdad under the watchful eyes of Shi'ite organizers, many armed with assault rifles, and of American military snipers posted on rooftops along the route. The crowd carried placards and banners reading, "No to the foreign administration," and "No, No, No USA." They needn't have worried about the "foreign administration," for in the wildly gyrating momentum of US postwar policy, Paul Bremer has now announced that there will be no interim government; and then, correcting himself the next day, that the "handover" to an indigenous Iraqi administration could be a year or more away.

That the "handover" is moving more slowly than American officials promised is no surprise. It's the speed with which the conflict between invader and invaded is unfolding that is noteworthy. The intensity of organized Iraqi resistance has forced the US to abandon the "neocolonial" stage, at least for now, and move immediately to direct administration by the American military.

Mr. Bremer is reduced to issuing promises to end looting and combat lawlessness, just like his predecessor, while new conflicts are breaking out between the Kurds and Muslims in the North, and between patrolling "peacekeepers" and unemployed Iraqis just about everywhere. As the American military presence increases, the first postwar casualties have begun; three American soldiers died on May 18 in mysterious circumstances which the

Pentagon calls "accidents." Iraqi casualties are not reported by CentCom, but independent sources place them at 3400 killed.

Rumsfeld's fey dismissals of the collapse of civil society no longer pass muster, even with his fans. It is not funny to call such conditions "untidy," and hope "that others can recognize that and accept it, and put it into some historical context." Asked at a Pentagon press conference about Osama bin Laden's whereabouts a few days before the deadly explosions in Riyadh on May 12 and Casablanca May 16, both of which were attributed to al Qaeda, Rummy shoots a quizzical gaze at his chief of staff, Richard Myers. "Why haven't we found him?" he asks; and shrugs: "The world is a big place …. He's either alive, or he's alive and injured badly, or he's dead. Who knows?"

Soon he will be asked the same question about Saddam Hussein, another creature from the lagoon of infinite potentialities with which the American empire traffics. What will he say then? And if the weapons of mass destruction are still not found, those deadly gases and biological agents that President Bush conjured up again and again and again in the march to war—"If we know Saddam Hussein has dangerous weapons today, and we do, does it make any sense for the world to wait to confront him as he grows ever stronger and develops even more dangerous weapons?"(October 7, 2002); "Intelligence gathered … leaves no doubt that the Iraq regime continues to possess and conceal some of the most lethal weapons ever devised" (March 17, 2003)— what then?

IS THE PENTAGON TRAPPED
IN THE WRONG WAR?

July 14, 2003, AlterNet.org

"Quit beating around the bush," snaps the *Wall Street Journal*: "America faces a guerrilla war." And so it does. But an odd paralysis still grips the US military command. While the number of American soldiers killed or wounded in ambushes multiplies by the day, Defense Secretary Donald Rumsfeld and proconsul Paul Bremer continue to speak of "remnants" and "bitter-enders" who can't get with the program, even as word spreads through the ranks that there is a well-organized resistance campaign underway in Iraq.

When Saddam Hussein spoke in March of letting Americans into Iraqi cities, especially Baghdad, and breaking their will, he meant it. After all, his government had been training civilians in combat techniques, and distributing firearms including AK-47 rifles and rocket-propelled grenade launchers, for a year before the invasion; and US planners knew it. But the Pentagon, trapped in a different scenario—where urban guerrilla warfare was to commence (if at all) immediately after US tanks entered the capital—didn't get the message. When heavy combat operations were followed by a pronounced lull, US commanders seemed to forget Saddam's warning. Now First Sergeant William Taylor, based near Tikrit, cites the lull as the period when the insurgents "got their cells together."

The Pentagon, in fact, has been feeding itself its own mistaken information. Unlike the faulty weapons intelligence the White House cynically used to sell the war, US military leaders seem to have believed what their analysts and Iraqi exiles were telling them. Saddam, the sources said, was incapable of participating in a guerrilla-style resistance campaign because he was accustomed to running a government, not an insurgency. "This is not a man who is an ascetic like Osama bin Laden who is willing to go live in a cave for a long period of time and be cut off from the outside world," said Vice President Dick Cheney on Meet the Press shortly before the war began. "This is a man who's used to his palaces and his luxuries." Indeed, some senior officials half-expected an Iraqi surrender before US troops even entered Iraq.

In prewar Pentagon estimates, this was to be a different war. Occupation forces would be quickly cut to 40,000 or 30,000. Small contingents of peace-keepers would remain to safeguard the reconstruction of Iraq's infrastructure, including oil pipelines and well-heads, and the building of four permanent American military bases (one, called "intelligence city," already underway in the north). The war itself was planned to knock out the Ba'ath regime to make way for a government compatible with America's long term interest in Iraq, which is (or was) to use it as a base of operations for bringing military and political pressure to bear on nations which are central to Bush's plans to dominate the Middle East. Thus it was important for US strategic goals to shock and awe not just the Iraqis but a wider Arab community with the terrifying spectacle of US military technology.

Defense intellectuals in the Pentagon speak of transforming the psycholog-ical architecture of the Islamic world. Neocon analysts, in particular, worry that the US withdrawal from Beirut in 1983, followed by early withdrawals from Somalia and Afghanistan, suggest that the United States, while powerful militarily, is incapable of resolute action. In Beirut and Somalia US troops with-drew after taking minimal casualties (casualties are always "minimal" in such formulations), while in Afghanistan the US halted operations after seizing a few major cities, apparently because it was unwilling to engage in a more extended conflict. The American invasion of Iraq was designed to change Islamic perceptions, to provoke anger in exchange for a greater fear.

Thus there is a grim irony to the fact that the first pillar of Middle East policy to fall in occupied Iraq is the credibility of American power. Iraqis express surprise, frustration, and fury that months after "victory" was declared the "Authority," as the Coalition Provisional Authority is called, is unable to bring order to Baghdad. Looting and sabotage continue; electricity runs only intermittently; water and sewage systems remain unrepaired; food distribution is spotty; and medical services, overloaded with mounting casual-ties from the fighting, are near collapse. Meanwhile, there are no jobs for a vast unemployed workforce, which includes hundreds of thousands of demobilized Iraqi soldiers and Ba'athist office workers dismissed by the Authority without pay.

Why are they here? Iraqis must wonder, as they queue up in hopeless lines behind the barricaded gates of Saddam's palaces where the Americans live. It's hard to imagine a set of conditions more conducive to the conversion of a desperate citizenry into partisans for resistance. Moreover, when you consider that civilian deaths from the three-week war are estimated at 5500 to 7000, with military deaths exceeding 10,000, and overall nonfatal casualties totaling 50,000—all together touching family and friends reaching into the millions—you have another condition feeding insurrection. Most of these casualties were sustained in the Sunni areas of Central Iraq where US bombing was heaviest, and where the present opposition is strongest. That the resistance will ultimately dwarf Ba'athist "bitter-enders" (who now include—another grim irony—Saddam himself) seems quite possible, especially if elements of the volatile majority of Shi'ites in the South enter the fray, along with increasing numbers of non-Iraqis.

No wonder many American soldiers are demoralized and angry. Some have written their Congressmen requesting repatriation. "Most soldiers would empty their bank accounts just for a plane ticket home," runs one such letter, quoted last week in the *Christian Science Monitor*. And another: "The way we have been treated and the continuous lies told to our families back home has devastated us all." And another: "We feel like pawns in a game that we have no voice [in]."

Naturally the V-word (Vietnam) is turning up frequently in reports from the front. The US command has certainly made some familiar moves. Outgoing General Tommy Franks, facing sharp questions July 9 from the Senate Armed Services Committee, admits the current number of US troops in Iraq, around 148,000, will remain for the "foreseeable future," while Secretary Rumsfeld doubled estimated military costs to $3.9 billion *a month*. Meanwhile, the US promises to Iraq cover a lie that appears more obvious each time Mr. Bremer squashes another attempt at self-governance that isn't limited to hospitals, water or electrical power facilities. Nor is the hand-picked Governing Council a substitute for homegrown representation. Washington doesn't want an independent and democratic Iraq to emerge, for one of the first moves its government would make is to order the US out.

Yet there are big differences between Iraq and Vietnam, starting with the fact that in Iraq the US has no indigenous support. There's no puppet army or friendly regime as there was in South Vietnam; and no counterinsurgency program with coordinated intelligence, pacification, and military arms aimed at separating the guerrillas from the population and rewarding the latter. Such operations were not in the plans, which saw "Operation Iraqi Freedom" as essentially a show of force whose finish would be greeted by a grateful population, ready to step aside while Halliburton and Bechtel raised a new Iraq.

The mix of falsehood and bad faith that feeds America's Iraqi venture is probably greater than it was at the start of the Vietnam war. But the major difference is that now all Iraq is under military occupation. The ultimate in-country authority is General David McKiernan, while Paul Bremer, Baghdad's de facto mayor, reports directly to Secretary Rumsfeld. A Texas millionaire and former Army officer, Roger "Buck" Walters, governs southern Iraq, and a career Army officer who served in Vietnam and Somalia, W. Bruce Moore, runs the north. Iraqis, an educated people with some experience of empire, are unlikely to kowtow to this kind of slapdash corporate-style administration.

What Team Bush faces in Iraq is more than a guerrilla war. It is the first crack in the larger Mideast campaign in which Iraq was the starting point. This is the vision that has intoxicated defense planners such as Paul Wolfowitz, Richard Perle, Douglas Feith, and Kenneth Pollack for a decade. It's the dream of imposing a Pax Americana on the Arab world that is modeled on the imperial order Britain imposed in an earlier era. And it's off to a bloody bad start.

The vision appears like Banquo's ghost in the July/August number of *Foreign Affairs*. Alas, for authors Kenneth Pollack, former director for Persian Gulf Affairs at the National Security Council, Max Boot, author of *The Savage Wars of Peace*, and Andrew Moravcsik, professor of government at Harvard, their articles each celebrate the indomitable victory in Iraq. With Pollack it's the "sweeping American and British military victory in Operation Iraqi Freedom," while Boot says the "US victory in Iraq makes the German blitzkrieg look positively incompetent in comparison," and Moravcsik concludes that the "American hawks were right. Unilateral intervention to coerce regime change can be a cost-effective way to deal with rogue states. In military matters, there is only one superpower—the United States—and it can go it alone if it has to. It is time to accept this fact and move on."

TRUTH IN LYING

August 11, 2004, AlterNet.org

This is not the first time that bogus allegations have helped the US go a-warring against another country. But it may be the first time so much lying about another nation has set the US up for disaster in precisely the kind of military engagement it is least prepared to fight.

During the Cold War, the CIA fed policy makers false information about target states and groups all the time. Not that analysts knew the facts were wrong—they did and they didn't. Just as neocons in the "bat cave," as former CIA counterterrorism chief Vince Cannistraro calls the Pentagon's Office of Special Plans, may or may not have known they were being conned by the shoddy weapons evidence supplied by Iraqi exiles. What matters in such instances isn't necessarily the truth. "Intelligence," General Richard Myers reminds us, "doesn't mean something is true." What matters is whether the intelligence advances a nation's security strategy, and the policies that flow from it.

President Bush provided an interesting variation on this principle at his last press conference when, in response to questions about the failure to establish links between Saddam and al Qaeda, he said: "Look, in my line of work, it's always best to produce results ... In order to, you know, placate the critics and the cynics about the intentions of the United States, we need to produce evidence." Evidence, in other words, isn't necessary to establish the validity of intentions, but to sell a doubting public a course of action the government has already chosen for reasons it does not share.

During the Cold War, the CIA's mission in the Third World, including the Middle East, remained fairly constant for forty years. It was, in the main, to determine whether indigenous opposition movements that upset the balance of power in a particular region were Communist-inspired. Foreign agents were trained to think in ideological terms of democracy versus totalitarianism, the US versus the USSR, and to evaluate local conflicts in the context of the global struggle against the Soviet bloc. Thus were governments overthrown and pro-American regimes installed, among them Iran in 1953 and Guatemala in 1954, principally on the grounds that an indigenous challenge to vital US interests (land reform in the coffee plantations of Guatemala, the nationalization of oil in Iran) was the direct result of Soviet penetration.

It was a strategy that, with the conspicuous exceptions of Cuba and Vietnam, two countries which really were led by Communists, tended to work. But the secret of America's leadership wasn't its ability to smash Communists so much as its willingness to exercise power within multilateral frameworks and alliances, which sometimes included backroom deals with Moscow.

What remains of this structure in the Bush doctrine is the substitution of terrorism for Communism, hence Iraq's alleged connection to al Qaeda and its supposed weapons of mass destruction.

The "cakewalk" Iraq was supposed to have been has turned into a nightmare for US forces, whose civilian leaders continue to broadcast a comic-strip fantasy of American power so remote from reality as to raise questions of competence. "We are going to fight them and impose our will on them and we will capture or ... kill them, until we have imposed law and order on this country," Paul Bremer said in July. "We will dominate the scene ...."

According to Rand Beers—the president's special assistant for combating terrorism until he recently resigned his post—Washington underestimates the real enemy which is terrorism. The obsession with Iraq has created serious fissures in US counterterrorism alliances, he believes. It's also breeding a new generation of al Qaeda recruits. As a result of the war, claims Beers, the "difficult, long-term issues both at home and abroad have been avoided, neglected or shortchanged ..."

Iraq is about something else: oil, the stability of the dollar, the security of the US's closest ally, Israel. The enemy in Iraq is not Saddam's regime either, which was easy enough to dispense with. "Every ten years or so, the US needs to pick up some small crappy little country and throw it against the wall, just to show the world we mean business." This remark, delivered by Michael Ledeen a decade ago to the American Enterprise Institute, has the virtue of underlining two singular features of America's national security strategy. First, the enemies it targets are weak, both economically and militarily; and second, the power it projects is grounded on force, the military force that is required to vanquish the weak in order to frighten the strong.

"It's like the bully in a playground," says Ian Lustick, a University of Pennsylvania professor of political science and author of *Unsettled States, Disputed Lands*. "You beat up somebody, and everybody else behaves."

The long-range goal of the national security strategy is to secure US global dominance by preventing the emergence of rival powers. Thus the rationale for the military campaign in Iraq was not that Saddam Hussein posed the biggest threat in the Middle East but, on the contrary, that he was the weakest, the least popular, and therefore the easiest to dispatch. The invasion was aimed at demonstrating America's political will and commitment to go to war unilaterally.

Now a real enemy has emerged in the form of the Iraqi opposition movement itself, which is determined to halt the gamble Washington has undertaken to make over Iraq in the image of a free enterprise paradise.

Iraq is a test case, as was Vietnam in another strategic context, for the Pentagon's plan to turn the country into a base for unilateral interventions throughout the Gulf. The plan, rarely addressed by the White House, emerged on July 30 when Bush asserted that "a free Iraq will help change the habits of other nations," making the US "more secure."

In any event, the scandal over tainted intelligence is misplaced. Blaming the intelligence community for the false evidence the government used to build its case for invading Iraq was a bad move for Bush. And his decision to accept responsibility for promoting the phoney Niger–Iraq yellowcake deal showed he understood this.

Popular support for the war never was dependent on the logic of the case so much as on the belief that a case existed, whatever it was, and that Saddam was a villain equal to the crimes that were committed on September 11. Parading evidence that the case is full of holes, while Saddam roams free and guerrillas knock off American soldiers, only enhances the aura of deception and incompetence that is fast closing in on this administration.

Every week brings new breaches in the firewall of executive privilege, ranging from the unraveling of the regulatory policy on media ownership favored by the Republican leadership, to Bush's inability to shield Condoleezza Rice from Congressional charges of lying concerning her account of pre-9/11 intelligence briefings at the White House. It's only a matter of time before a grim assessment of the future of the Iraqi conflict set forth by the influential Center for Strategic and International Studies in Washington percolates through Bush's "critics and the cynics" to a wider public. Citing twenty-six "avoidable problems," CSIS military expert Anthony Cordesman writes: "Unless this situation changes soon, and radically, the United States may end up fighting a third Gulf war against the Iraqi people ... It is far from clear that the United States can win this kind of asymmetric war."

Meanwhile, the military is struggling to adjust to the new reality. On August 6, US Army Chief of Staff John Keane announced that the Army is planning to deploy an "experimental force" consisting of Special Forces, regular infantry, military police, and civil affairs troops. Its purpose will be to combine counter-insurgency capabilities with pacification forces in one package. A time warp back to Vietnam. But as in Vietnam, it misses the heart of the problem, which is the American presence in Iraq.

7

THE POLITICAL ECONOMY OF DEATH

I

Nothing is more important in the face of war than cutting taxes.

TOM DELAY, Majority Leader of the House of Representatives

It's time to look more closely at the relationship of power and violence, or "*la agresión*," as the Spanish writer Pep Subiros puts it in "Utopias imperiales," an interesting little essay in *El Pais*. Speaking of a perverse logic of empires, together with America's obsession with security following September 11, and the subsequent war in Iraq, Subiros argues that "there is no power more precarious than that sustained by continuous aggression and brute force." And then: "no weapons are as 'intelligent' as a fanatical human being full of hate and bent on vengeance."[1] This last is inspired by al Qaeda's successful attacks on the Pentagon and the World Trade Center, and could be countered by citing the obliging distraction of the intelligence agencies. Subiros makes a stronger case for the fragility of Pax Americana when he turns to the wartime economy.

A "virtual economy," he calls it, living an "immense fiction" of wealth and power, it lacks direction, is pregnant with catastrophe, and rewards only a slender financial elite inside the United States at the expense of other elites abroad.[2] For these reasons, and especially the last (he's not the first European to observe how the Bush administration has raided multilateral institutions such as the International Monetary Fund and the World Bank to pad out oil and gas deals), US global interests are accompanied by an ever more confrontational praetorian guard.

The damage of course cuts two ways. Enormous military expenditures have robbed the domestic economy of its ability to meet fundamental fiscal obligations, finance basic services, and patch what remains of a tattered safety net for a growing underclass. This we know, and can but wonder at the ease with which the populace seems to adjust to the general lowering of standards in health care, education, and environmental protection codes, already low by comparison to Europe's; along with the loss of jobs (3.2 million since March 2001, when the recession began), of retirement funds, even of police services and the protections the US Coast Guard once provided coastal communities before these agencies were roped into Homeland Security. The *Wall Street Journal* reports that "the US is experiencing the most protracted job-market downturn since the Great Depression. It has left behind a remarkably broad swath of workers—from young to old, and from high-school dropouts to the highly educated."[3]

Indeed, the sense of powerlessness and the fear of impending disaster which the Bush administration has skillfully bred into the mass mind feeds, in part, on a growing anxiety engendered by losses in the domestic economy. For many, the American dream, curdling into nightmare, reinforces the president's pessimistic image of the world, *and helps sell his message of world domination.* "I will not forget this wound to our country or those who inflicted it," Bush proclaimed in the wake of September 11. "I will not yield, I will not rest; I will not relent in waging this struggle for freedom and security for the American people."[4] With its false despair and empty bravado, it's the cry of the loon in the swamp of good intentions: *I will not ... I will not ... I will not.* ... But the words touch a deeper, politically inexpressible wound that many Americans have sustained in the collapse of traditional expectations for the future.

Bush speaks bluntly of the new objectives. The budget for 2004, he declares, "meets the challenges faced by three national priorities: winning the war against terrorism, securing the homeland, and generating long-term economic growth."[5] Yet none of these goals has an end or even a plan, except "economic growth," which is tied with gossamer thread to increased tax cuts for corporations and wealthy investors, and whose logic convinces nobody, not even the rich. A report commissioned by the Treasury Department in tandem with the budget, but suppressed until after the $350 billion tax cut passed Congress, shows that in addition to 2004's $450 billion deficit,* the United States faces a future of cascading federal budget deficits—as the baby boom generation reaches its sen-iority—whose dire consequences have not been faced. Over the next ten years, the tax cuts alone will add $1 trillion to the deficit.[6] The federal Treasury, once full, has been looted. It was a mission impossible; and even the taciturn Federal Reserve Chairman, Alan Greenspan, was moved to protest what he called Washington's "deafening" silence concerning the future crunch. But the Bush administration has pulled it off, reasoning no doubt that had the money remained, it would be used to fund social programs of no use to the favored sectors of the economy.

Each of Bush's three priorities is designed, in effect, to secure the finan-cial health of the godfathers of the administration's political fortunes, chiefly the warlords of the energy and defense industries that batten on the "virtual economy"and serve as patrons and beneficiaries alike. Among the thirty members of the Pentagon's Defense Policy Board (DPB), at least nine are directors or officers of companies that were awarded *$76 billion in*

---

* Now over $500 billion.

defense contracts in 2001 and 2002.[7] These include Retired General Jack Sheehan, vice president of the Bechtel Group, the giant engineering firm that bagged the $680 million prime "capital reconstruction" contract to rebuild Iraq, and stands to dole out fistfulls of subsidiary contracts to corporate entities, not all American. At the other end of the spectrum, there is the colorful James Woolsey, CIA chief under Bill Clinton, and vice-chairman of the board of Crescent Investment Management, a New York-based hedge fund trafficking in national security technologies which is directed by a shadowy financier of Pakistani origin named Mansoor Ijaz.[8]

Woolsey, whose Middle East connections are not untypical of the DPB, is a talk-show guest adept at rendering US military objectives in the blood-baked tones of the Apocalypse. Asked on PBS whether the truck bombing of UN headquarters in Baghdad on August 19, 2003 indicated that a wider war was underway, he replied: "This has always been a wider war. It's always been about dictatorship, Islamism, and weapons of mass destruction and terrorism coming out of the Middle East. ... This is really all one big fight ... like the fight against the Nazis, it's a war to the death."[9]

Jim Woolsey is a propagandist. The Bechtel connection is more significant; for it reflects an institutional partnership between the defense industry and government—both Ronald Reagan's secretary of defense, Caspar Weinberger, and his secretary of state, George Schultz, came from Bechtel—which has come a long way from the "military–industrial complex" that Eisenhower warned of forty years ago. Then it was a matter of influence-peddling in high places where issues of war and peace were at stake; and for good reason the anti-democratic implications of the growing power of industry lobbyists have concerned both liberals and conservatives (some, anyway) for decades.

Indeed, the danger is still commonly measured by the purse that wins politicians to a corporate pitch for a multimillion dollar weapons system or a high-priced mopping up contract for a distant battlefield. James Ridgeway points out that Bechtel gave $1.3 million in campaign contributions during the 1999–2000 cycle, mainly to Republicans.[10] Working alliances continue to be oiled in the free and easy pastures of party (especially Republican) fundraisers, golf games, turkey shoots, and duck hunts, where social alliances are forged without which business doesn't get done. Looked at from a systems point of view, however, a transformation has occurred. The old-fashioned cronyism has matured as it has been institutionalized in the Pentagon in recent years, and today in Vice President Dick Cheney's office where energy policy is set, cronyism has achieved a higher level of efficiency.

With all three branches of government currently dominated by the conservative wing of the Republican Party, these partnerships have largely done away with the pesky middlemen and regulators traditionally rooted in Congress and the Supreme Court. High-end lobbyists ignore the democratic pretense that they are pressing for programs in an open market where all comers are welcome to argue their interests. Now that they're free to cut to the chase, the back-room talk has changed. At a 1999 conference organized by the Project for the New American Century, Bruce Jackson, the Lockheed vice president who served as financial chair and chief fundraiser for George W. Bush's first presidential campaign, bragged that he would personally "write the Republican platform" on defense if the Texas governor made it to the White House.[11]

Meanwhile, 2004's $2.2 trillion budget, a 4.2 percent increase over 2003's spending, called for $41 billion for Homeland Security, thereby doubling the funding of a barely functional department over what it was two years ago, and creating a porkbarrel for a proliferating array of security companies—which may or may not include former DPB chairman Richard Perle's Trireme Partners, another outfit with Middle East ties, "whose main business," according to a letter of intent, "is to invest in companies dealing in technology, goods, and services that are of value to homeland security and defense."[12] At the same time, the $41 billion appropriation, equipped with liability protection for security services, as well as for the pharmaceutical giants standing by with mass inoculations, falls drastically short of funding the antiterror measures which the administration has imposed on state and local governments. "We are asking our firemen, policemen, Customs and Coast Guard to do far more with far less than we ever ask of our military," observed the special assistant to the president for combating terrorism, Rand Beers, who quit the Bush administration in disgust in April 2003 over its lack of genuine concern for domestic national security needs.

Defense spending, which jumped 4.3 percent to $373 billion, includes stepped-up military assistance to twenty-five "frontline states" that have joined the war on terror. Pay-off money, one might say; but looking ahead, one suspects they will need it, especially Pakistan and the Philippines, if only because of the ever-present threat of blowback. Four leaders of a July 27, 2003 coup attempt against the Arroyo government in Manila were trained by US Special Forces. They received sniper, night fighting, and counterterrorism training, and previously fought against the Islamist separatist group Abu Sayyaf on Basilan Island.[13] As for Pakistan, despite evidence that General Pervez Musharraf struck a deal with President Bush *not* to seize Osama bin Laden after the Afghan War, for fear of inciting trouble with Islamic radicals in his own country, the failure to catch bin Laden, who in August 2003 was said to be hiding in the northern Pakistani province of Baluchistan, has emboldened surviving al Qaeda forces.[14] Given reports that same month of open recruiting by al Qaeda and the Taliban in the Baluchistan city of Quetta—along with fresh inroads the rebel groups have made in southeastern Afghanistan— it appears that the double-edged deal Bush made with Musharraf has backfired. The agreement to ignore bin Laden in exchange for Pakistan's help in destroying the Taliban regime during the Afghan campaign has devolved into a reestablishment of Taliban power sufficiently widespread to lead Hamid Karzai to invite Taliban participation in a future coalition government. And in February 2004, sensing trouble with his presidential campaign, President Bush has sent Defense Secretary Rumsfeld's chief covert action group, Team 121, to the Hindu Nesh mountains to catch Osama bin Laden.

The State Department reports a substantial increase in foreign affairs spending which targets "security assistance" to the same countries that have signed on to the antiterror campaign. $4.7 billion has been set aside for counterterrorism as compared to $2 billion for programs linked to the "war on poverty." $1.3 billion of the latter goes to the Millennium Challenge Account (MCA), an aid fund that was first set at $5 billion in March 2002 for a select group of countries deemed by the president to be "ruling justly, investing in their people, and establishing economic freedom." The fund was further cut in the House to $800 million without a peep from the White House, whose aid promises, like the multibillion dollar State of the Union pledge to fight AIDs in Africa, are generally knocked off their pedestals when abandoned to the vicissitudes of the Republican dominated Congress. MCA, nonetheless, is worth a closer look for what it reveals of Bush's original plan to restructure foreign aid; "to reform US aid requirements," a Heritage Foundation memorandum explains, "as work requirements changed welfare."[15] For one thing, it seeks to include private sector firms as "development partners," and to operate independently of the existing aid bureaucracy through a Millennium Challenge Corporation.

MCA embodies a familiar formula. This is the holy trinity of privatization, deregulation, and trade liberalization that led to the collapse of the Argentine economy in December 2001, and has furthered a kind of development-in-reverse throughout Latin America, whereby beggar nations, already indentured to the World Bank, the IMF, or the Inter-American Development Bank, have been gradually stripped of control over their national resources. Today, commercial banks such as Citigroup (previously Citibank) and J.P. Morgan Chase (previously Chase), which profited from the governance rules of the 1980s and '90s by loaning money to companies with mandates to scoop up "failing" dams, power projects, telephone companies and the like, or by floating bonds and issuing stock to raise long-term money to grow new businesses, have by and large pulled back from such ventures. They didn't pay out; or, as in Argentina, the banks and their brokerage houses are no longer welcome. Nor, for the most part, did the investments deliver the promised goods or services, and they have since been picked up mainly by the Inter-American Development Bank, which seeks to involve venture capitalists from Spain and Chile. ("Vulture capitalists," they're called in Bolivia.)

Like the go-go deals of the last decade, MCA yokes development aid for capital-starved countries to "governance indicators" favorable to investors: adherence to the rule of law, opening national markets, etc.[16] But it plans to extend the free trade formula to a new set of target economies, presumably more amenable to private-sector guidance. Thus a formula that stalled in Latin America, and was rejected in Southeast Asia, is being trotted out by President Bush as a condition of foreign aid in the Gulf.

If this exercise of "soft power" lacks substance, it's because the heart of the Bush doctrine lies elsewhere—with "hard power," with preventing war by waging it. And preemptive war recasts the definition of sovereignty in a way that undermines the prospects for bolstering marginal economies. If terrorist groups are by definition not subject to deterrence, because as subnational entities they can slip from state to state, the United States must be prepared to strike anywhere at any time to destroy an actual or potential threat. How then can investors, much less regional governments, count on the stable social and political conditions that traditionally underpin growth?

The answer is they can't; and if initial reactions to the free trade zone the Bush administration has promoted in the Middle East are any indication, they don't. At an economic forum held in Shuneh, Jordan in late June 2003, US Trade Representative Robert Zoellick presented plans for a Middle East Free Trade Area (MEFTA), and dangled the possibility of $1 billion in economic aid to cooperating countries. Washington's proconsul in Baghdad, L. Paul Bremer, arrived to tout the opportunities for private enterprise in Iraq, where the United States plans to privatize nearly every-thing, not just oil production (whose privatization comes later, after the ravaged infrastructure has been secured and modernized at public expense), but also water purification, telecommunications, transportation, postal services, etc. Arab participants, however, mainly factory owners from Jordan and Lebanon, weren't buying into either Bremer's promises or the MEFTA. The problem was more than the nasty postwar war in Iraq—it was a trade agreement already signed with Jordan which stood as a disturbing model for future deals with other Arab states.

Like most such agreements, NAFTA included, Jordan's trade deal benefits local elites, or is intended to (Mexican shipping companies are still waiting for the US to let their long-haul trucks cross the border, as promised under NAFTA). But many Gulf area elites are oil-dependent, and oil trades freely on world markets with no significant customs bar-riers. Why would the region's businessmen commit to a trade zone that offers no additional benefits? Some Lebanese manufacturers have expressed interest in expanding exports to America, but the US charges a 17 percent import duty on Lebanese textiles and garments. And worse, under Jordan's agreement, Washington requires that at least 7 percent of all duty-free exports to the US must originate in Israel[17] (a variation on the old mercantilist principle which held that you could export to the US pro-vided the exports used American products rather than those of its competitors). With terms like these, and no indication they will be signif-icantly modified for an area-wide trading regime, the Bush administration has shown that it's not seriously interested in negotiating viable trade agreements in the Middle East.

The US has long imposed higher tariffs, averaging 13 percent, on less developed countries than does the EU, whose comparable tariffs average 2 percent. This helps explain why revenues collected on imports from Bangladesh, for example, are roughly equivalent to those collected on imports from France, even though the latter are twelve times greater.[18] The truth is that alongside the Bush administration's dismissal of international arms control accords and multilateral security arrangements inherited from the Cold War, the sacred cows of economic development and free trade have, in effect, been demoted as well. With the doctrine of preemption, the very concept of the state and of the sanctity of its borders has fallen prey to the imperial dystopia—which is partly why the Bush team never did plan seriously for peacekeeping in Afghanistan or nation-building in Iraq.

America disdains the "long tail" of burdens and commitments that great powers customarily undertake in the wake of major military actions. Winning is all, and then profiteering from the spoils. Hence the Pentagon is stymied in Iraq, not only because it is unable to stabilize the battlefield, and establish a political authority and regulatory environment conducive to business, but because it failed to imagine a serious postwar obstacle other than catastrophes that did not occur, like widespread oilfield fires and large-scale refugee flows. Defense Department experts never studied the country they expected to subdue, or listened to voices that challenged the premises behind a vision of conquest and transformation which is as remote from the realities of the Arab world as any chapter in the history of Western incursions into the Middle East. It's no surprise that the government has failed to craft a wartime aid package or trade deal (apart from one pending with Morocco) which has any practical chance of success.

Even the administration's strategic interest in Middle East oil has foundered on the procrustean bed of a fantastical foreign policy, and on the prolonged occupation of a hostile Iraq. Oil was supposed to finance postwar reconstruction, whose initial cost was set at $2.4 billion before it jumped to $100 billion, and then, according to a CSIS estimate in August 2003, to $200 billion, until by summer's end—after Paul Bremer acknowledged that because of repeated sabotage of Iraqi pipelines, it would be months if not years before the country's oil production reached *prewar* levels—figures as high as $500 billion began to circulate in the press.

Iraqi oil won't come close to meeting the costs of repairing and pro-tecting the antiquated pipelines, much less covering the ballooning expenses of reconstruction, which will have to be met the same way Washington usually finances deficit spending: by increased borrowing, mainly from foreign investors. And that assumes the bond markets will continue financing America's mounting debts; or, to put it another way, that foreign investors will keep covering the government's obligations to the defense industries that are its most powerful creditors—though this, of course, is not how US allies or future competitors, such as China, see it. From their point of view, if the US garners an ever greater share of world savings, it's to finance American consumption, which in turn guarantees increased exports from abroad. Especially in East Asia, financing the US debt is still justified if it secures unrestricted access to the US market.

According to Niall Ferguson, author of *Empire: The Rise and Demise of the British World Order and the Lessons for Global Power*, international financial claims on the US Treasury now amount to about $8 trillion of its financial assets, which is the result of ever larger US balance-of-payments deficits, totaling nearly $3 trillion since 1982. What if, he asks, investors choose to reduce their stakes in the American economy, and trade in their dollars for the increasingly dynamic euro?[19] An important question. Empires are not built on debt, says Stephen Roach, the chief economist at Morgan Stanley who argued that the explosion of the US asset bubble in the late 1990s revealed the fundamental unsoundness of a "US-centric world." "Can a savings-short US economy continue to finance an ever-widening expansion of its military superiority?" he asks today; and answers with a "resounding no."[20]

Both American and European investors, in fact, have already started selling nondomestic stocks and bringing their money home, mainly to obtain debt relief. So far the move is largely aimed at emerging countries like Brazil, once the vanguard of globalization. But the trend in Europe could turn on a dime, and savage America's economy. According to the *Economist*, this is already underway; total foreign direct investment in the

US fell a phenomenal 77 percent (to $30 billion) between 2001 and 2002.[21]

The Bush team's larger strategic interest in Iraq, which had already gone for the euro in November 2000, was to get Iraq back on board; and to ensure American access to the Gulf region's oil at favorable prices, thereby undercutting OPEC's power. The idea was not only to meet growing US energy needs, but to shape the distribution of oil and gas to rival European powers, and to Russia and China. As a result, the primary focus of the new national security strategy—to preserve American hegemony by actively resisting the rise of alternative centers of power (which is to say euro-power) could be pursued by timely applications of economic pressure. It's a sophisticated theory—in theory; an expression of *realpolitik* worthy of Mr. Kissinger, especially if one is prepared to ditch the global economy; but it too has fallen on hard times.

In the hierarchy of objectives that lie behind America's imperial dreams, neither trade liberalization, foreign economic development, and least of all, domestic prosperity, rates very high. Even Homeland Security was cut back from $41 billion to $29.4 billion after Congress had its way with it in September 2003. (Defense spending, by contrast, went from $373 billion to $368 billion, a minor drop.) The deeper the US sinks into the quicksand of combat in the greater Middle East—from northern Africa to the Levant, from the Persian Gulf to Afghanistan—the more grievous is the damage which these traditional indicators of American power will sustain. There will be the usual ups and downs for economic prophets to chew over; especially those who maintain (with Mother Courage) that "wars are inherently stimulative [because] they are financed by government borrowing, which increases demand. ..." Like the Texas-based forecaster STRATFOR, author of this remark, they will cite John Maynard Keynes in defense of the idea, and find it "ironic and laughable that Democrats now attack Keynesian economics while Republicans embrace them."[22]

In the meantime, a slide of this dimension carries profound implications for the future stability of the United States—whose business, after all, is business. Or was. Now that both the defense and energy industries, having thrown off nearly all vestiges of regulation, regard the US government as their best customer, they have implanted themselves at the helm to guide the ship of state. There is no longer much government left to defend the interests of lesser institutions, including other businesses, or the welfare of mere citizens, *or the actual security of the nation.* In the past, American prosperity typically followed America's armed expansion into new markets—first, after "winning the West"; later, with the defeat of the Spanish armada in Cuba and the Philippines, by seizing coaling stations in the Pacific, and further opening the China trade; and then building the Panama Canal, thereby linking America's seaborne trade from coast to coast, and cutting a path to Central American coffee and bananas. After American victories in World War II, the United States invested in a war-ravaged Europe, and reaped the rewards for years to come. Even today, more than half of all US foreign direct investment is based in Europe—compared to a trifling 1 percent in the Middle East.[23]

In each instance, expanded economic opportunities were established in the wake of military intervention, although the public face of war has traditionally been one of surprise and horror at the unexpected infamy of the foe, whether it be marauding Indians, or Spain's "Butcher" Weyler in Cuba, or a real villain like Hitler. The "myth of the 'reluctant super-power'," Andrew Bacevich calls it in *American Empire*, which is "the pattern of evil spurring the United States into action."[24] The two major thrusts behind American foreign policy—the constant need to expand markets, and the use of military force to secure policy objectives—have generally gone hand-in-hand. In fact, it wasn't until the US intervention in Vietnam that the economic motive dropped behind. In Vietnam the US was engaged in "a new kind of war," as the saying went. A precursor of Iraq in this sense, the war was intended to redraw the geopolitical map of Southeast Asia in America's favor, and to demonstrate to Moscow and Beijing that the US military's ability to defeat guerrilla wars of national liberation was incontestable.

Like Iraq—which some economists call a "monetary Vietnam," because its costs account for nearly 15 percent of annual budget deficits— the Vietnam War sapped the economic health of the nation. But while the war in Southeast Asia ended the promises that Lyndon Johnson's Great Society extended to disenfranchised communities, the widening war in the Middle East, pursued in tandem with massive tax cuts and reduced social spending, threatens to derail Social Security and Medicare on which all Americans depend. As the creditworthiness of America's economy tumbles, so too will the bets that half the industrial world has placed on its Midas touch, and on its infinite capacity to consume.

"A fiscal train wreck," and perhaps a deliberate one, *New York Times* columnist Paul Krugman calls the wartime budget. "[I]t's no secret," he writes, "that right-wing ideologues want to abolish programs Americans take for granted." In support of this idea Krugman invokes the staid *Financial Times*, organ of British business opinion—which greeted Bush's tax cuts with the famous line: "The lunatics are now in charge of the asylum"—to the effect that "extreme Republicans" actually want a train wreck. "Proposing to slash federal spending, particularly on social programs, is a tricky electoral proposition," the *FT* reasons, "but a fiscal crisis offers the tantalizing prospect of forcing such cuts through the back door." Krugman, who wonders when the American public will wake up to what's going on, agrees.[25]

Yet this view grants rhyme and reason to a reality where mainly chaos and greed hold sway. True, right-wing ideologues would like to destroy most vestiges of the New Deal; and yes, Americans take their social programs for granted, just as they take most privileges and rights for granted, including civil liberties, forgetting, as Woodrow Wilson said: "The history of liberty is a history of resistance." But that doesn't mean that gutting the economy to serve the private interests of fat cats from Texas and Virginia is part of a grand plan to sabotage liberalism. Liberalism is quite capable of doing itself in; and indeed, has made a career out of sacrificing public for private interests under the last three Democratic administrations. It's the price liberals have paid, not always happily, to sit down with the big boys at the gaming tables of national politics.

If the train is running off the track, it's more likely because the engineer and the conductor are back in the boiler room counting gains.

8

THE POLITICAL
ECONOMY OF DEATH
II

The center did not hold.

PAUL KRUGMAN[1]

There's no question that the United States has entered a permanent state of war, one that is being fought overtly and covertly throughout the Middle East and beyond. With it has arrived a permanent war economy, whose footing in the eroding sands of America's historic wealth and power has begun to slip. You won't hear Pentagon service chiefs tell their commanders that "we are posturing for the long haul. For all the forces heading home, our mission now is to re-cock this force," as Admiral Vern Clark said following "victory" in Operation Iraqi Freedom.[2] Instead, the chiefs are squabbling again, as they did in March 2003 when the long supply lines were interdicted by the Fedayeen, and as they do whenever the battlefield news goes sour, for they suspect that the civilian leadership's goals, whatever they are, are unattainable.

As American soldiers continue to be picked off, and the targets of unseen and unidentified foes in Iraq expand from oil pipelines, power stations, and police stations to include UN headquarters and international aid organizations—and, on August 29, the Shi'ite shrine of Imam Ali in the holy city of Najaf, whose bombing killed and wounded hundreds of worshippers, including Ayatollah Muhammed Bakr al-Hakim himself— even Secretary of Defense Rumsfeld has resorted to shuffling paper "studies" in public to back up a "midcourse correction." Rumsfeld is grasping at alternatives to committing more American soldiers to the battlefield, as well as for arguments to back up an emergency appeal to Congress for an additional $87 billion for the upcoming fiscal year (this on top of the $79 billion Congress approved six months ago). The defense secretary's sharp opposition to troop increases is commonly attributed to his desire to reserve US soldiers for combat, and not use them for constabulary duties. Others point out that American forces are already stretched thin, with some 370,000 troops deployed in 120 countries, and that Rumsfeld must keep his options open for an engagement with North Korea. But there is another, unspoken, reason for the aversion to tying down more GIs. With their continuing vulnerability to sniper fire from the widening resistance in Iraq, and their tendency to write families and Congressmen about the true face of the war, the awkward fact is that American soldiers have emerged as an unexpected Achilles heel in Washington's master plan to subdue the Middle East.

The issue that Pep Subiros raises is not whether the United States can afford to remain on the offensive. Very likely not, for both economic and strategic reasons; but the decisions have been made, and they don't include an exit strategy. No amount of warnings from the persuasive Mr. Ferguson—that being the world's largest debtor nation leads to a fragile Pax Americana—can make much difference as long as the ideological armature underpinning America's historic inability to pull out of a losing military proposition remains firmly in place. Even if the Bush regime is thrown out of office in November 2004, Congress is still dominated by "extreme" Republicans. And if their dominance should give way, and a

Democratic president rides into the White House on a wave of antiwar sentiment and populist resentment of corruption in high places, the roots of Washington's fear of being caught with a white flag in hand are too deeply ingrained in the nation's martial psyche, and too heavily fortified by a hungry defense establishment, to give way to a mere changing of the guard. ("It is part of the general pattern of misguided policy that our country is now geared to an arms economy, which was bred to an artificially induced psychosis of war hysteria and nurtured upon an incessant propaganda of fear." That's General Douglas MacArthur, of all people, speaking in 1951.)

The leading Democratic candidates, who originally hoped for UN cover to sanction a war many opposed but voted for anyway, are united in arguing that the US should seek a UN blessing so that international forces may come to the rescue of American troops in Iraq. Only Dennis Kucinich calls for outright withdrawal. But the *Wall Street Journal*'s Max Boot also promotes the idea that America can't go it alone, and must seek UN assistance. Where liberal Democrats will take the lead is in squelching popular support for getting out by arguing that *it's too late*. Indeed, they're already at it. "Reality has poked ideology in the eye," writes Christopher Marquis in the *New York Times* of August 31, referring to the suddenly "widespread recognition" that the US must make a "midcourse correction." "For liberals—many of whom opposed the invasion," he observes, "it may mean admitting there can be no swift departure because the stakes have become too high. Leaving now would place Iraqis under violent usurpers, and set a precedent that could haunt Washington for years."

Here's how Secretary of State Dean Rusk put it in 1965, not long after the Marines landed at Danang, and the antiwar protests began. "The integrity of the US commitment is the principal pillar of peace throughout the world. If that commitment becomes unreliable, the Communists would draw conclusions that would lead to our ruin and almost certainly to catastrophic war." Substitute *terrorists* for "Communists," and you have the mantra now rising out of the fog of war.

To return to dollars and cents, what Subiros suggests is that the wartime economy spawned by "continuous aggression" *is itself destabilizing*, not just for target regions, or for those sectors of the international economy— principally French, Russian, and British interests—invested in Middle Eastern petroleum and non-petroleum industries, but for the national economy, whose core programs rest on taxes and a sound dollar. As for the substantial part of the American economy whose foreign investments have traditionally depended on predictable political climates, the free flow of Federal Deposit Insurance funds, and assured markets, this piece of economic tradition is no longer intact.

The Bush administration, in effect, is practicing economic warfare on its own economy, including a significant sector of the investor class. And it's doing so with a powerful but risky instrument of late capitalist development. This is the privatization of military, energy, and foreign policy-making by a small group of people who move back and forth between the corporate boards of Halliburton, Bechtel, Lockheed-Grumman, the Fluor Corporation, Phillips Petroleum, Booz Allen Hamilton, et al., and the upper echelons of government. In the present war administration, this includes most top officials, led by Vice President Cheney whose former chairmanship of Halliburton gave its subsidiary Kellogg Brown & Root (KBR) the inside track on the Iraqi oilfields contract—one that Democratic Representative Henry Waxman reports will ultimately be worth $7 billion. (Without the political influence of Halliburton—whose first Iraqi oilfield contract was signed in December 2001, *fifteen months before the war started*—it's possible, some argue, that the US would not have gone to war.[3]) But the exchange goes deeper than mere influence, as writer Dan Baum demonstrates in a prescient appraisal of US reconstruction efforts in Iraq. "KBR didn't need any help [from political connections]," he states. Why? Because it was by then "so enmeshed with the Pentagon that it was able essentially to assign the contract to itself."

Baum cites an Army base, Camp Arifjan, which KBR conjured out of nothing in the Kuwaiti desert in October 2002, while the war was still being debated at the UN and in the streets. Had the Army built it, reservists would have been mobilized, thereby generating untimely TV coverage of men and women leaving home in uniform before Congress had approved the war. (Thanks to a classified timeline of events which was leaked on September 3, 2003, we know that Bush formally approved "Iraq goals, objectives and strategy" on August 29, 2002. Three months before that, the Pentagon began a series of regional war exercises called "Prominent Hammer."[4] But on September 17, 2001, a few days after the terrorist attacks, Bush told the Pentagon to go to work on Iraq.) "It's a political decision to use contractors," a logistics commander reminds Baum. "The Army can get a delicate job done quietly." Camp Arifjan may look like an Army base, but it's effectively a subsidiary of Kellogg Brown & Root, and the Army, according to the resident KBR project chief, is actually the "client."[5]

When Dick Cheney was secretary of defense in 1992, the Pentagon hired Halliburton to report on the feasibility of privatizing Army functions worldwide, from building camps and airbases to running food, laundry, and mail services. And when it finished, the Defense Department chose KBR to start implementing the recommendations. From 1994 to 2002, the Pentagon entered into 3016 contracts, valued at more than *$300 billion*, with twelve of twenty-four US-based private military companies (PMCs), of which 2700 were divided between KBR and the management and technology consulting firm Booz Allen Hamilton. PMCs sell their wares abroad through the Defense Department's Foreign Military Sales program, under which the Pentagon pays the contractor for services offered to a foreign government. Altogether by 2002, the companies had carried out operations in fifty countries, from Bosnia to Sierra Leone to Columbia.[6] Like lawyers, some work only for "ethical" clients, while others make money from less savory types, and still others—one thinks of Douglas Feith in the former Office of Special Plans, whose off-the-books operations in the Middle East were run by Manchur Ghorbanifar, the arms merchant of Iran-Contra fame—do business with both.

PMCs (trade group: the International Peace Operations Association) may lease out whole battalions of commandos, or run live-action war games, or undertake training and recruiting duties for ROTC at over 200 American universities, or train the new army the US has promised for Iraq.[7] A San Diego company, Cubic, has contracts from the State Department and the Pentagon to train the armies of prospective NATO members from "emerging Europe": Romania, Hungary, the Czech Republic, etc.[8] This arrangement has a special irony. First the Bush administration sabotages NATO's global authority, both in practice and via the National Security Doctrine; then, in order to convert it into a police force to protect US defense and energy interests abroad, it turns to the private sector to get the delicate job done quietly.

Another big player in Iraq, the Virginia-based DynCorp—which flies planes against guerrillas in Columbia (as does Northrop Grumman)—trains the Iraqi police and also fields its own personnel, known in-country as Dyn-a-Cops. DynCorp (a subsidiary of the giant Computer Sciences Corp.), which has a State Department contract to protect Afghan leader Hamid Karzai, saw revenues rise 18 percent in 2002, to $2.3 billion.[9] Other PMCs maintain weapons systems and oversee fuel supplies for mechanized Army units. Indeed, the increasing complexity of military hardware has made the armed services more dependent on them. Experts estimate that as much as one-third of the monthly $3.9 billion cost of keeping US troops in Iraq goes to private companies. P.W. Singer, author of *Corporate Warriors*, sets the number of contract workers in Iraq at 20,000, or about one for every ten soldiers,[10] a figure likely to rise sharply as Rumsfeld struggles with limited reserves of qualified troops. And that doesn't include British security firms like Erinys which protects Iraqi oil installations, and commands a 14,000-strong armed force in Iraq.[11]

Never has a war—or a national security strategy—appeared more perfectly suited to the task of succoring an industry. Shortly before Operation Iraqi Freedom was launched, business magazines churned with excitement. Speaking of the coming war, *Fortune* allowed that "[w]e wouldn't be so crass as to describe that crisis as a business opportunity—too many lives are on the line. But the fact is that if America goes to war, private companies are going to be deeply involved both in supporting the troops during the fighting and in whatever peacekeeping and reconstruction efforts follow."[12]

Halliburton, which hired Dick Cheney's former chief of staff from his Pentagon years, David Gribben, to be chief liaison with the Defense Department, remains the kingpin of the growing army of defense contractors. When Cheney, who was Halliburton's CEO from 1995 to 2000, left to become Bush's mentor and running mate, Gribben went with him to direct Congressional relations for the new administration. At Halliburton, Gribben was replaced by former commander-in-chief of US forces in southern Europe Joe Lopy, a retired four-star general and Cheney's close friend. This particular node of the buddy system that drives *L'Amérique d'outre mer* includes Richard Armitage, current assistant secretary to Colin Powell in the State Department, who once consulted for Halliburton. Since Cheney's gang streamed into the Bush administration, KBR has brought home billions for its military services, not all from the Middle East, for the Balkans remain a lively market, and Central Asia has come up fast.

The Lockheed-Grumman node, which Bush's former fundraiser Bruce Jackson represents, centers on Air Force Secretary James G. Roche, who before his nomination in the summer of 2002 was for seventeen years a top executive for Northrup Grumman. In October 2002 he awarded Lockheed-Grumman a $250 billion contract to build 6000 supersonic Joint Strike Fighter combat planes. The order, expected to provide forty years of work and revenue, calls for the development and manufacture of 3000 fighter planes to be used by the Air Force, Navy and Marines. A similar number is to be sold to other countries, such as Turkey, Israel, and Canada. Toward the end of Roche's tenure at Northrop Grumman, he was president of the Electronic Sensors and Systems Sector, a division which is now a key subcontractor for the fighter deal. In the meantime, *on the day before Roche's nomination hearing*, Northrop Grumman made two donations to the

Republican Party: $100,000 to the president's 2001 Dinner Committee and an additional $15,000 to the Republican National State Elections Committee.

Other aircraft company men and women include Navy Secretary Gordon England, who was president of Lockheed's Fort Worth division, which builds the fighter planes. Bush later appointed him second-in-command to Tom Ridge at Homeland Security. Bush's Secretary of Transportation, Norman Mineta, jumped his term as a Congressional representative to join the Lockheed team back in 1995. Undersecretary of the Air Force Albert E. Smith was a Lockheed vice president who oversaw the company's space program. And Vice President Dick Cheney's wife, Lynne, served on Lockheed's board of directors from 1994 to 2001.

Lockheed made headlines in the mid-1980s when the Pentagon found the company was producing $640 toilet seats. Such scandals provoke conflict of interest charges from watchdogs like William Hartung at the New School's World Policy Institute. "The Constitution says that civilians should be in charge of the militia, but the Bush administration has put a lot of corporate and military people in charge of the Pentagon," he observes,[13] as if what the Constitution says matters a fig without an alert citizenry prepared to defend it. "The defense industry is one of the major industries that enjoys close ties with the US government," echoes Peter Eisner of the Center for Public Integrity, lamenting the "long-standing practice of [the] revolving door," whereby industry CEOs move in and out of Defense Department positions without significant public oversight. (And former soldiers from Delta Force are recruited to sell their military skills to PMC recruiters for big bucks, while more ex-employees of the elite Special Air Services [SAS] regiments run and man British firms than their American counterparts.)

But Hartung and Eisner grant too much authority to government. In reality, the revolving door is simply a recycling of established business relationships. *Industry and government function as two branches of the same operation*—a military-industrial-congressional complex, if you will—

which in this instance sells off military stock to private cartels engaged in amassing power on many more levels than critics have recognized. The Pentagon, busy with war—the US Army has deployed troops thirty-six times since the end of the Cold War—provides both cover and value. But with $30 billion, or 8 percent of 2004's defense budget going directly into the corporate sector—to companies which are, in some cases, private armies themselves, directed by ex-military officers in uniform—it can no longer be said that the state has a monopoly over the use of force. Business is making a killing too.

Meanwhile, when Dan Baum says KBR could write its own ticket in Iraq, he refers to a ten-year contract signed in 2001 with the Army Logistics Civil Augmentation Program, known as LOGCAP, which ordered the company to provide an unlimited range of logistical services to the US Army, mainly in the Middle East. In this way KBR both continues to define Army needs, and assigns them in no-bid contracts which are issued more often than not to KBR. Outsourcing, it's called; and its chief advocates are Dick Cheney and Donald Rumsfeld. It was Rumsfeld who declared in May 2003 that "more than 300,000 uniformed personnel" were doing jobs that civilians could do; but nobody really knows the full extent of the turnover, not even the Pentagon. In a preliminary report to Congress in April 2002, the Defense Department guessed that the Army had contracted out the equivalent of *between 124,000 and 605,000 persons in 2001.*[14]

Selling off military services is the hidden side of what Rumsfeld means when he speaks of "modernizing" and "transforming" the Defense Department. It has nothing to do with cost-cutting but is the razor's edge of the administration's push to expand the privatization of government; to place as many as 850,000 government jobs, according to one projection, up for bid to private contractors. *In budgetary terms, this is another massive diversion of taxpayer dollars from the public to the private sector,* one over which there is little control. A September 2002 report by the General Accounting Office (GAO) found that effective oversight of KBR's contract in the Balkans was impaired by the government's confusion over the extent of the GAOs authority and by the inadequate training of Army auditors. From 1996 to 2000, the company had collected more than $2.1 billion in additional costs for its contracts, nearly twice the amount agreed to originally.[15] Given the absence of Congressional oversight, and the fact that defense contracts are notorious for cost overruns, especially when skyrocketing insurance premiums for war-zone assignments are added to cost-plus fees, US taxpayers are staring at a bill they cannot possibly pay.

And more. They are looking, or not looking, at a more complex problem: by using mercenaries, the executive branch can evade Congressional limits on both troop strength and military interventions abroad. At the same time, outsourcing advisory and training services, along with logistical support and combat operations, places a major foreign policy tool in the hands of private companies whose primary interest is profit. When PMCs sell services to a foreign state, it's the company, not the US government, that establishes the relationship, one in which the foreign government thereby becomes another customer in a worldwide shell game: an ally of fortune.

Looked at within a larger political context, the true nature of this phenomenon snaps into view. It is the modus operandi of a fascist state to privatize governing institutions; and further, to secure the ruling political party's place in the seat of government. The F-word has been hurled in anger and frustration at too many targets to retain the structural significance it once had. But here, in the ongoing privatization of the Pentagon—and of the National Security Agency as well, where Computer Science Corp. holds a ten-year $2.5 billion contract to run its technology services, *thereby turning 1000 NSA employees into Computer Science employees*—sits the workshop of the classic fascist regime.

Both the structural and political ramifications of Rumsfeld's attempt to break the back of the traditional armed services remain largely unexamined outside the military, even by veteran government reporters. "It might just as well be the British East India Company," laments James Ridgeway, referring to the "colonial corporations [that have] become an instrument of the nation-state, in this case to undertake the reconstruction of Iraq. They, not the government, are the purveyors of laws and customs and democratic ideals."[16] Maybe so. But this misses a more profound reversal, which is that to an unprecedented degree, *the nation-state has become an instrument of the defense industry*—and of the energy industry, as well.

On his tenth day in office, President Bush launched the secret energy task force led by Vice President Cheney that developed national energy policy. According to a GAO report issued August 25, 2003, energy secretary Spencer Abraham privately formulated Bush's policy "with chief executive officers of petroleum, electricity, nuclear, coal, chemical and natural gas companies, among others." The GAO had previously sued for access to Cheney's task force records, and lost. Now the Energy Department released e-mails, letters, and calendars reflecting the heavy input from corporations, including private sessions with Kenneth Lay, then chairman of Enron, and the man who financed the lion's share of Bush's run for president; but the contents of the exchanges remained sealed. Comptroller General David M. Walker told reporters the standoff called into question the existence of "a reasonable degree of transparency and an appropriate degree of accountability in government."[17] An understatement if there ever was one.

Nevertheless, it's possible to reconstruct from other sources something of the strategic import of the pre-9/11 meetings, both for national and for international policy. A report prepared by the influential James A. Baker Institute for Public Policy, and submitted to Cheney's task group in April 2001, asserted that "the US remains a prisoner of its energy dilemma. Iraq remains a destabilizing influence to ... the flow of oil to international markets from the Middle East." This was an unacceptable risk, the Baker report maintained, and it concluded that "military intervention" was necessary.[18] Other task force exchanges reaching similar conclusions, albeit via different routes, also found their way to the press. But unpublished was why Iraq was a "destabilizing influence"; or why Saddam Hussein's switch from the dollar to the more multilateral euro for the UN-monitored oil-for-food program was a rebuke to Washington's hard line on the sanctions.

In the *Guardian*, Michael Meacher, MP, the former environment minister who maintains that the "so-called 'war on terrorism' is being used largely as bogus cover for achieving wider US strategic geopolitical objectives," came close to naming the problem when he traced the Iraqi oil thesis back to the blueprint prepared in September 2000 by the Project for the New American Century (PNAC) for the creation of a global Pax Americana. Entitled "Rebuilding America's Defenses," it was presented to Vice President Cheney, Secretary of Defense Rumsfeld, Rumsfeld's deputy Paul Wolfowitz, the new president's younger brother Jeb Bush, and Cheney's chief of staff Lewis Libby—most of them founding members of PNAC. The import of the plan, according to Meacher, is that it shows that Bush's cabinet intended to take military control of the Gulf region from the beginning. "[W]hile the unresolved conflict with Iraq provides the immediate justification," the blueprint stated, "the need for a substantial American force presence in the Gulf transcends the issue of the regime of Saddam Hussein."[19] This was before Iraq went on the euro, which would have refocused attention on Baghdad.

As it was, the focus was on OPEC; on the weakening leadership of Saudi Arabia prior to September 11, and with it the other Gulf monarchies who faced a growing rebelliousness among their educated classes. But by 2002 attention was back on Iraq, when a second Baker Institute report concluded: "After two major wars and a decade of sanctions, [the Iraqi oil industry] is in desperate need of repair and investment." Behind the Baker Institute stood the former secretary of state under Bush Sr., James Baker, and the Houston-based oil-services company Baker Hughes, which was competing with Halliburton for the massive repair contract.[20]

But by 2000 the oil linkage was already an *idée fixe*. PNAC's white paper was built on the Defense Planning Guidance that Wolfowitz and Libby had prepared in 1992 for then Secretary of Defense Dick Cheney. This was the document that said the US "must discourage advanced industrial nations from challenging our leadership or even aspiring to a larger regional or global role." It maintained that "even should Saddam pass from the scene, US bases in Saudi Arabia and Kuwait will remain permanently," because "Iran may well prove as large a threat to US interests as Iraq has." The Guidance already called for an alliance with the UK, as "the most effective and efficient means of exercising American global leadership."

Britain had paved the Anglo-Saxon road to empire in the Gulf, though empire-building is not exactly what the Pentagon's directives convey. Something more like the seizure of coaling stations in the Philippines a century before, writ large, shadowed by concern for the strategic needs of America's chief ally in the region, Israel, come closer to indicating what Wolfowitz and Libby were after. Iran and Iraq, standing outside the US sphere of influence, were prime impediments to the consolidation of greater Israel's expansion into the West Bank.

But asserting America's unilateral leadership in a world that had become infinitely more problematical to defense planners after the fall of the Soviet Union, when the *raison d'être* for constant military preparedness disappeared, was the common thread that linked all the documents. That, and the subsidiary right to preempt potential threats via unilateral military action, laid the groundwork for a continuous expansion of American military strength. To make sure the new strategy operated without international interference, "peacekeeping missions," PNAC declared, required "American political leadership rather than that of the UN" or of any multilateral alliance. After September 11, the argument became a rallying cry: America cannot leave the safety of its homeland hostage to the decision-making of another power!

Such were the strategic principles of an administration that owed its existence to an odd coupling of ideologues and oilmen, the first bending to power and the second to money, and all of them dreamers when it came to international politics. It was the Sunshine Warrior, Wolfowitz of Arabia, who first sold President Bush on the vision of a Middle East reborn in the image of all things good, especially free trade and cooperative relations with Israel. Bush was the dreamer-in-chief, and in Wolfie, as he called the house intellectual, he found the big, bold, activist ideas that history's great presidents have always espoused. Besides, Wolfie was a man who didn't talk to his pockets like George's Texas cronies did; he was a man of faith, like himself.

It's touching to imagine the scene at Camp David's Laurel Lodge the weekend after September 11, when the war council assembled, and Wolfowitz reportedly couldn't stop talking about bombing Iraq, until a White House aide asked Rumsfeld to restrain his deputy. At that moment, in virtual time, a film director would have Wolfowitz see the light, and Vulcan-like (he was one of the Vulcans who had advised Republican administrations since Ford), he would commence romancing the poor president, who never knew what hit him, either before or after the horrible September attacks, but smelled public-relations trouble from the start. "I think he really believes in them," Wolfowitz later told a reporter; speaking of the visions he conveyed to Bush of an Arab reformation and a vast shake-up of the Middle East.[21]

Behind this coupling, of course, stands the age-old American imbroglio that historian Brooks Adams warned of in 1900. This is the presence of great wealth, cheek to jowl with the Executive, which exerts only private power and is incapable of recognizing, much less exercising, public responsibility. Meanwhile, what Cheney's task force accomplished, with the help of the Vulcans, was to pound out the geopolitical cornerstone of Middle East policy, around which the defense industry and the Pentagon flew into formation, like filings to a magnet.

No wonder the energy meetings were kept secret. In addition to evidence of their influence on the decision to go to war in Iraq, scattered through the cyber-trail were institutional reports and meetings that led to the gutting of the Clean Air Act, and the decision to allow power plants, refineries, and other industrial sites to spew more pollutants into the air. This last was just one of the assaults on the global environment that have been sustained under the stewardship of the captains of sludge.

Another Bush–Cheney energy crony was Anthony Alexander of Ohio's FirstEnergy Corporation, the company that helped trigger the massive August 2003 blackout in the US and Canada by failing to properly upgrade its transmission system following deregulation. Alexander, like many in the group, was a Bush Pioneer, having raised over $100,000 for the 2000 campaign,[22] while the electric utilities industry as a whole contributed $4.8 million. The payoff, in this instance, came one week after the blackout, when energy secretary Spencer Abraham (a record holder for auto-industry campaign contributions) refused to separate grid modernization from the rest of the energy bill and place it on the fast track, thereby reversing Bush's promise to take action to "determine whether or not our grid needs to be modernized."[23]

9

THE POLITICAL ECONOMY OF DEATH

III

We wanted something different for our people; not to find ourselves an old, reactionary republic, full of ghost-fears, the fears of death and the fears of birth. We want something else.

MURIEL RUCKEYSER, *The Life of Poetry*

On September 12, 2003, US forces shot and killed ten freshly trained Iraqi policemen and a Jordanian hospital guard near Fallujah. There had been other large-scale killings by American troops in and around Fallujah, as there have been throughout central Iraq; for such "accidents," far from aberrations, are part of what the American occupation is all about. But this attack, whose aftermath turned up not a single Iraqi shell fired in self-defense, set off a powder keg of fury among the local Sunni population. And it marked a turning point of sorts for the US, when the Bush team, after slouching toward the UN in search of money and troops, returned empty-handed (but for a lone offer of military assistance from *Bangladesh*).

The sticking point was France and Germany's resolve that the UN take charge of the pace and manner in which Iraqis regained political control of the country. The Bush administration wanted a UN mandate over an international peacekeeping force under US military command, which left control over Iraq's political development in American hands. At first, the argument appeared to be moot; for the United Nations, suffering what Colin Powell called "donor fatigue," and still stunned by the attack on UN headquarters in Baghdad on August 19 (which killed twenty-three people, including the chief UN envoy, Sergio Vieira de Mello) was fast losing interest in either fielding troops or establishing UN authority over the increasingly uncertain road to Iraq's political renovation—all, that is, but France.

On the day of the Fallujah massacre, French Foreign Minister Dominique de Villepin presented an eloquent brief for convening an "international conference" as soon as Iraq's sovereignty was reestablished, in order to "tackle together all the problems linked to reconstructing Iraq. It would aim to *reestablish* the coherence and efficiency of international action on Iraq's behalf." This pertained to both the contributions that UN members would make to a peacekeeping force, which Villepin agreed should operate under US command, as well as to the "formation of the army and the police"—the latter suggesting that responsibility for domestic security was not to be turned over to a sovereign Iraq. More important, insofar as French (and other) geopolitical interests were concerned, the conference "would have to define the financial aid commitments and *assistance modalities* to be brought to restoring the Iraqi administration back to order" (emphasis added).[1]

"Reestablish" and "assistance modalities" were code words that infuriated the Bush administration, which suspected they were related to the euro issue; and it denounced Villepin for politicking outside Security Council channels. What the buzzwords pointed to first was the US seizure of monopoly control over Iraqi oil, and the return to the dollar (which was formalized by President Bush on May 22, in UN Resolution

1483); this threatened to toss former French and Russian and even British investments into the dustbin, along with some $130 billion in Iraqi loans, mainly owing to Russia and France.[2] Second, the words referred to the dominant position which the Halliburton/Bechtel cartel held over the myriad concessions tied to reconstruction. France, in effect, was promoting a division of the spoils as the price for helping the US out of the hole it had dug for itself.

In Washington that same day, Powell and Rumsfeld told the US Senate that the bill for postwar reconstruction would probably run to *$55 billion more* than the $87 billion the president had called for the previous Sunday. When Senators asked how they thought they could "fill the gap" this would leave in the budget, the two men, according to a Senate official, "looked at each other and there was a sort of embarrassing pause before Powell said 'maybe we'll get a few hundred million from Europe and maybe a little help from Japan'."[3] Clearly they hadn't a clue; or perhaps the question hadn't occurred to them. A few days later, the staff director of the House Appropriations Committee pointed out that the $87 billion was "really just a down payment."[4]

Catfights began to break through the lockjaw consensus on military policy, which was in such deep disarray that leaders began contradicting each other and themselves. First Rumsfeld, Cheney, and Paul Bremer seemed to be pitted against Bush and his right-hand woman, Condoleezza Rice; with Cheney, in closed-door Senate meetings, calling for a hasty exit, and Bush still pining for a reborn Iraq capable of radiating "democracy" throughout the Middle East. A task for "a generation," Rice explained; and for a moment, the whole war in Iraq was up for grabs. "We're on a glide path out of town," vied with "We're here for the long term."[5] Then Cheney was summoned to tell Meet the Press that Iraq remained the central front in the war on terror, as the president had declared on September 9, and therefore America wasn't leaving any time soon. But he sullied the message by dragging out long-discredited arguments, like the "Czech connection," alleging that Mohammed Atta once met with a senior Iraqi intelligence official in Prague. And Bush, playing straight, publicly corrected him by saying the administration *never* had evidence of a link between Iraq and 9/11, thereby negating a line they had all worked assiduously to implant in the public mind. This correction, duly echoed by Rumsfeld, was issued for the record, so to speak, for the record was beginning to matter, and critics, not all of them Democrats, were chipping away at the edifice on which the war and the afterwar rested.

Of all the discredited arguments, only the antiterror one remained—originally the most "disingenuous" of all, James Steinberg observed from the Brookings Institution—and Bush pumped it for all it was worth. "We have carried the fight to the enemy. We are rolling back the terrorist threat to civilization, not on the fringes of its influence but at the heart of its power."[6] And lo, the hand of God descended from the heavens to fulfill the prophecy. The revelation was memorialized by Garry Trudeau in "Doonesbury":

Roland Hedley, CNN, interviewing a masked terrorist: "So where has your cell been operating, Commander?"

Terrorist: "Chechnya, Afghanistan, Kosovo—You name it. ... But then we heard about Bush's challenge to the Jihad community to 'Bring 'em on' in Iraq. What kind of commander invites fire on his own troops? A few days later, we took Bush up on his dare."

Roland: "Why the delay?"

Terrorist: "No one believed it. I had to get it re-translated."[7]

On September 22, seeking the UN mandate, which he knew by then would be pasted like a fig leaf over his nakedness, *sans* money and *sans* troops, Bush delivered a peculiar speech to the General Assembly. All the outworn

arguments were trundled out, as if nothing had happened since his previous address the year before (so much for the record); and not an inch of
ground was given to the ominous reality the US now faced in Iraq. The
occupation authority is doing good work in Iraq, he said; you should come
help us; and if you don't, you're on the side of the terrorists. He spoke
murkily of the "clearest of divides: between those who seek order, and
those who spread chaos. ..."[8] It was the preemptive war party's answer to
the lost simplicities of the Cold War, invoked by neocons and neoliberals
alike. "Today's world is also divided," is how *New York Times* columnist
Tom Friedman put it, "but it is increasingly divided between the 'World of
Order' ... and the 'World of Disorder'." The latter, he writes, "is dominated by rogue regimes like Iraq's and North Korea's. ..."[9]

American diplomacy had suffered a major defeat, in spite of the money
Washington dangled before its prospective pawns: especially Pakistan,
Turkey, and India, whose troops it coveted for the mythical multinational
division. Even Japan withdrew a pledge to contribute to reconstruction,
which was now widely viewed as America's burden for having botched its
duties to the international community. In two speeches bracketing the president's address, UN secretary Kofi Annan and French President Jacques
Chirac charged that it was the US doctrines of unilateralism and preemption that threatened to spread chaos across the globe. Both leaders spoke
bluntly, and were roundly applauded, while Bush's remarks received a
lackluster response, even in the home press. Two days later, Kofi Annan
announced that the 600-member UN delegation in Iraq would be cut back
to eighty-six, and further if security under the US occupation continued to
worsen. On September 29, thirty more UN workers were withdrawn.

In its quest for international support, the administration had hit an air
pocket with no apparent end. At the same time, from inside its own ranks
came the rumblings of a Deep Throat capable of throwing a monkey
wrench into the already irregular workings of the White House political
machine. On September 25, former US ambassador Joseph C. Wilson IV
charged Bush's chief adviser Karl Rove with leaking the name of Wilson's

wife, Valerie Plame, a CIA agent specializing in WMD, to journalist Robert Novak in revenge for Wilson's exposure of the phoney Niger–Iraqi uranium deal some months before. The White House, said Wilson (who later contended Rove only "condoned" the leak), was seeking to intimidate government employees from challenging its war policy. Such critics—who were not averse to politicking via leaks themselves (without, however, exposing undercover agents)—were proliferating in the intelligence services and the State Department.

On September 27, the *Washington Post* cited "a senior administration official" who confirmed "that before Novak's [July 14] column ran, two top White House officials called at least six Washington journalists and disclosed the identity and occupation of Wilson's wife." Wilson had just revealed his Niger mission for the CIA in the *New York Times*, and stated that he'd found no evidence to back up Bush's repeated references to Saddam's uranium deal. The account had touched off "a political fracas," and the unnamed senior official was quoted as saying of the leak: "Clearly it was meant purely and simply for revenge."[10]

The intentional disclosure of a covert operative's identity is a serious violation of federal law. Apart from destroying Plame's effectiveness in the field, and endangering her life and possibly the lives of others, it very likely destroyed whatever counter-WMD operation she was involved in. For the authors of the Patriot Act, this represented an astonishing breach of security. And it raised the interesting question of why the Bush team chose to sabotage a CIA effort in the war against terror.

The administration promised an in-house investigation to uncover the culprit. But the CIA had already notified the Justice Department of the security breach, as it was legally bound to do, presumably after Novak's July column. Now with Wilson upping the ante, CIA Director George J. Tenet stepped forth to reinforce the seriousness of the case, while Attorney General John Ashcroft, dodging conflict-of-interest charges from the Democrats, deputized FBI Director Robert Muller to commence the investigation. The cover-up was on.

Nobody asked why Wilson waited until September to throw down the gauntlet (on August 21, he told a public forum outside Seattle that it was of keen interest to him "to see whether or not he could get Karl Rove frog-marched out of the White House in handcuffs"[11]). Clearly he had decided to become a player in an attempted take-down of an administration that had heretofore swatted its domestic opponents away like flies. Steadily mounting US casualties in Iraq, and the open frustration of military commanders who now spoke of the hydra-headed enemy with a certain professional respect—together with the corrosive power of that $87 billion working its way through Congress—were taking their toll. Or so it seemed. "The Bush administration is not at risk of damaging its credibility in Iraq," editorialized the *Los Angeles Times* on September 26; "it's in danger of destroying it." What better moment to strike.

Meanwhile, CIA weapons inspector, David Kay, esteemed leader of the much-publicized 1200-man Iraq Survey Group, on which the White House and the Pentagon placed high hopes, returned from Iraq empty-handed. Not only was there no evidence of active programs to develop or produce chemical or nuclear weapons, but the interim report refuted another of the administration's justifications for going to war: the argument that UN inspections didn't work:

> Information found to date suggests that Iraq's large-scale capability to develop, produce, and fill new CW munitions was reduced—if not entirely destroyed—*during Operation Desert Storm and Desert Fox, 13 years of UN sanctions and UN inspections*. [Re Saddam's intention to develop nuclear weapons] to date we have not uncovered evidence that Iraq undertook significant post-1998 steps to actually build nuclear weapons or produce fissile material [emphasis added].

The same appeared to be true for the biological weapons program and the missile program, though Kay suggested there was more to be learned about those efforts.[12]

With a negative WMD report, the chief framing tale on which the administration had hung its war finally seemed to collapse. And everyone leapt into the fray, including the hawkish Democratic presidential candidate, Joseph Lieberman, who called for a special prosecutor to lead the investigation of the White House CIA leak even before the liberal Minority House leader Nancy Pelosi did. From the forecaster STRATFOR came the acerbic observation, apropos *le scandal*, that the "only winner in all of this is Osama bin Laden. It's beginning to look like his analysis of the United States was shrewder than it might originally have appeared. The United States is self-destructive. Just give it a little push, and Washington will tear itself apart."[13]

On the battlefield, debates over whether coalition forces were besieged by outside "terrorists" or by a homegrown Iraqi guerrilla army suddenly seemed irrelevant. The answer was obviously both, with domestic resistance groups multiplying by the week. It was the diversity of targets—the sabotaged pipelines, power stations, water and sewage systems; the ransacked museums, hospitals, and schools; the daily attacks on US and British troops, international aid workers, American contractors, journalists, Iraqi policemen, translators and chauffeurs working for Americans, and, on September 25, with the death of Akila al-Hashemi, the Governing Council itself—that sowed terror and confusion among Iraqis and foreigners alike.

In the United States, more observers were reminded of Vietnam, as they were in Iraq where every afternoon the CPA's spin-doctors addressed the press in a large auditorium at the Baghdad Convention Center in what reporters called "the 3 o'clock follies," after the "5 o'clock follies" in Saigon. The numbers, writes Christian Parenti, were mumbled as in a Latin Mass, reinforcing the sense that the driving force behind the war was pure faith:

In the last 24 hours, coalition forces have detained 149 individuals, conducted over 1000 patrols and 20 raids ... confiscated 110 diesel-smuggling trailer trucks, and destroyed more than 20 IEDs [improvised explosive devises]. Coalition forces completed four civic action projects in the Basra area. ..."[14]

And on and on. American deaths by hostile fire were duly noted, but not the increasing numbers of wounded, or the accidental deaths, or the suicides, or the female troops sent home pregnant, or the US soldiers busted for looting. There was, and remains, no official US attempt to calculate the number of Iraqi dead and wounded.

In spite of the echoes of Vietnam, however, Iraq is a different kind of war. Meaner, more desperate, with no quarter given by any party to winning support from other nations. The guerrillas show little interest in prying apart the enemy's fragile alliances; or reaching out to America's and Britain's opposition movements; or assuring Iraqi civilians that they, and not the Coalition, with its puppet council, represent the true welfare of the nation. There is no publicly articulated vision of a social revolution. Once US strategists handed Iraq the opportunity to rally militant Islam to the challenge of defeating the American empire on the battlefield, how could these fighters refuse the call of the wrecking ball? They do not, after all, represent an insurgent nation in embryo. Not yet. While the US is setting the stage for a new phase of Iraqi resistance—one in which Sunni, Shi'ites, and even Kurds may unite around a common goal, which is getting the US out of Iraq—there is no Ho Chi Minh on the horizon.

Among frightened Iraqi citizens are those who say the solution is to bring Hussein back, if "he only do security. [If] Saddam gave one speech," the director of a small private hospital in Baqubah told a *Los Angeles Times* reporter on September 26, "security would be improved." This was shortly after a mortar attack had missed a US military compound in the busy market town thirty miles north of Baghdad, killing nine Iraqis and wounding many more. "We would like to see action from the Americans," the man added; but another civilian, wounded in the attack, said the only solution was to have Iraqis take care of law enforcement, and not US-trained Iraqis. "The Americans want to apply their laws to us. They are too soft," he said. "There is something inside ourselves that we do not like, but we need a strong central authority." He didn't blame the Americans for the attack, but others in Baqubah did, while still others blamed "outsiders" from Iran and Saudi Arabia. US military sources blamed former regime supporters, mainly the paramilitary group Fedayeen Saddam.[15] Not long after, they blamed Islamist outsiders.

It's not hard to understand the wrecking of the country's oil infrastructure—whose oversight was transferred on September 23 from Phillip J. Carroll, one-time head of Shell Oil Co., to Robert E. McKee III, a former ConocoPhillips executive. McKee's selection as Bush's energy czar in Iraq has drawn fire on Capitol Hill because of his ties to Halliburton. "The administration continues to create the impression that the fox is in charge of the hen house," comments Representative Waxman. "Given Mr. McKee's close relationship with Halliburton"—he is chairman of Enventure Global Technology, an oilfield joint venture owned by both Halliburton and Shell—Waxman finds him to be "an odd choice to hold [Halliburton] accountable for the billions of dollars they are charging American taxpayers."[16] Because McKee, who took home $26.2 million last year (placing him second in the *Houston Chronicle*'s list of 100 highest-paid executives), is responsible for establishing energy policy for Iraq's "new" oil industry, and for running the very large petroleum operation of a semi-conquered nation, it would be passing strange if anti-occupation forces didn't hit the pipelines over and over again.

Looked at from afar, however, it's harder to understand the laying waste of the infrastructure that underpins civilian life. Some, mainly US officials, still attribute this to the criminals Saddam Hussein released from Iraqi prisons, working alongside the storied Ba'athist "dead-enders" who want to stir up sentiments not unlike those expressed by the anxious hospital director in Baqubah; while many Iraqis blame the damage on both sabotage and on America's April blitz of Baghdad, and more importantly, on the failure of the CPA to make a priority of restoring public services. Whatever the reasons for the continuing break-downs, there's no denying the rapidity with which a majority of Sunnis and minority of Shi'ites have rallied around the demand that the US withdraw from Iraq. Moreover, when one contemplates the isolation of the guerrilla forces arrayed against the United States—their lack of great power support, such as North Vietnam and the Vietcong drew from China and the Soviet Union, along with the debilitating history of ethnic conflict in Iraq—one marvels at their ability to keep the American behemoth on the run.

After Joseph Wilson's rabbit punch and David Kay's bad news, the White House tried to kill two birds with one stone by turning the hounds loose on the CIA, and on George Tenet, in particular. There was blood in the water, and Bush's guardians wanted to make sure it wasn't their leader's that would feed the growing hunger for blame. Tenet, who had supervised Kay's work, had already taken the rap for Bush a few months earlier, when he agreed to accept responsibility for not removing the false uranium statement from the State of the Union Address. Now he and his agency were pegged to take it again; and it was Tenet's head that seemed poised to roll in the sudden shake-up of US Iraqi strategy that the White House announced on October 6. Tenet's head, and maybe Lord Rumsfeld's, too.

The new entity was called the Iraq Stabilization Group, and it would oversee "counterterrorism" (which conflated guerrillas with terrorists, something the military command had avoided), economic issues, the development of political infrastructure, and communications (public relations). Interestingly, the new group's oversight also extended to Afghanistan, which undercut the State Department's authority, just as the reorganization seemed to undercut Pentagon authority in Iraq. The Stabilization Group, which included obscure representatives from State, Defense, and Treasury, but not the CIA, would be centered in the White House, and led by National Security Adviser Condoleezza Rice. Rice had recently presented a convoluted version of her boss's "Bring 'em on!" line when she stated on the Today Show that a "transformed Iraq would be the death knell for terrorism [which was] why foreign fighters are now coming to Iraq. ... [T]hey clearly understand that a victory for the peace in Iraq, like the military victory we've had there, will mean that their goals and their strategies will be severely undermined."[17]

The White House pretended to take over both the war and reconstruction, along with the task of repackaging America's manifold defeats. Guided leaks initially assured reporters that contrary to appearances the president was satisfied with the war's progress, and with the leadership of Rumsfeld and Paul Bremer, both of whom were said to have been directly involved in forming the new group. ("Not true!" Rumsfeld snapped a few days later.) In fact, their future roles remained undefined, as did George Tenet's. It was a shot across the Pentagon's bow by Bush and "First Chum" Condi Rice (as Maureen Dowd calls her). Rice in fact had overnight become the most powerful national security adviser since Henry Kissinger. "She has all the tools," said STRATFOR; "all she needs now is a strategy."[18]

For a White House desperate to rid itself of the Iraqi nightmare, so it could throw itself into the pressing business of running a political campaign, this was an odd move, akin to rearranging the deckchairs on the *Titanic*. In the face of the president's troubles, tradition dictated that the commander-in-chief seize control of the runaway war, or seem to, and thus neutralize the negative publicity surrounding his person, and reverse the downward course of his ratings. But if there was any substance to the shake-up, it threw the Oval Office open to the stream of chaos and confusion emanating from Iraq which was previously sectioned off in competing bureaucracies. Theoretically anyway, the White House was now accountable. Hunkered down with his First Chum, and with a third-rate group of overseers that included his mother's former press secretary, nothing was likely to come of the move but more trouble.

Business, meanwhile—the sort that springs from liaisons between the Pentagon, industry, and Congress—had begun to wobble. The challenge of turning war-ravaged Iraq into a cash cow for the brotherhood of investors who were supposed to be standing by to crack open the closed markets of the Arab world was a challenge to which the president and vice president had paid special heed. Reconstruction policy, in fact—the part that covered US business—was always run from the White House; and was responsible for the sophomorisms that plagued dispatches from Mr. Bremer's office, like the opening sentence of a fall 2003 timetable on nation-building: "Now that Saddam Hussein's regime has been removed," it read, "the Iraqi people have the opportunity to realize the president's vision of a stable, prosperous and democratic Iraq." Which prompted Senator Patrick Leahy, top Democrat on the Senate Appropriations Foreign Operations Subcommittee, to reflect that "Some, considering [Iraq's] civilization is a bit older than ours, might consider that a bit condescending. Some might think the Iraqi people might want to be asked if they want an American president to determine what their vision would be."[19]

The president's vision of prosperity is the flame that burns behind the dreamy invocations to a peaceable Iraq galvanizing the rest of the Middle East. It inspired Ahmed Chalabi's pitch to the UN on October 2, when he entreated international lenders and investors to "Place your confidence in Iraq. Take from it stability and prosperity, and you will see it spread into the region and the entire world."[20] Faith in the fantastical vision led the *Wall Street Journal* to hype Iraq, against all reason, as "the largest government reconstruction effort since Americans helped to rebuild Germany and Japan after World War II."[21]

To jump-start the miracle, which has had few takers outside state-funded behemoths such as Halliburton and Bechtel, the Coalition Provisional Authority unveiled a set of policies on September 21 that formally threw open the entire Iraqi economy to foreign investment and potential ownership. The exception was the oil industry, still under nominal Iraqi ownership while American taxpayers secured and repaired the hardware. What income oil produced—and according to an estimate from George Soros, it produced $1 billion between August 12 and September 2, 2003—was reportedly used to finance Iraqi aspects of the occupation, such as public-service salaries and running the Governing Council and its ministries.[22] According to the new laws, announced by Finance Minister Kamel al Keylini, foreign owners could control 100 percent of any enterprise in which they invested, in sharp contrast to the rest of the Arab world, where foreign ownership is tightly restricted.

The new regulations, fresh from CPA drawing boards, invited investors to enter Iraq post-haste, without having to be screened by the government (assuming one existed). All profits could be immediately remanded overseas, without having to pass through an Iraqi institution. Real estate could not be foreign-owned but could be leased for up to forty years. Corporate and personal income tax rates would range from 3 percent to 15 percent after a tax holiday expires in 2004. To boost trade, Iraq would levy a flat tariff of just 5 percent on all imports except relief supplies. The law, Order 39, permitted six international banks to take complete control of local banks within the next five years, after which there would be no limits on the entry of foreign banks into Iraq.[23]

The delivery of this remarkable document ("setting the most far-sighted investment climate in the Middle East," said the CPA[24]) was timed to coincide with a World Bank and International Monetary Fund meeting in Dubai, and to anticipate a donors'conference in Madrid, where the White House planned to follow up another request for a UN mandate on October 17 (successful, as it turned out) with yet another appeal to US allies for UN financial involvement (unsuccessful). The latter was buttressed by a concession from the administration, which agreed to cede control over aid to Iraq in certain sectors (electricity, sewage, health services) to an agency run by the World Bank and the United Nations. Even so, substantial commitments of aid or troops were not forthcoming. The new agency was snagged on the issues of Iraq's outstanding debts to Russia and France, and the billions of dollars in reparations still owing from past wars, but more important, on the mounting resistance to occupation. "Quite simply, we cannot do what we would want to do," said a UN official, "if security does not improve."[25]

One after another, the Bush administration's government-to-government negotiations had failed. Secretary of State Powell was no more successful in selling administration policy on his beat than his counterpart at the Pentagon had succeeded in turning the promised quick and easy war into a clean slate on which Mr. Bremer could work his magic. For the White House, it was easier to talk shop with CEOs. Should any doubt remain that Iraq was to be sold off at cut-rate prices, rather than rebuilt, a meeting of 100 multinationals organized in London on October 13 made it clear enough. The corporations—principally oil (ExxonMobil) and banking, but also McDonald's, Delta Airlines, and the American Hospital Group—discussed investment opportunities with US officials, who encouraged them to start up in Iraq as soon as satisfactory levels of security were restored, levels which, despite President Bush's latest "good news from Iraq" campaign, kept dropping.

Sponsored by the US–Iraq Business Alliance, which claimed to have close contacts with the Pentagon, the London meeting, called "Doing Business in Iraq: Kickstarting the Private Sector," was part of the "virtual economy" to which Pep Subiros refers; the one that lives an "immense fiction" and speaks in tongues. Viz. Tony Blair's trade representative, Brian Wilson, addressing the kickstarters: "Let me say straightaway that this conflict in Iraq, now thankfully behind us, was not about business or about oil. It was about liberating the people of Iraq and giving them the choice to enjoy a life free from tyranny."[26] The wonder of such assertions is not how foolish they sound but how neatly they invert the facts, and in so doing pay them a weird homage. They are the truth upside down, the truth that offends. They cannot draw a breath without it.

The conflict in Iraq, far from over, had in fact taken off, sweeping the president's visions before it like rubbish in a hurricane. "The enemy has evolved. [It's become] a little bit more lethal, a little bit more complex, a little bit more sophisticated," according to the commander of US and allied forces in Iraq, Lieutenant General Ricardo S. Sanchez. "As long as we are here," he added, "the coalition needs to be prepared to take casualties."[27]

For independent reporters still on the beat, there was only desolation. *Smoke rising from Karrada Street, an electronics district popular with soldiers, where a Humvee was blown to bits by a remote-activated mine ... sidewalks jammed with refrigerator and air-conditioning boxes; a military transport truck and another Humvee idling in the street, near the smoldering hulk ... a few US soldiers crouched behind the truck.* Two wounded GIs, writes Christian Parenti, are sprawled on the ground while a medivac helicopter circles above, unable to land because of the snarl of overhead wires. A desultory firefight ensues until several Bradley fighting vehicles roll up and start pounding a building with 25-millimeter cannon shells. A typical scene. Two Iraqi civilians lie dead on the sidewalk and a few more are wounded. A cigarette stand has been knocked down, its packs of smokes strewn everywhere. An Iraqi shopkeeper leans on a wall and sobs while his store goes up in flames. The GIs crouched among the smashed appliances seem neither scared nor courageous, only tired and numb. With all their firepower, they can rarely dominate skirmishes like this (which may or may not have started as an ambush), but only ride them out and hope to emerge intact.[28]

Not far from Karrada Street is the air-conditioned oasis of trophy palaces known as the "green zone," which is home to the CPA and Iraq's Governing Council with its ministries of this and that. The latter are staffed by members of the Iraqi Reconstruction and Development Council (IRDC), which was established in Virginia and composed of dissidents hastily recruited a month before the war began. It was the US government's first attempt to "put an Iraqi face" on the postwar administration of Iraq; but while it has an Iraqi face, the IRDC has an American paymaster. This is SAIC (Science Applications International, Co.), which AP calls "the most influential company most people have never heard of," and *Asia Times* describes as "the most mysterious and feared of the big 10 defense giants."[29]

Kamel al Keylini, the finance minister, was drawn from these ranks, which have begun to buckle under the strain of serving masters who have nothing for Iraq. Why, the Governing Council demands, did the occupation authority issue a $20 million contract to Jordan to buy new revolvers and Kalashnikov rifles for the Iraqi police when the US military has confiscated hundreds of thousands of these weapons from Saddam Hussein's abandoned arsenals? Most are said to be in mint condition, and would cost nothing. Another deal with Jordan, resented for the large payment the Hashemite monarchy will draw from the dwindling Iraqi treasury—and for the close ties it enjoyed with Saddam's regime—angers Council members even more. This is the US decision to spend $1.2 billion to train 35,000 Iraqi police officers in Jordan when the training could be done in Iraq at a fraction of the cost. Germany and France, moreover, have offered to provide such training for free.

Iraqi officials and businessmen charge that millions of dollars in contracts and subcontracts are being awarded without competitive bidding, most to Americans while those to Iraqis include former cronies of Hussein's government, such as the powerful Bunnia family. Mahmoud Bunnia, meanwhile, director of the company that secured a Bechtel contract to repair forty-nine damaged bridges, complains that work has begun on only three. "It's peanuts," he says of the money trickling in from Bechtel, arguing, as many do, that all the damaged bridges were quickly rebuilt after the 1991 war, as were the damaged roads. "Saddam would have done better," is a common refrain.[30]

"There is no transparency," laments Mahmoud Othnan, a Kurdish member of the twenty-four-member Governing Council, speaking of contractors large and small. Othnan, who will soon learn, if he hasn't already, that transparency is expected only of subject institutions, sees "mismanagement right and left," and wishes the GC could "sit with [the US] Congress face to face to discuss this"—*imagine!*—because, he declares, "we are victims and the American taxpayers are victims."[31] How ironic that the puppet council is demanding more autonomy and control over the affairs of state, while in Washington Congress is demanding, and receiving, less and less.

Congress, alas, has approved the $87 billion for Bush's war chest, raising overall military spending to an amount equal to what the federal government spends on education, public health, housing, unemployment, pensions, food aid and welfare *put together.*[32] The CPA will keep doling out contracts like sugar candy, often by simply phoning favored companies and announcing, "I have a contract for you"—as an American businessman who received such a call in October told the *New York Times.*[33] These practices, however, while typical of crony capitalism, betray the hot breath of desperation that now accompanies the selling of Iraq. But it wasn't for lack of trying that the US originally hoped to draw subcontractors to the marketplace through more orthodox channels.

In his story on KBR's operations in Iraq, Dan Baum reported that much of Halliburton's global business would depend on US and foreign subcontractors and customers getting loans from US banks, *loans which were automatically guaranteed by the government's trade-promoting Export-Import Bank.*[34] Baum didn't explore this provision, but it's a tasty carrot the Bush administration extended to vassal states and the American banking community. Under an ExIm warranty, defense-related loans are safe, safer than the capital expenditure and M&A (merger and acquisition) loans of the go-go years, and far safer than trade-related investments, much less infrastructure ventures of potential use to an undeveloped nation. Endlessly self-perpetuating, as conflict breeds conflict, and free of liability risks, defense loans offer the US government a tool for roping client states into presumably mutually rewarding alliances, while sending new business to Wall Street financial institutions. Jordan, not exactly a client state, but a vassal scrambling for lordship in America's Arab Brigadoon, is a case in point. (Jordan, the monarchy, that is; in March 2004, eight out of ten Jordanians said that suicide attacks against Americans and other westerners in Iraq were justified.[35])

No doubt the tool has sweetened many deals, but not enough to satisfy the administration, which has directed Bremer's MBAs to see that Iraq rolls over dead, in effect, to attract recalcitrant investors. In the meantime, the president has dispatched a squad of personal barkers to pump for customers. Joe Allbaugh, Bush's campaign manager in 2000, who spent most of his career in Texas politics before being awarded control of the Federal Emergency Management Agency, heads the most chesty of the new operations, New Bridge Strategies. Allbaugh was rotated out of government in the spring of 2003 and into the private sector assignment to advise companies looking for taxpayer-financed business and licenses to sell products in Iraq. While Allbaugh has spent most of his career in the political arena, John Howland, another officer (and former president of the Texas-based American Rice Co., once a major exporter to both Iraq and wartime Vietnam), reminds us that "there's a lot of cross-pollination between that world and the one that exists in Iraq today." Indeed, the company's website notes that its partners have served in the Reagan and both Bush administrations, making them "particularly well-suited" to deal with the White House, Pentagon, and Congress.[36]

New Bridge Strategies has its counterparts among regional partnerships hoping to profit from the war. Among them is the Iraqi International Law Group (IILG) which brings together the former Israeli law partner of Defense Undersecretary Douglas Feith, L. Marc Zell, and the nephew of Ahmed Chalabi, Salem Chalabi. IILG touts its ability to offer clients the advantages of close contacts with the CPA and the Governing Council, but it's a sign of the unrest developing among

America's hand-picked Iraqi leadership that a member of the elder Chalabi's inner circle sees fit to call the operation "greedy, careless and stupid."[37]

The multibillion dollar reconstruction effort has unleashed what an American adviser in Iraq calls a "gold-rush mentality" among corporations eager to get in first and fast. The principals talk of the seemingly limitless opportunities involved in rebuilding an economy shattered by three wars, not to mention twelve years of punishing sanctions. Baghdad, exclaims a New Bridge partner, has "not one single recognizable brand name, not one single oasis of quality, no brass, glass and steel office building, or a retail store you're familiar with—nothing. ... One well-stocked 7-Eleven," he exults, "would put 30 Iraqi shops out of business."[38] It's a vision that recalls a speculative operation from the gaming tables of the boom years—the buy-out of bankrupt companies, often by mutual fund directors who turned their bargains (or tried to) into cash cows for stockholders via "restructuring" (cutting wages, firing employees, busting unions, outsourcing). Substitute bankrupt countries for bankrupt companies and you can see the larger picture.

In December 2002, STRATFOR cited Arab League estimates that the total GNP of Arab countries ($712 billion) accounted for only 2 percent of world GNP in 2001, just above sub-Saharan Africa's estimated 1 percent of the world economy. Measuring the crisis differently, the UN-assisted Arab Human Development Report for 2002 concluded that Arab deficits in education, democratic representation, and women's empowerment had left the region so far behind that the combined Gross Domestic Product of the twenty-two Arab states was less than that of a single European country: Spain.[39]

Already near the bottom of the global pyramid, the Middle East, according to STRATFOR, would slip even further during and after the war. The political and security upheavals caused by US-led operations against Iraq, along with new threats by al Qaeda, would deter traditional investors. But the "biggest winners," it predicted, "will be the investors *who are willing and able to scoop up cheap assets. Foreigners familiar with the region and its business practices, who have contacts there and an ability to tolerate risk will find a host of investment opportunities in everything from telecommunications to manufacturing"* (emphasis added).

In a report entitled "War Will Restructure Investment in the Middle East," STRATFOR explains how it works:

> The US wars against Iraq and al Qaeda will devastate the already troubled economies of the Middle East. Investment into non-petroleum industries will fall in most countries—with Iran a possible exception—and increased security risks and mounting political instability will plague traditional FDI [Foreign Direct Investment] destinations. ... For governments and citizens, the consequences will be disastrous—but for savvy investors who can take a risk, the opportunities will be sublime.[40]

"Sublime" is not a word one normally associates with investment opportunities, unless they bear promises of salvation. Looked at from the perspective of the present global economy, where international divisions in foreign affairs and military strategy have spilled into an economic sphere already beset by the falling dollar, spreading deflation in Asia, and simultaneous recessions and near stagnant growth in North America, Japan, Russia, and much of Europe, salvation may well be what Washington's brokers are after—especially if they can count on the White House and the Pentagon's broad shoulders to protect them from the risks.

For the United States, the master template for doing business in the Middle East is the Carlyle Group, the private equity firm associated with George Bush, Sr. and James Baker which manages vast sums in the Middle East, including, until recently, a large chunk of bin Laden family wealth. On the day al Qaeda attacked the US, Shafiq bin Laden, Osama's estranged brother, was attending an investment conference in Washington with both Baker and Bush *père* which was hosted by the Carlyle Group. Such are the syndicate's enduring connections that immediately following the attack, when no one was allowed in or out of the US, most of the extended bin Laden clan in America were spirited home to Saudi Arabia. The burst of defense spending that followed September 11, meanwhile, greatly increased the value of the Carlyle Group's significant investments in defense companies, which are less well known than are its ties to Saudi sheiks.

Carlyle got its start in 1987 by exploiting a bizarre tax loophole that allowed profitable American companies to claim a large tax break by buying the losses incurred by Eskimo-owned companies in Alaska. The scheme brought together the dealmaker, long gone, with David Rubenstein, a former aide to Jimmy Carter who is said to be the brains behind the venture. According to the company's unauthorized biographer, Dan Briody (*The Iron Triangle: Inside the Secret World of the Carlyle Group*), Carlyle stumbled into some bad deals, including buying shares in Caterair International, a company that tanked under the weight of its junk-bond financing. But it introduced the partners to a Caterair director, George W. Bush.

Carlyle took off in 1989 when it hired Frank Carlucci, a former defense secretary and deputy director of the CIA, who was able to open doors in Washington, allowing it to participate in many lucrative deals. The group's contacts spread throughout the "iron triangle" where industry, government, and the military converge, to embrace the former President Bush, former British prime minister John Major, and former South Korean prime minister Park Tae-joon, "all of whom," sniffs the *Economist*'s reviewer, "have taken the Carlyle nickel." Bush Sr. continues to get private intelligence briefings not available to ordinary investors, which prompts the magazine to wonder whether this "inside knowledge of, and possible influence over, the administration's political strategy towards, say, North Korea and Saudi Arabia directly benefits Carlyle?" There might be less reason to worry if there were "rival clubs of ex-political heavyweights competing within the iron triangle." But alas, there aren't. Carlyle seems to be an "aspiring monopolist, hoovering up former public officials from across the political divide and, increasingly, from across the world. It is becoming more ambitious in Europe, and is keenly eying China." And recently, in collaboration with James Baker, it opened an office in Azerbaijan to oversee Caspian oil deals. Oil interests in Russia led it to hire two oligarchs, Platon Lebedev and Mikhail Khodorkovsky, both of whom were arrested by Putin in July and October, 2003, respectively, thereby putting on hold Carlyle's plan to initiate a buyout of part of the oil giant Yukos. Shortly after that, Bush resigned as a Carlyle adviser.

"Asset capitalism," as the *Economist* calls such high-level cronyism, "is for ghastly places like Russia, China or Africa, not the land of the free market."[41] But the plain truth is the reverse. So-called free markets are for subject nations, not for the rich and certainly not for the United States which eschews the rules demanding transparency and accountability that it expects from its competitors and demands from its prey.

If there is an underlying value system that unites the free trade realm it is, as Subiros observes, that the "concept of liberty is only applicable to doing business ... not to people." For the people is reserved "a concept of happiness based on the maximization and constant replenishment of the possession of objects."[42] Such thinking animates the Washington Consensus on world trade that flourished under Clinton, and, in slightly different form, tinged by the moralism of Bush *fils*, appears in the current national security strategy. "We will actively work to bring the hope of democracy, development, free markets, and free trade to every corner of the world," states the strategy; and lists among its guidelines lower marginal tax rates and pro-growth legal and regulatory policies. "The concept of 'free trade'," it argues,

arose as a moral principle even before it became a pillar of economics. If you can make something that others value, you should be able to sell it to them. If others make something that you value, you should be able to buy it. *That is real freedom, the freedom for a person—or a nation—to make a living* [emphasis added].

The passage is quoted by economist William Tabb in "The Two Wings of the Eagle," a reflection on the good cop/bad cop strain in American diplomacy. "To any honest observer this is not an ideology of freedom or democracy," writes Tabb. "It is a system of control, an economics of empire."[43]

Where free market myths prevail, syndicates like the Carlyle Group and the smaller fixers and hedge funds spawned by the war in Iraq will very likely prosper. But not necessarily in happy juxtaposition; for while Carlyle is out for the long buck, and the stable international partnerships such a vision requires, the Bush administration's schemers are grabbing the main chance as if there is no tomorrow. In the war on terror the Bush team has found a "a shield of impunity," as Naomi Klein calls it; "an idea that can be easily franchised by any government in the market for an all-purpose opposition cleanser."[44] It's also a formula for promoting constant instability which, while it may justify expanding the power of the sword, appears to diminish the power of the purse.

Perhaps it's a sign of the threat this formula poses to the larger imperial ambition pursued by the Carlyle Group that the First Father gave a treasured prize, the 2003 George Bush Award for Excellence in Public Service, to the outspoken antiwar Democrat Ted Kennedy, of Massachusetts. ("An inspiration to all Americans ..."; a man who "consistently and courageously fought for his principles. ...") The event unleashed reams of purple prose about the rift between father and son; with the architect of Gulf War I commended for living "a life in the service of moderate and intelligent internationalism," who brought the Middle East "to the verge of peace for the first time in history ...," while the "son seems to have made posturing against his father's accomplishments and beliefs his life's work ... and led the Middle East to the nadir of its hope and possibilities, and ... the US to a moment in history in which we face asymmetric warfare from one end of the globe to another."[45]

This is over the top. More likely, the award to Senator Kennedy, which caught Washington by surprise, was a bolt from the multilateralist wing of the American eagle, a warning that the latter-day Wise Men, tainted as they are, viewed the war in Iraq as a menace to global security, *their* global security. For while it's Dick Cheney, Douglas Feith, and Bechtel's Jack Sheehan—even Bremer in his Baghdad hot seat—who now wear the triangle's three hats and deal the deadly hand, it's the blue-chip racketeers at Carlyle who will reap the bitter winds of change.

10

THE *CONSIGLIERI* IS BACK

There are two ways to regard the installation of James Baker in Bush Jr's White House. Either the president has finally found a temporary assignment that persuaded his old retainer to rescue him from his Middle East hot seat. Or Baker found a job, as special envoy in charge of reducing Iraq's $130 billion debt, that met his need for a White House cap with which to carry out continuing private conversations over oil and gas deals in Eurasia. Or both. In which case Baker has done it again. He's found a way to prove that George W. Bush is not a unilateralist but a multilateralist (when necessary), and thereby rescued a troubled political campaign, for the moment.

You never know with Baker, who may be representing his law firm Baker Potts, which represents Halliburton; or Baker Hughes, the oil services company that was promised the second tier of oilfield restoration contracts in Iraq after Halliburton's KBR took its share; or the Carlyle Group, of which Baker is senior counselor. Carlyle is where former top government officials come to roost alongside powerful business leaders, to raise funds and identify takeover targets; a giant hedge fund, if you will, with offices in twelve countries, managing $17.5 billion in assets, mostly in the areas of energy, aerospace, and defense.

In any event, the job of Iraq debt emissary to the presidents of seven nations cuts close enough to Baker's business interests that he renounced his partnership share of fees in "client matters" with both Carlyle and Baker Potts if they conflict with his official duties.[1] It's a standard move in such assignments, and irrelevant to the inestimable long-term value for a company like Carlyle of the contacts Baker has established. With his drop-the-debt tour, he has woven an astonishing web throughout the world: a network of pledges, mainly centered on Iraq, and confirmed at the very highest reaches of power. Public attention, however, was swiftly drawn to Paul Wolfowitz's petulant reminder, issued on the same day Baker's appointment was announced, that Russia, France, and Germany had forfeited their access to America's $18.6 billion in reconstruction contracts. "It's understandable that the Bush team wouldn't rush to give reconstruction contracts to France, Germany and Russia," grumbled Tom Friedman in the *New York Times*, "but why shove that in their faces while we're asking them to forgive Iraq's debts?"[2] Or was Wolfowitz's directive a bargaining chip placed on the table as part of Baker's negotiating strategy—the two wings of the American eagle, each bending to catch a different breeze, beating in tandem?

In the days before the tour, there was widespread agreement that the former secretary of state under Bush *père* had been embarrassed by Deputy Defense Secretary Wolfowitz. It was partly the liberal media's fascination with the radical right, and the susceptibility of American journalists to the takeover theory, in which the good sense of government was (once again) subverted by an alien ideology. Commentators such as J. M. Marshall, Jim Lobe, and the *New York Times'* Paul Krugman, agreed that Baker had been crossed, with Krugman adding that when he issued the reminder, Wolfowitz's hopes for becoming secretary of state in a second term took a nosedive. Marshall wondered whether we're "trying to get retribution toward these countries by stiffing them on the contracts, or are we trying to come to some sort of agreement ... to refinance and restructure Iraq's mammoth foreign debt?"[3] As if these goals, so close to the bad guy/good guy beat of American diplomacy, were in mortal conflict.

Lobe saw the problem as a continuation of the battle between neocons and realists going back to 1992, when Wolfowitz and Scooter Libby, now Cheney's powerful chief of staff, co-authored the Defense Department Guidance that so alarmed then secretary of state Baker, not to mention the first president Bush, that it took former defense secretary Cheney's promise to overhaul the text to save the authors' jobs. Baker, like other realists, in Lobe's view, was "deeply skeptical, not to say incredulous, about neoconservative ambitions to 'remake the face of the Middle East' by exporting democracy." Baker, in a word, had become a hero, or hero enough to rid the war of the right. He was Big Oil, and would see radical change in the region as "unacceptably risky and destabilizing."[4]

The moment Jim Baker returned to the White House, the tables had turned; or so it seemed. Baker, longtime *consiglieri* to the Bush family— whose last mission on its behalf was to secure Florida's votes for W in 2000, regardless of the state's voting laws, and thereby win the election for Bush (which he had failed to do as campaign manager for Bush's father's second term)—stood for a different Middle East than did neocons or hawks like Donald Rumsfeld. He had made no secret of his opposition to waging unilateral war on Iraq, though he was more discreet than was former national security adviser Brent Scowcroft (who is another Carlyle adviser). But the challenge posed by Baker's presence went beyond personal score-settling. "We went into Iraq to overturn the geopolitical dynamics of the region," said Marshall. "Now Baker, an opponent of everything the architects of the war stand for, is being sent in to reach an accommodation with the status quo powers to pave the way for our departure."[5]

Behind these statements lies the belief that President Bush wants out; that the turnaround announced on November 15 was real, and that the timetable for ending the civil occupation in July 2004 is genuine. It's a dangerously wrongheaded view, and not only because it ignores the continued presence of America's 130,000-man occupation army, bolstered by a new $3 billion Special Forces group, Task Force 121, whose numbers will not be reflected in troop totals. This is the secret force run by the CIA, with help from Israeli advisers, which includes Iraqi exile groups, Kurdish and Shi'ite militias, and former senior intelligence agents under the Ba'ath regime, that finally caught Saddam Hussein. In fact, it was the group's Kurds who found Saddam, and set him up for the on-camera capture by US forces. Like the Phoenix program in South Vietnam, the CIA's cadre are trained to ferret out and assassinate Iraqi and Afghan insurgents, and thereby allow the US to maintain control over the direction of the country when sovereignty is passed to the Iraqis. A loyal secret police, says John Pike, a military expert in Washington, means "the new Iraqi political regime will not stray outside the parameters that the US wants to set." It will "reign but not rule."[6]

Meanwhile, power is supposed to remain with the Coalition Provisional Authority and its retinue of Republican appointees and lobbyists in Washington and in Baghdad, where it will be absorbed into a 5000-man American Embassy in July—minus Paul Bremer, who is rumored to be a candidate for Bush's next cabinet. Here is where Baker's deals will be nailed down, the reconstruction contracts parceled out, and the privatization of the Iraqi economy—what's left after Bremer gave in on the state industries and Saddam's nationwide food rationing program (too risky to change)—implemented. That is, if security can be maintained; a big *if* over which Baker has no more control than Bush. And Bush, it appears, has even less control since the capture of Saddam which, far from triggering a diminution of the insurgency, has become a liability for the American leadership, demonstrating just how little influence Saddam Hussein had over the galloping resistance to the takeover of Iraq.

While the administration was strong enough to ride roughshod over the cracks in the public argument for war—the absence of WMDs, of

Iraq's links to 9/11, of any Iraqi threat to the region (much less to the US) after twelve years of punishing sanctions—it's not strong enough to turn the country into an American client state, even with British help. And however many conferences are convened on how to rebuild Iraq and get a piece of the $18.6 billion makes little difference. The occupation of Iraq has entered another critical phase, with a new set of blinders, centered on the so-called acceleration of the American withdrawal. According to an unnamed American diplomat: "Ideology has become subordinate to the schedule."[7] And the schedule is set by the presidential elections.

No longer will it take the promised two years to transform the political system and the security forces. Half of the 40,000 Iraqi soldiers the administration hoped to train by next October for use in light infantry battalions has already deserted, citing lack of adequate pay and fear of reprisals from insurgents. The US has concentrated instead on the police, who can be deployed much faster. "If you build a strong police force, you have a republic," says Steve Casteel, the CPA's security adviser. "If you build a strong military, you have a banana republic"—which is a good line, albeit wrong for Iraq, even when followed by the question: "when have you ever seen the police lead a coup?"

As for the political system, whose conversion to a secular, pluralistic, market-driven "democracy" was the neocons' contribution—that never got off the ground. Their real public was in America. "If there's one thing the Wolfowitz/Baker dust-up makes clear, it's that the ideology of the Bush White House is not neoconservatism; it's old-fashioned greed," Naomi Klein said in the *Guardian*;[8] and she was right. The Bush team never had a serious stake in the politics of postwar Iraq—so long as it didn't interfere with the geostrategic goals for which it was fighting. "Plans for Post-Saddam Iraq"—one of ex-Treasury secretary Paul O'Neill's documents from his Bush years—is a secret memo discussed early in 2001, months before 9/11, which envisioned peacekeeping troops, war crimes tribunals, and the divvying-up of Iraq's oil wealth.[9] Not much changed as Operation Iraqi Freedom drew closer.

The Iraq war is the wrong war against the wrong enemy at the wrong time, and the Bush administration is doing its best to hide the facts. Only it can't keep up with the breaking news—with, for example, the demand by the Grand Ayatollah Ali al-Sistani for direct elections by July 1—except with compromises which concede very little. On January 16, a top aide to the leading Iraqi cleric said that "in the coming days and months, we're going to see protests and strikes and civil disobedience, and perhaps confrontations with the occupying force [if it] insists on its colonial and diabolical plans to design the country's politics for its own interests."[10] Two days later, on the eve of Bremer's attempt to get the UN to send its people back to Iraq as part of a hairbrained scheme to persuade al-Sistani to withdraw his demand, a truck bomb exploded at the CPA's entrance, killing twenty-three and wounding ninety-five.

Karl Rove, not Condoleezza Rice—and not Dick Cheney or Donald Rumsfeld either—deals this corner of the game, one of whose objectives is to rebrand the president as a man of peace. Thus, the White House has retreated from preemptive and preventive war with either Iran or North Korea, and has ratcheted back to conventional multilateral diplomacy to persuade Iraq's former lenders to forgive the debt. Not that such a sum would ever be paid out, but the goal is to invite the nations that bought into Iraq's prospects when the United States did to restructure—in other words, reduce—debt payments. Which is where Jim Baker comes in, with his initial stops in Paris, Berlin, Moscow, London, Rome, Tokyo, and Beijing; and—now that Bush has extended the list to the Middle East—to Damascus, Kuwait City, and Riyadh, when he's ready. Riyadh, where Baker will be right at home, defending the Saudi sheiks against the September 11 survivors who have sued them (a Baker Potts case), is owed a cartoonish *$30 billion*, mainly for Gulf War I, for military services rendered the US.

On the first day, Baker won pledges from both France and Germany to reduce their Iraqi debts with the Paris Club, which is a group of nineteen Western-based creditor nations, including the US, that coordinates policy on problem loans made by their governments. (The debt that Iraq owes the

US, some $4 billion, is one to which Secretary of State Baker personally gave critical support in 1989.) Even countries that weren't in the Paris Club, like Japan and China, will abide by its rules, one of which is that negotiation take place only with a sovereign government; one elected by the people, not selected, via the US plan, by caucuses with the eighteen governorates. No wonder the doors of Old Europe flew open to Baker's touch. Even Russia promised to forgive 65 percent of the $8 billion (with interest) owing from Iraq. In exchange, then Governing Council president Abdul Aziz al-Hakim announced that Russian business would be "welcome" to invest in Iraq. And the head of the Kurdish PUK, Jalal Talabini, another GC member, then in Moscow, told the press that "Russia was willing to consider writing off the rest if it received beneficial treatment in terms of oil contracts."[11]

Iraqi oil has always been more important than the reconstruction contracts. "More important for France than the back debt would be oil contracts. ... The French oil giant Total has been negotiating to explore and develop two sites [in Iraq]," the *Washington Post* took note on December 17. In Berlin, Baker won a vaguer commitment, perhaps because the oil interest was less clear. Asked about its "incentives," US State Department spokesman Richard Boucher ventured that Baker "can be very effective in that regard" because he was "working with all the tools at his disposal in the US government."[12] And so, on December 22, the contract bidding was suspended, followed by columnist Robert Novak's suggestion that the administration was actively considering lifting the ban against the three countries. When the bidding starts (in March 2004), the winning bidders are expected to hire hundreds of thousands of Iraqis to toil on 2311 projected construction projects that are to be completed in two years.

Like the military's 3 o'clock follies in Baghdad, the new plan is full of numbers. "Numbers sanctify," says Charlie Chaplin in *Monsieur Verdoux*, speaking of Bluebeard's body count, and of the hundreds of thousands killed in World War I; but numbers are used differently now. "If you put as much money in as we are," says David J. Nash, a retired Navy admiral who heads the rebuilding effort in Iraq, "you can't help but make a difference."[13] Nash, a former top executive with the US construction firm Parsons Brinckerhoff, is in charge of the enormous logistical ballet.

On one level, it's a formula for disaster. With airports expected to remain off-limits because of security concerns, arriving contractors and supplies will be fighting for the same dock slips and highway lanes as the US military, which will be in the midst of its largest troop rotation since World War II. Contractors will compete for the same labor pool, the same supplies of concrete and pipe, the same trucking fleets. Slow-moving convoys are fat targets for Iraqi guerrillas, who are expected to disrupt and discredit the US rebuilding effort, as they have disrupted the military occupation. Contractors must hire their own private armies, and write the costs into their bids; for the US military, busy defending itself, won't protect them. But this will bring more business to private military companies, another industry that has ballooned alongside the expanding American oil industry, together with engineering and construction, transportation and telecommunications. So, on another level, it's a formula for success. As Naomi Klein says, "if it helps our friends get even richer, do it."[14]

But if the rebuilding effort breaks down, and the renovation of the oilfields is blocked, what will our *consiglieri* have accomplished? Given the fragility of the American position, why did so many countries buy in, if indeed they did? In June 1992, ABC broadcaster Ted Koppel said on Nightline that it's "becoming increasingly clear that George [H. W.] Bush, operating largely behind the scenes through the 1980s, initiated and supported much of the financing, intelligence, and military help that built Saddam's Iraq into the aggressive power that the United States ultimately had to destroy." Not once, but twice. And in the second round there was a comeback, and the second Bush has entered a country that was ready for him.

One of the last things this administration has publicly considered is the possibility that the resistance might prove successful; that the US will be unable to secure the oilfields or the construction sites, or its own green troops. Jetting from one Middle East capital to another, Jim Baker may succeed in doing whatever he's doing—building a multilateral consensus perhaps for a war that's already lost—while down below on terra firma in Iraq, the guerrillas will continue to get the last word.

EPILOGUE

George W. Bush has done more to undermine US dominance of the global system that underpins world stability than any other American president. He has lost the respect of the European powers; he has failed to exercise traditional US control over the UN; he has presided over the largest trade deficit ($46 billion in March 2004) and the highest oil import prices since 1983; he has totally aligned himself with Ariel Sharon's anti-Palestinian strategy; he has belittled the war against al Qaeda; and suffered massive tactical losses in Iraq which leave the United States facing a strategic defeat in the confrontation with radical Islam.

In Iraq Bush has revived the country's deep-seated nationalism, uniting both Sunni and Shi'ite partisans in acts of resistance. Beyond that, the occupation has provoked a new pan-Islamic nationalism, one that transcends sectarian divisions. Bush's administration has achieved this by occupying Iraq primarily for the purpose of exploiting it. Exploitation got in the way of the larger goals of securing an oil base in the Middle East to supplant Saudi Arabia, and controlling Iran and Syria for the benefit of Israel. Exploitation, as embodied in Order 39, assures the full privatization of public and private enterprises, full ownership rights by foreign firms, full repatriation of foreign profits. "For many conservatives," wrote the *Wall Street Journal* on May 1, 2003, "Iraq is now the test case for whether the US can engender American-style free-market capitalism within the Arab world." One year later, the answer is clear.

For the top ten US contractors in Iraq and Afghanistan—Halliburton, Bechtel, International American Products, Perini Corporation, Contract International, Fluor, Washington Group International, Research Triangle Institute, Louis Berger Group, Creative Associates International—all fed on tax-payer dollars, the road has been hell. In fact, control of the roads has been the most striking loss for the coalition. US forces, military and civilian, have been unable to hold on to the supply and communications lines on vital roads leading out from the capital. Insurgents have blown up key bridges, rocketed fuel convoys, maintained a steady kill ratio of US soldiers, and seized hostages. Since March 31, when four security guards were mutilated in the western city of Fallujah, fifty civilians have been kidnapped and an untold number of contractors killed. According to Aon, the insurance broker, Iraq has become the most dangerous place to do business in the world, and hundreds of contractors have left the country, including the giant German company, Siemens, and General Electric, whose work on the power stations was necessary to many of the others.

Halliburton, the backbone of the US Army's supply chain, has cancelled truck convoys after lethal grenade attacks made the roads too dangerous to travel. Like Fluor, the US construction company with contracts valued at more than $500 million, Halliburton uses aircraft to transport heavy equipment and supplies—which increases the cost of the contracts, 50 percent of which now go to pay for insurance and security. Half of Bechtel's staff has decamped to Kuwait and Jordan, and for those who remain in Iraq, ArmourGroup, a British security company, provides two guards for every employee. The consequences of such disruption are showing up on Baghdad's streets where untreated sewage is backed up and electricity is more sporadic than it was. With Iraqis weary and casualties mounting, the question for coalition officials is whether the delays can be overcome, or whether they have, as many fear, already fatally compromised reconstruction.[1]

Fallujah was the turning point for US military policy in Iraq. The recent rebellion in Fallujah, a Sunni stronghold, appears to have been sparked by the Israeli assassination of the Hamas leader Sheikh Ahmed Yassin on March 22. In retaliation a local Islamist group named after Yassin killed the four security guards, and the townspeople desecrated their bodies.[2] On April 5, the US took its revenge. Throughout the Middle East, the sight of decapitated children and rows of dead women and old people in Fallujah's soccer stadiums, along with Marines occupying hospitals and snipers firing from rooftops to keep the wounded away, led the Israeli newspaper *Haaretz* to charge US forces with "war crimes." "The one-ton bomb that was dropped on an apartment building in Gaza in order to assassinate Salah Shehadeh, which also killed 14 civilians," was almost nothing, wrote Orit Shohat, "compared to the number of bombs the Americans dropped on the houses of the residents of crowded Fallujah"[3]—which was shocking unless one recalled that Israeli advisers had been brought in to teach Marines, Rangers, and Navy Seals the sophisticated curriculum of sniper and demolition teams, with heavy armor and overwhelming airpower, so ruthlessly employed by Israeli Defense Forces in Gaza and the West Bank.[4] Meanwhile, even British commanders in Basra asked if the US response to low-grade guerrilla insurgence with massive force was drawing it into the commission of war crimes. Nearly 600 Iraqis were killed in the city, most of them civilians; a figure drawn from four clinics and a hospital which excludes the bodies buried in the soccer fields, and an unknown number buried in people's houses.[5]

A different face of war reached the United States, as it nearly always does. Only one American reporting team was embedded with the soldiers who invaded the city of 300,000, and that team's work was shared with the other networks. For three weeks in April, Marines carried out retaliatory operations for the killing of the guards, using tanks, artillery, F-16 fighter planes, assault helicopters, and deadly C-130 gunships in a pattern of continuous bombing. The single reporting team made it easier to control the story; but the networks had long ago learned to narrow the war news to something roughly compatible with the remoter violence of the entertainment industry. No close-ups of dead bodies, and never, ever, any dead Americans—of which 151 were killed in April alone. But it was the sudden halt in the US bombing, and the handover to Saddam Hussein loyalists—first, the portly General Jassim Mohammed Saleh, in his chauffeur driven Mercedes, and then, when Saleh was identified by angry Shi'ites on the Governing Council with the suppression of the Shi'ite uprising in 1991, to General Mohammed Latif—that marked the turning point. The Ba'athist "Fallujah Brigade" was greeted with open relief in the city, and quickly signed up recruits from amidst the Sunni townsmen who had previously fought the Marines. There were no foreign operatives in Fallujah, Latif said—indeed, "there are no insurgents," he told the Americans. The US had to immediately withdraw; swallow an earlier demand for weapons and the surrender of an estimated 2000 insurgents; and surprisingly enough, it did.[6] It was "a microcosm of what we want to happen all over Iraq," announced the chairman of the Joint Chiefs of Staff, General Richard Myers.[7] For the time being.

The sudden resort to cooptation instead of confrontation ignored the Pentagon's "Special Analysis" that had appeared a week before, and attributed many attacks on the Americans, including guerrilla raids in Fallujah, to Saddam Hussein's secret service who had planned for the insurgency before the fall of Baghdad.[8] The turnabout was attributed to the top marine commander, Lieutenant General James T. Conroy. "These were military professionals [who] spoke a language ... that was very similar to how we perceived the problem," he said of the generals picked from the elite Revolutionary Guard—which was the same outfit that, according to the intelligence report (completed on March 26), supposedly melted away in Fallujah. The generals asked for security responsibilities, Conroy said, not for money or equipment.[9] That the plan had support from White House and Pentagon authorities signaled the depth of American desperation;

for the US had finally realized that it lacked the resources to govern Iraq if the Ba'athist personnel were excluded.

The plan also reflected the American withdrawal of support from Ahmed Chalabi, and all that implied. Chalabi, who had dropped his alliance with Israel, and heightened his ties to Tehran, had nonetheless seen to it that key posts in Baghdad went to family and friends; so that when the national security adviser to the Governing Council and the defense minister called the Fallujah "auxillary" force a temporary unit and not a template for the rest of Iraq, they were speaking for Chalabi. It was one of many cracks in the Iraqi political leadership the US had constructed, and it reflected the cracks in American leadership, in which the neocons, all present (save Perle), were—in the manner of Karl Rove's administration, where everybody stayed—still occupying their posts but no longer making policy.

Fallujah had a special significance for Arabs. As Eric Margolis writes in the *Toronto Sun*, in 1948, during the rout of Arab troops in Palestine by Jewish forces, "an isolated Egyptian brigade held out against heavy attacks in the Palestinian village of Fallujah. The so-called Fallujah pocket was one of only two honorable Arab military actions during the 1947–49 Arab–Israeli war. Its defenders, including young army officer Gamal Abdel Nasser, became national heroes." At Fallujah, Nasser began his book, *Philosophy of the Revolution*, which shaped pan-Arab politics for the next generation.[10] In Iraq at Fallujah, the withdrawal of American troops was deemed a great Iraqi victory, all the more so because of the participation of the Shi'ites.

In short, the reason for the rehabilitation of the Revolutionary Guard was the revolt of the Mahdi Army, led by the rebel Shi'ite cleric Moqtada al-Sadr in early April, first in the Baghdad slums, then in Karbala, Najaf, and Kufa, and in Shi'ite strongholds throughout the south. The US had provoked al-Sadr by shutting down *Al Hawsah*, his anti-coalition newspaper, and arresting key aides, but the majority Shi'ites had been increasingly restive since the Grand Ayatollah Ali al-Sistani had called for direct elections in January, and scorned the interim constitution produced by the Governing Council. Ahmed Chalabi had originally advised Paul Bremer to fire all the Ba'athists and dismiss the army, decisions that were soon discredited. "Paul Bremer and his Pentagon masters, far from steering Iraq towards freedom and democracy," the *Financial Times* said of such moves, "have brought it just beyond the brink of anarchy."[11] Now it was clear that only by pulling back from Fallujah, and turning the battles against the Sunni over to the Iraqi generals, could the Americans take on the Shi'ites, whose uprising was wider and deeper than US commanders conceded. Al-Sadr had "hijacked the political process," said an Iraqi expert, and more moderate clerics and politicians dared not oppose him.

It was widely believed among the Shi'ites that the US was determined to uproot Islam in Iraq, to steal its oil, and to deny them a voice commensurate to their numbers in the country's future governance, beliefs that were not off the mark. Even the Badr Brigade, the powerful militia that backed the Ayatollah Sistani, was supporting the Mahdi. But the event that drove the Americans to reverse course was the emergence of the Sunni–Shi'ite alliance in Baghdad. It wasn't the first since the nineteenth-century Ottoman sultan, Abdullah II, and the reformer, Sayyid Jamal al-Din al-Afghani, launched a pan-Islamic movement uniting Sunni and Shi'ite forces against European imperialism, but then no senior American commander would have known of that. After the British takeover of Iraq in 1920, there was a full-scale revolt which began in Baghdad mosques, spread to the Shi'ite holy center of Karbala, and reached as far as Kirkuk; another rebellion that was unknown to the Americans. Contrary to the British expectations, Sunnis, Shi'ites, and even Kurds had acted together; but as Niall Ferguson has observed, "[t]heory looms surprisingly large" in US policy. "Neo-conservative theory ... stated that the Americans would be welcomed as liberators, just as economic theory put privatisation" at the top of the list. History's lessons are overlooked in American exceptionalism, and the precedent for privatisation, it turns out, is Eastern Europe.[12] This time it was the predations of the US hyperpower that led the Mahdi militiamen to join forces with the radical Sunni in the Baghdad neighborhood of Azamiuyah, and raise a convoy of sixty trucks of relief supplies for Fallujah.

The Board of Muslim Clergy, a hardline Sunni group, issued a communique on April 17 announcing its support for Moqtada al-Sadr, and calling on all Iraqis "to expel the occupation." Sectarian groupings no longer saw their religious identities as superseding their national ones. Shi'ite political parties, such as al-Dawa, were much persecuted under Saddam, whose nationalism glorified Iraq's civilization through the persons of Hammurabi and Nebuchadnezzar, and sought to replace Cairo with Baghdad as the center of the Arab world. Al-Dawa had cooperated with Ahmed Chalabi in his attempts to put together an alliance of expatriate Iraqi parties, but it broke with Chalabi's Iraqi National Congress over the issue of semi-autonomy for the Kurds. Al-Dawa wanted a strong, centralised national government that encompassed Sunnis and Shia, Arabs and Kurds. A similar view was put forth by Sistani, who recalled the Great Rebellion of 1920, the first national uprising in modern Iraqi history that, though led by Shi'ite notables and clerics, was joined by other sections of the population. "Division of the people is treason," he held.

Moqtada al-Sadr had gone up to Kirkuk in August 2003, and again in December and January 2004 when ethnic tensions broke out over Kurdish plans to incorporate the city into a semi-autonomous Kurdish canton. He fielded 2000 members of the Mahdi army in a demonstration to support 300,000 Shi'ite Turkmen residents who were on strike, thereby using the presence of the Shi'ites throughout Iraq, even in the north, to broaden his stage.[13] In early May 2004, al-Sadr moved back and forth from his heavily-guarded headquarters in Najaf and Karbala, while at first the US nibbled at the edges of the holy cities, taking out sizable numbers of his men, along with a few Pakistani pilgrims, while promising Shi'ite leaders in Najaf and from the Governing Council that they would not enter the sacred core of Najaf, which is the theological center of many Shi'ite communities world-wide. To attack it would be a final act of suicide for the United States, one that would set it against the heart of Islam, provoking the rage of Shi'ites and numerous Sunni Arabs throughout the Middle East. Yet in mid-May, working behind the screen of the terrible photographs from Abu Ghraib, American forces escalated their attacks on Karbala and Najaf.

On May 12, US tanks, helicopters, and jets attacked Karbala, destroying the Mukhaiyam mosque, many shops, the central market, and setting seven hotels afire. Twenty-two people were killed, "militants," said Brigadier General Mark Kimmit in Baghdad; but US snipers fired at anyone that moved. At dusk the call for evening prayers rang out from the Imam Hussein mosque, one of the most sacred shrines of Shi'ite Islam. Mahdi militiamen took up new positions near another holy site. They acknowledged they lost control of the Mukhaiyam mosque. "We put up a very stiff resistance," a young militiaman said. Late that night US forces probed Najaf, where the thirty-one year old al-Sadr was holed up. He spoke to reporters in the afternoon. "I appeal to the fighters and mujahedeen in Karbala to stand together so that none of our holy sites and cities are defiled. We are prepared for any American escalation and we expect one," he said. He spoke of Vietnam, and of how the Iraqi people have "faith in God, and his prophet and his family. The means of victory that are available to us are much more than what the Vietnamese had." Which was problematical, but then American forces in 2004 were more vulnerable, if only because they were joined by the monumental detritus of "American-style free-market capitalism," which was not welcome in Iraq. Al-Sadr spoke also of the abuse of the prisoners at Abu Ghraib prison, which had enraged the Middle East. "Look at the torture they have committed against our detainees. Could anyone who came to rid us of Saddam do this?"[14]

The newly US-appointed mayor of Najaf said he would give another week to the efforts of Shi'ite leaders to end the standoff in the city. "If you assess US military movements in terms of territorial gains, then US forces a week from now will enter certain areas of the city that will ... make the prospect of a peaceful settlement very weak," he said.[15] Fajullah wasn't mentioned, but on May 16 political and tribal leaders in Najaf said al-Sadr would end the standoff if the coalition postponed its legal case against him (he was charged with being an accessory to the murder last spring of another cleric close to the Americans), *and established an Iraqi force to patrol the city*. The Shi'ites hoped to save Najaf the same way the Sunnis had saved Fallujah, if not by bringing in the Revolutionary Guard then by introducing Shi'ite peacekeeping forces. The offer hinged on an agreement that US forces pull out of both Kufa and Najaf, and that al-Sadr's militias lay down their weapons. The next day, political leaders in Karbala named a major general in Saddam's army, but al-Sadr wasn't satisfied.

It's not hard to predict how this will play out. Some months ago, when the Americans believed the Shi'ites took their orders from Iran—where Sistani was born—they were deep in negotiations with the Iranian clergy. Now that the radical Shi'ites in Iraq have declared themselves, and Sistani has not broken ranks, and the beginnings of a Shi'ite–Sunni alliance against the occupation is underway, US policy will revert to military form. It is all America knows how to do, and it will fail again. The great temples of Najaf and Karbala will go down, and join the ruins of the Iraqi museums in the ashes from which a new Iraq will be built. And US forces, having demolished the citadel, and perhaps killed Moqtada al-Sadr, will try to remove themselves from the day-to-day ordeal of fighting in Iraq in time for the "handover" on June 30, and maybe for the American elections; but they will fail at that, too.

Those of us who watch television and read newspapers will be led to hope for something else, but it will not be. The myth that has ruled the United States, beginning with the City on a Hill and moving on to Manifest Destiny, and to Woodrow Wilson's belief that we are "to show the way to the nations of the world how they shall walk in the paths of liberty…," has ended. It has blown itself up in Bush's empty recitations of how America will bring "freedom and democracy to the Middle East." In the current "story," William Pfaff writes, the exalted destiny is fatefully challenged by rogue nations with nuclear weapons; failed states, riddled with the menace of Islamic extremists—something like Samuel Huntington's war of civilizations. National mobilization has taken place, and years of struggle lie ahead. But our principal allies no longer believe in the national myth, Pfaff says. They have been courteous about it even as skepticism grew. They are alarmed by what has happened to the country under the Bush administration, and see no good coming from it. They are struck by how impervious Americans seem to be to the notion that September 11 was not the defining event of the age. Most have had their wars with "terrorism"—the British with the IRA, the Spanish with the Basque separtists, the Germans, Italians, and Japanese with the Red Brigades, the French with Algerian rebels. They are inclined to believe that the international condition, like the human condition, is in fact very much the same, and that it's the United States that has changed. They're disturbed that American leaders seem unable to understand this. "[I]t has been like discovering that a respected, even beloved, uncle has slipped into schizophrenia," a French writer says. "When you visit him, his words no longer connect with the reality around him. It seems futile to talk about it with him. The family, embararassed, is even reluctant to talk about it among themselves."[16]

It is astonishing to realize how shallow is the US government's commitment to the reasons put forward for the invasion of Iraq. There's nothing backing it up like the Cold War backed up Kennedy's and Johnson's reasons for invading Vietnam. September 11 can go only so far. The substance of reconstruction, which is privatization, was never put forth as a reason for war, but it was the very heart of the matter: the partnership between the Agency for International Development and the CIA that would use private contractors to economically reconstruct Iraq in a way that would create a favorable business climate for US interests. When a former US Middle East analyst observed that "the Iraqis are a proud people, and if they get a sense that big multinationals are bagging and tagging their institutions and oil fields, we may get another Nasser," he spoke too late. The Iraqis have figured it out.

In the end, Bush's "Trust me," almost sufficed, almost held the thin majority of votes he needs for November 2004; but it failed utterly to explain the pictures of American soldiers laughing at the naked, hooded, and shackled prisoners. Speaking of Abu Ghraib, *Army Times* wondered why "the prison wasn't razed in the wake of the invasion as a symbolic stake through the heart of the Ba'athist regime." But of course it wasn't; for Abu Ghraib was where the US could freely exercise its contempt for the Arab enemy. Full of low-level people who were warehoused to keep them off the streets, it wasn't a prison so much as a secret place for perpetrating unspeakable crimes against Iraqis. That the images validated the other negative images and charges against the US, Israel, and the West for actions in Iraq and Palestine is why they are so potent, and won't go away. It's why the solution is not to release some prisoners, or to rediscover the Geneva Conventions in time for media attention—long after the Bush administration dismissed Geneva as irrelevant for military prisoners it called "unlawful combatants."

At the Pentagon, said *Army Times*, the enlisted soldiers at the heart of the furor were called "the six morons who lost the war." But they were "the wrong morons," it declared in an editorial on May 10 that also ran in the *Air Force*, *Navy*, and *Marine Corps Times*. "While responsibility began with them," it concluded, "it extends all the way up the chain of command to the highest reaches of the military hierarchy and its civilian leadership." To Richard Myers and Donald Rumsfeld. For if there is one thing that soldiers know it is to follow orders, and from the wake of September 11 the administration pushed to free itself from constraints that the rule of law imposes on states, both domestically and internationally. In Guantanamo, Afghanistan, Iraq, and elsewhere, prisoners have been denied the most basic legal protections. This created the climate that permitted the lawless behavior we have witnessed.

As for the beheading of Nick Berg on May 11, one thing is sure. "Despite the further slide in popularity, Mr. Bush now appears to have a better chance of surviving than he did," according to Christopher Caldwell, senior editor of the *Weekly Standard*, "better perhaps than either Britain's Tony Blair or Italy's Silvio Berlusconi." It was the link to al

Qaeda which made this a bigger story for the American public than the American prisoner torture, Caldwell believed. All the US networks led their morning programs with the execution, while *Le Monde* ranked it the fourth war bulletin on its website. The identification by the CIA of the "terrorist mastermind," al-Zargawi, as the man who carried it out was the clincher; for Berg's beheading restored the link in the public mind between al Qaeda and Iraq that was part of the justification for war in the first place. Even if there was little to it, Roy Blunt, Republican Congressman from Missouri, could say that it "jolted everybody's memory about why we were in Iraq and who we're dealing with"; while Charles Schumer, liberal Democrat from New York, could add that "if they think this is going to make us cut and run, they are dead wrong."[17] And Kerry, who is panting heavily to match Bush, described Berg's killers as "people who have no values system," and softened his denunciation of the abuses at Abu Ghraib.

Caldwell came close to identifying the beheading as a setup, as did Tom Englehardt when he found Nicholas Berg's murder "grisly beyond imagining, literally staged as the al Qaeda equivalent of an MTV-style recruitment video ... certainly when it comes to the Bush Administration, the phrase 'wish fulfillment' has gained new meaning."[18] But neither called it that, and so I will. The citation of the Jordanian-born militant al-Zargawi, for months a name on the lips of every US commander who has wished to implicate al Qaeda in Iraq—like General Kimmit who said on May 17 that the car bombing of the Governing Council head, Izzadine Saleem, had the "classic hallmarks" of Zargawi—is enough to raise grave doubts about the provenance of the dreadful deed. As for Saleem's murder, an unknown group, the Arab Resistance Movement, took responsibility on a website associated with Anbar province, a stronghold of Sunni resistance that includes Fallujah.

It's hard to tell when things started to fall apart, for mutiny was underway at least since the terrorist bombing of Madrid in March when Spain announced that it would withdraw its troops. Since then Honduras, the Dominican Republic, Nicaragua, Kazakhstan, and New Zealand have left, while South Korean and Bulgarian troops were pulled back to their bases. El Salvador, Norway, the Netherlands, Thailand—even Japan, whose medical and engineering teams were pledged to aid the US so long as America offered protection against a rapidly expanding China—were tottering. Iraq's civil defense forces, those that remained, had laid down their arms in Fallujah, and 10 percent had joined the other side. An Iraqi policeman was said by US government and industry sources to have alerted local resistance fighters of the arrival of the security guards.

Four members of the Governing Council had resigned in protest, and half the Iraqis with jobs in the heavily secured Green Zone were staying home. Fifty-two former British diplomats wrote Tony Blair that "there is no case for supporting policies which are doomed to failure," while on May 4, 2004, fifty-three US diplomats, including the former ambassadors of Qatar, India, Saudi Arabia, Syria, and Egypt, accused the White House of sacrificing America's credibility in the Arab world and the safety of its diplomats and soldiers because of the Bush administration's unqualified support for Ariel Sharon. Bush had invested in Sharon's proposal for an Israeli withdrawal from the Gaza Strip, and gone two steps further to endorse continued Jewish settlements of the occupied West Bank, and deny the Palestinian right of return to the occupied territories. The overwhelming rejection of Sharon's withdrawal from Gaza by the Likud Party afterwards was seen as a direct snub to the president.

Such broadsides from American diplomats haven't been delivered since the Vietnam war, and it was particularly unusual for former US government officials to criticize policy on Israel, but more unusual still for Bush to kowtow to Sharon without measuring his authority. He took another fall, one of many in his Middle Eastern sheherazade, where the stories he was told never panned out, and the people who sustained him began to break up—and there he was with the last thing he understood, which was the presidential campaign.

NOTES

PREFACE

1 Régis Debray, *Revolution in the Revolution* (New York, 1967), p. 19.
2 April Glaspie, "Transcript of Meeting…, July 25, 1990," *New York Times International*, 23 September, 1990.
3 Doyle McManus, "Iraq Setbacks Change Mood in Washington," *Los Angeles Times*, 23 May, 2004.
4 Center for American Progress, 24 May, 2004; progress@American progress.com.
5 Nicolas Pelham, "Saddam's Men Quietly Regroup," *Financial Times*, 14 May, 2004.

1
STARTING OVER IS NOT
AN EASY THING TO DO

1 Philip Stephens, *Financial Times*, March 5, 2004.

2   Roy quoted by Jacob Heilbrunn, "Forgiving Their Own Vision of Empire," a review of *The Rise of the Vulcans* by James Mann, *Los Angeles Times Book Review*, March 7, 2004.

3   Javad Yarjani, head of OPEC's Petroleum Market Analysis Dept., "The Choice of Currency for the Denomination of the Oil Bill," speech delivered in Oviedo, Spain on April 14, 2002.

4   Roula Khalaf and Guy Dinmore, "Reforming the Arab World," *Financial Times*, March 23, 2004.

5   Neil Dennis, "Rising Gasoline Prices Boost Crude Oil Futures," *Financial Times*, March 24, 2004.

6   Robert Fisk, "Happy First Birthday, War on Iraq," *Independent*, March 13, 2004.

7   *Financial Times*, March 20–21, 2004.

8   Naomi Klein, "Terror as a Weapon of Occupation," *Guardian*, March 24, 2004.

9   Ibid.

10 Hannah Arendt, *On Violence* (New York: Harcourt, Brace & World, 1969), p. 87.

11 Ibid., p. 56.

12 Elisabeth Young-Bruehl, *Hannah Arendt: For Love of the World* (New Haven: Yale, 1982), p. 98.

13 Gore Vidal, *Dreaming War* (New York: Nation Books, 2002).

14 Andrew Kopkind, "A Sense of Crisis" (March 23–30, 1970), in *The Thirty Years' War* (London: Verso, 1995), p. 211.

15 David Lamb, *Vietnam, Now* (Cambridge, MA: Perseus, 2002), p. 255.

16 Kopkind, "The Return of Cold War Liberalism" (April 23, 1983), in *The Thirty Years' War*, p. 358.

17 Lamb, *Vietnam, Now*, p. 177.

18 Said quoted by Tomeditor@aol.com, November 15, 2002.

19 Cordesman quoted by Pauline Jelinek, "Pentagon Won't Give War Costs," *Arizona Daily Sun*, March 11, 2004.

20 "America's Election Battleground," *Financial Times*, March 11, 2004.

21 "Spanish PM-elect Vows to Pull Troops Out of Iraq," AFP, March 15, 2004.

22 Jelinek, "Pentagon Won't Give War Costs."

23 Ibid.

24 William Clark, "The Real Reasons for the Upcoming War With Iraq," Information Clearing House, February 20, 2004.

25 Henry C.K. Liu, "US Dollar Hegemony Has Got to Go," *Asia Times*, April 11, 2002.

26 Senator Tim Ferguson, "A New American Century? Not," iraqwar.com, January 19, 2004.

27 Gerard Baker, "This Year's Will Be the Most Sustained and Serious Debate...," *Financial Times*, March 12, 2004.

2
HOW IT WAS

1 Antonia and Anthony Lake, "Coming of Age Through Vietnam," *New York Times Magazine*, July 20, 1995.

2 *The Party For You*, 1956 official program, Democratic National Convention.

3 Kennedy quoted by Carol Brightman, "The Weed Killers," *Viet-Report*, June–July 1966.

4 *The Party For You*.

5 Rusk quoted in "The Weed Killers."

6 *The Party For You*.

3
SECURING THE REALM

1 Robert Kagan, "Power and Weakness," *Policy Review*, No. 113, June 2002.

2 *New York Times*, November 24, 2002.

3 Ibid.

4 Mandelbaum quoted by Thomas L. Friedman in "The New Club NATO," *New York Times*, November 17, 2002.

5   *New York Times*, April 16, 2003.

6   Jude Wanniski, "Wolfowitz and the Axis of Evil," *Jude Wanniski's SupplySideInvestor*, July 2002.

7   *Los Angeles Times*, October 27, 2002.

8   Jane Mayer, "Contract Sport," *New Yorker*, February 16 & 23, 2004.

9   *Forbes*, January 6, 2003.

10   Hazel Henderson, "Beyond Bush's Unilateralism," InterPress Service, June 2002.

11   Ibid.

12   Charles Recknagel, "Iraq: Baghdad Moves to the Euro," *Radio Free Europe*, November 1, 2000.

13   William Clark, "The Real Reasons for the Upcoming War With Iraq," Information Clearing House, February 20, 2004.

14   "Saudis Face Greater Difficulty in Extracting Oil," Middle East Newsline, February 27, 2004.

15   Sean Naylor, "The Lessons of Anaconda," *New York Times*, March 2, 2003.

16   Dexter Filkins, "Flaws in US Air War," *New York Times*, July 21, 2002.

17   Thomas E. Ricks and Vernon Loeb, "Afghan War Faltering," *Washington Post*, November 8, 2002.

18   Kate Clark, "Revealed: The Taliban Minister, the US Envoy and the Warning of September 11 that was Ignored," *Independent*, September 7, 2002.

19   Syed Saleem Shahzad, "US Turns to the Taliban," *Asia Times*, June 14, 2003.

20   *Oil and Gas International*, August 11, 2002.

21   Matthew Reimer, "Caspian Region Likely to Remain Critical for Foreseeable future," Power and Interest News Report, 11 January, 2004.

22   Patrick Martin, "Oil Company Adviser Named US Representative to Afghanistan," World Socialist Web Site, January 3, 2002.

23   Michael T. Klare, "Oil Moves the War," *Progressive*, June 2002.

24   Meyers quoted from "Novak, Hunt, and Shields," CNN, April 5, 2002.

25   *CounterPunch*, January 10, 2002.

26   Jordan Green, "Halliburton: To the Victors Go the Markets," *Southern Studies*, February 1, 2002.

27   *Oil and Gas International*, January 28, 2002.

4
MAKING WAVES

1 "Voice of the People," *Portland Press Herald*, October 13 , 2003.

2 Pariser quoted by George Packer in "Smart-Mobbing the War," *New York Times*, March 9, 2003.

3 Tomeditor@aol.com, January 10, 2003.

4 Todd Gitlin, "The War Movement and the Peace Movement," Open Democracy, December 2, 2002.

5 "Rumsfeld Unmuzzled," *Maine Sunday Telegram*, February 16, 2003.

6 A Buzzflash Reader Commentary, by Stephen V. Kane, buzzflash.com, February 10, 2003.

7 Susan Sontag, "Fast-forward War," Tomeditor@aol.com, March 23, 2004.

8 Muller quoted in AlterNet.org, March 24, 2003.

5
MOUNTING WAR

1 Thompson quoted in *St. Louis Post Dispatch*, March 23, 2004.

2 Reuters report,TomEditor@aol.com, March 24, 2004.

3 Ibid.

4 Eric Margolis, "The Moment of Truth for Iraq," *Toronto Sun*, March 23, 2003.

5 Danny Schecter, News Dissector Weblog, March 24, 2003.

6 David Carr, "Reporting Reflects Anxiety," *New York Times*, March 25, 2003.

7 MSNBC staff and wire reports, March 27, 2004.

8 Vernon Loeb, *Washington Post*, March 30, 2003.

9 Catherine Belton, "Why Not Price Oil in Euros?" *Moscow Times*, October 10, 2003.

10 "The Future of Iraq," *Wall Street Journal*, April 7, 2003.

11 AFI Research Intelligence Briefing, April 10, 2004.

12 *New York Times*, May 13, 2004.

13   *New York Times*, April 9, 2003.

14   *Wall Street Journal*, April 11, 2003.

15   *Maine Sunday Telegram*, July 6, 2003.

16   *Wall Street Journal*.

17   *Portland Press Herald*, April 10, 2003.

18   Firas Al-Atraqchi, "Before You Cheer," YellowTimes.org, April 14, 2003.

19   Joel Brinkley, "American Companies Rebuilding Iraq Find They Are Having to Start From the Ground Up," *New York Times*, February 22, 2004.

6

VIETNAM REDUX

1   Mike Hume, www.spiked.com, April 10, 2003.

2   Van Riper quoted in Sean D. Naylor, "War Games Rigged?" *Army Times*, August 16, 2002.

3   Marilyn B. Young, from a talk given at the annual meeting of the Organization of American Historians on the topic "Historians and the War"; April 5, 2003.

4   Mary McCarthy, *Hanoi* (New York: Harcourt, Brace, Jovanovich, 1968), p. 123.

5   Mary McCarthy, *The Seventeenth Degree* (New York: Harcourt, Brace, Jovanovich, 1974), pp. 212–213.

6   Susan Sontag, *Trip to Hanoi* (New York: Farrar, Strauss & Giroux, 1968), pp. 69–70.

7   Ibid., p. 77.

8   Staughton Lynd and Thomas Hayden, *The Other Side* (New York: New American Library, 1966), p. 77.

9   Harrison E. Salisbury, *Behind the Lines* (New York: Harper & Row, 1967), p. 102.

10   Pham Van Dong quoted by Carol Brightman in untitled travel journal from North Vietnam, January–February 1967.

11   Donald Kagan and Frederick W. Kagan, *While America Sleeps*, quoted in the

Defense Association National Network's News, Vol. 7, No. 3, Winter 2000.

12 McCarthy, *Hanoi*, p. 505.

13 Evan Thomas, "Why Were We in Vietnam? He'll Tell You," review of *Ending the War*, by Henry Kissinger, *New York Times Book Review*, March 23, 2003.

14 Salisbury, *Behind the Lines*, pp. 196–97.

15 Ed Vuillamy, "Israel Seeks Pipeline for Iraqi Oil," *Observer*, April 20, 2003.

16 McCarthy, *Hanoi*, p. 301.

17 Michael Ledeen quoted in William O. Beeman, "Who is Michael Ledeen?" Pacific News Service, May 8, 2003.

18 Hannah Arendt, "The Ex-Communists," *Commonweal*, March 20, 1953, p. 597.

19 Malcolm Cowley, in Warren Susman's *Culture as History* (New York: Pantheon, 1984), p. 169.

20 Weinberger quoted by Frances FitzGerald in *Way Out in the Blue* (New York: Simon & Schuster, 1995), p. 473.

21 Ibid.

22 The authors include two officials responsible for strategic planning in Bush's National Security Council, as well as Stephen A. Cambone, deputy under-secretary of defense.

23 Norm Fruchter quoted by Harry Mauer in *Strange Ground: Americans in Vietnam, 1945–1975* (New York: Henry Holt, 1989), p. 437.

24 Marilyn Young explores how this worked with America and Japan at the turn of the last century, in *The Rhetoric of Empire: American China Policy 1895–1901* (Harvard, 1968). See p. 231.

25 At an Asian Scholars conference in Singapore, August 21–26, 2003, Vietnamese panelists addressing "Vietnamese Foreign Relations" still saw an American commitment to Southeast Asia as a counterweight to Chinese ambitions in the area, especially since China's economic importance in the Pacific, once low, has grown fast. However, according to Pham Ngoc Uyen, "the unilateral hawkish tendency in Bush's foreign policy has stirred up past concerns in Southeast Asia, in Vietnam and China."

7

THE POLITICAL ECONOMY OF DEATH

I

1   Pep Subiros, "Utopias Imperiales," *El Pais*, May 15, 2003.

2   Ibid.

3   Jon E. Hilsenrath, "Why for Many This Recovery Feels More Like a Recession," *Wall Street Journal*, May 29, 2003.

4   Bush quoted by Renana Brooks in "Bush Dominates a Nation of Victims," *The Nation*, June 24, 2003.

5   Bush quoted by Emad Mekay in "Global Economy," *Asia Times*, February 5, 2003.

6   Peronet Despeignes, "White House Shelved Deficit Report," *Financial Times*, May 29, 2003. Three months later the CBO increased 2004's budget deficit to $480, a record shortfall that it said could top $500 when new Iraq war spending requests are included. "Deficit Could Top $500 Billion in '04," MSNBC, August 26, 2003; "GAO Grim on Deficit Outlook," *Atlanta-Journal Constitution*, September 14, 2003.

7   Dan Baum, "Nation Builders for Hire," *New York Times Magazine*, July 22, 2003. Baum's source is the Center for Public Integrity.

8   "Inside Story of the Hunt for Bin Laden," *Guardian*, August 23, 2003. According to the *Guardian*, Ijaz has contacts in Pakistan's intelligence service, and has served as an intermediary in past negotiations with bin Laden.

9   Woolsey quoted on PBS Online NewsHour, August 20, 2003.

10 James Ridgeway, "Corporate Colonialism," *Village Voice*, April 23–29, 2003.

11 Jackson quoted by Geoffrey Cray, "USA: Inside Lockheed's $250 Billion Pentagon Connection," *Village Voice*, March 19, 2003.

12 Seymour M. Hersh, "Lunch With the Chairman," *New Yorker*, March 1, 2003.

13 Reported by AFP July 29, 2003, and cited in STRATFOR'S MORNING INTELLIGENCE BRIEF the same day.

14 "Inside Story of the Hunt for Bin Laden," *Guardian*, August 23, 2003. A major source for this information is the financier Mansoor Ijaz.

15 Paolo Pasicolar, Executive Memorandum #892, Heritage Foundation, July 15, 2003.

16 Mekay, "Global Economy."

17 Reese Ehrlich, "Arab Thumbs Down on Free Trade," AlterNet.org, July 15, 2003.

18 Kevin Watkins, "Trade Hypocrisy—the Problem with Robert Zoellick," Open Democracy, December 27, 2002.

19 Niall Ferguson, "True Cost of Hegemony: Huge Debt," *New York Times*, April 20, 2003.

20 Stephen Roach, "Worldthink, Disequilibrium, and the Dollar," speech given in New York, May 12, 2002.

21 *Economist*, June 28, 2003.

22 STRATFOR, August 29, 2003.

23 Ferguson, "The True Cost of Hegemony."

24 Andrew J. Bacevich, *American Empire* (Harvard: Harvard University Press, 2002), p. 8.

25 Paul Krugman, "Stating the Obvious," *New York Times*, May 27, 2003.

8
THE POLITICAL ECONOMY OF DEATH
II

1 Paul Krugman, *The Great Unraveling: Losing Our Way in the New Century* (New York: Norton 2004).

2 Clark quoted by Thom Shanker and Eric Schmitt in "Latest Mission by Armed Forces," *New York Times*, April 30, 2003.

3 See the US Army Corps of Engineers' website for contract details; also Michael Dobbs, "Halliburton's Deals Greater than Thought," *Washington Post*, August 28, 2003.

4 Rowan Scarborough, "US Rushed Post-Saddam Planning," *Washington Times*, September 3, 2003.

5   Baum, "Nation Builders for Hire."

6   Mafruza Khan, "Business on the Battlefield," Corporate Research E-Letter No. 30, December 2002. Much of this information was gathered by the International Consortium of Investigative Journalists.

7   P. W. Singer, "Military Privatization," *New York Times*, July 23, 2003. In a $2.2 billion contract with the Pentagon, the Iraqi Army is being trained by the Vinnell Corp., a subsidiary of Northrup Grumman. Alex Berenson, "Iraq's New Army Gets Slow Start," *New York Times*, September 21, 2003.

8   Nelson D. Schwartz, "The War Business," Reason Policy Institute, RPPI.org, March 17, 2003 (first appeared in *Fortune*).

9   Ibid.

10 Michael Dobbs, *Washington Post*, September 28, 2003. During Gulf War I the proportion was roughly 1 to 100.

11 *Economist*, March 27, 2004

12 Schwartz, "The War Business."

13 Geoffrey Gray, "USA: Inside Lockheed's $250 Billion Pentagon Connection," *Village Voice*, March 19, 2003.

14 Khan, "Business on the Battlefield."

15 Ibid.

16 James Ridgeway, "Corporate Colonialism," *Village Voice*, April 23–29, 2002.

17 Mike Allen, *Washington Post*, August 26, 2003.

18 *Sunday Herald*, October 6, 2002, cited by Michael Meacher in "This War on Terrorism is Bogus," *Guardian*, September 6, 2003.

19 Quoted by Meacher, "This War on Terrorism is Bogus."

20 Stephen Pizzo, "Divvying up the Iraq Pie," AlterNet.org, October 8, 2003.

21 Wolfowitz quoted by Bill Keller in "The Sunshine Warrior," *New York Times Magazine*, September 22, 2002.

22 Maureen Dowd, "Who's Losing Iraq," *New York Times*, August 31, 2003.

23 "Bush Fails on Promise to Update Electricity Grid," daily.misleader.org, October 15, 2003.

9

THE POLITICAL ECONOMY OF DEATH

III

1 Dominique de Villepin, "Iraq: The Paths of Reconstruction," *Le Monde*, September 12, 2003.

2 Re Iraq's $130 billion debt, see "Skimping on the Peace," *Wall Street Journal*, September 30, 2003.

3 Sonni Efran, Robin Wright, and Janet Hook, *Los Angeles Times*, September 12, 2003.

4 *Washington Post*, September 15, 2003.

5 David Sanger, "Trying to Figure Out When to Say it's Over," *New York Times*, September 14, 2003.

6 Steinberg and Bush quoted by Greg Miller, *Los Angeles Times*, September 11, 2003.

7 Garry Trudeau, "Doonesbury," *Portland Press Herald*, September 26, 2003.

8 Bush quoted by Glenn Kessler in the *Washington Post*, September 24, 2003.

9 Thomas L. Friedman, "Vote France Off the Island," *New York Times*, August 12, 2003.

10 Mike Allen and Dana Priest, "Bush Administration is Focus of Inquiry," *Washington Post*, September 28, 2003.

11 Ibid.

12 John Cirincione, "The Kay Contradiction," *Carnegie Analysis and Commentary*, October 3, 2003.

13 STRATFOR, September 14, 2003.

14 Christian Parenti, "The Progress is Disaster," *In These Times*, September 11, 2003.

15 Alissa J. Rubin, "With Each Attack, US Image in Iraq Erodes," *Los Angeles Times*, September 27, 2003.

16 Waxman quoted by David Ivanovich, *Houston Chronicle*, September 23, 2003.

17 Rice quoted by Greg Miller in "Perception Grows that Iraq has Become the 'Central Front' in War on Terror," *Los Angeles Times*, September 11, 2003.

18   STRATFOR Geopolitical Diary, October 7, 2003.

19   Leahy quoted by Alan Fram, *Los Angeles Times*, September 24, 2003.

20   Chalabi quoted in Colin Lynch, *Washington Post*, October 3, 2003.

21   Quoted by Stephen Pizzo in "Divvying up the Iraq Pie," AlterNet.org, October 3, 2003.

22   David Ignations, "Minding Iraq's Business," *New York Times*, October 17, 2003. The figures are drawn from "Iraq Revenue Watch," a project sponsored by George Soros' Open Society Institute.

23   Timothy L. O'Brien, "Iraq Offering Laws to Spur Investment from Abroad," *New York Times*, September 22, 2003.

24   "Iraq's Reconstruction: Cleaner, But Still Bare," *Economist*, October 4, 2003.

25   Steven Weisman, "US Set to Cede Part of Control Over Aid to Iraq," *New York Times*, October 20, 2003.

26   Wilson quoted by Ewen MacAskill, *Guardian*, October 14, 2003.

27   Sanchez quoted by Michael R. Gordon in "Reality Check in Iraq," *New York Times*, October 20, 2003.

28   Parenti, "The Progress is Disaster."

29   Pizzo, "Divvying up the Iraq Pie."

30   "Iraq's Reconstruction," *Economist*. Bechtel claims the $680 million it receives from USAID is less than 5 percent of its $16 billion assessment of Iraq's civilian reconstruction needs, enough for "critical" projects only.

31   Patrick E. Tyler and Raymond Bonner, "Iraq: Millions Misspent for Contracts," *New York Times*, October 3, 2003.

32   George Monbiot, "States of War," *Guardian*, October 14, 2003.

33   Tyler and Bonner, "Iraq: Millions Misspent."

34   Baum, "Nation Builders for Hire."

35   Salamander Davoudi, "Survey of Attitudes Makes Disturbing Reading for US," *Financial Times*, March 16, 2004.

36   Douglas Jehl, "Insiders' New Firm Consults on Iraq," *New York Times*, September 30, 2003.

37   Craig Gordon and Knut Royce, "Israel–Iraqi Boom Ties Raise Questions," *Newsday*, October 5, 2003.

38 Ibid.

39 Cited by Thomas L. Friedman in "Courageous Arab Thinkers," *New York Times*, October 19, 2003.

40 STRATFOR, "War Will Restructure Investment in the Middle East," December 6, 2002.

41 "The Carlyle Group: C for Capitalism," *Economist*, June 28, 2003; a review of Briody's *The Iron Triangle*.

42 Pep Subiros, "Utopias Imperiales."

43 William K. Tabb, "The Two Wings of the Eagle," *Monthly Review*, July–August 2003.

44 Naomi Klein, "A Deadly Franchise," AlterNet.org, September 8, 2003.

45 Georgie Ann Geyer, "Bush, Sr.'s Message to Bush Jr.," *Boston Globe*, October 18, 2003.

10
THE *CONSIGLIERI* IS BACK

1 Terence Hunt, "Baker Gets Backing as Iraqi Debt Emissary," *Portland Press Herald*, December 12, 2003.

2 Thomas L. Friedman, "Hearts and Minds," *New York Times*, December 14, 2003.

3 Joshua Micah Marshall, Talking Points Memo, December 9, 2003.

4 Jim Lobe, "Baker's Return—Cheney's Heartburn," Antiwar.com, December 13, 2003.

5 Marshall, Talking Points Memo.

6 Julian Coman, "CIA Plans New Secret Police to Fight Iraq Terrorism," *Telegraph*, January 14, 2004.

7 Rajiv Chandrasekaran, "Ending Occupation Gets Higher Priority," *Washington Post*, December 28, 2003.

8 Naomi Klein, "It's Greed, Not Ideology, That Rules the White House," *Guardian*, December 23, 2003.

9   "Iraq War Planned Pre-9/11?" CBS News, January 11, 2004.

10   Robin Wright, "Bremer: A Will on Iraq, Not a Way," *Washington Post*, December 23, 2003.

11   Keith B. Richburg, "France, Germany Agree to Lighten Iraq Debt Load," *Washington Post*, December 1, 2003.

12   Jim Krane, "Squabble Over Aid," *Portland Press Herald*, December 22, 2003.

13   Ibid.

14   Klein, "It's Greed, Not Ideology."

EPILOGUE

1   Nicholas Pelham, Joshua Chaffin, and James Drummond, "In the Line of Fire ...," *Financial Times*, May 6, 2004.

2   Juan Cole, "US Failure Helps Revive the Old Pan-Islamic Project," *Le Monde Diplomatique*, May 2004.

3   Orit Shohat, "Remember Falluja," *Haaretz*, April 28, 2004.

4   Mike Davis, "The Pentagon as Global Slumlord," in www.TomDispatch.com, April 19, 2004.

5   Rory McDonald and Julian Borger, "US Says 95% of Fallujah Dead Were Military Age Males ... Hospital Director Says Vast Majority Were Women, Children and Elderly," *Guardian*, April 12, 2004

6   Rajiv Chandrebaran, "Old Iraqi Army Reborn in Fallujah," *Washington Post*, May 7, 2004.

7   Nicholas Pelham and Roula Khalaf, "Creation of ex-Ba'athist Force 'Strictly One-off' Plan, Say Officials," *Financial Times*, May 4, 2004.

8   Thom Shanker, "Hussein's Agents Are Behind Attacks in Iraq, Pentagon Finds," *New York Times*, April 19, 2004.

9   Conroy quoted by Chanbrebaran, "Old Iraqi Army Reborn."

10   Eric Margolis, "Déjà Vu All Over Again," *Toronto Sun*, May 2, 2004.

11   Quoted by Arnaud de Borchegrave, in *Washington Times*, May 1, 2004.

12 Niall Ferguson, "Viet Nam Generation of Americans Has Not Learned Lessons of History," *Telegraph*, April 4, 2004.

13 Cole, "US Failure Helps Revive the Old Pan-Islamic Project."

14 Associated Press, "Karbala Wracked by Battles With al-Sadr Supporters," *Portland Press Herald*, May 13, 2004.

15 Ibid.

16 William Pfaff, "The American Mission," a review of Zbigniew Brezinski, *The Choice* (Basic Books), *New York Review of Books*, April 8, 2004.

17 Christopher Caldwell, "America's War to Sway Opinion," *Financial Times*, May 14, 2004.

18 Englehardt quoted by Danny Schecter in News Dissector Weblog, May 18, 2004.

INDEX

'60s radicalism 15–20
9/11 (World Trade Center attack, 11 September 2001) 2, 15, 17, 22, 25, 46, 56, 61, 144–5, 193, 238
    Commission 9
    Bush's reaction 166–7
    Iraq and 198, 224
    survivors' law-suit 225
    threat ignored 59

abortion 13
Abraham, Spencer 6, 63, 190, 194
Abrams, Elliot 49
Abu Ghraib 236, 239
Adams, Brooks 193
ADB (Asian Development Bank) 62
Adleman, Kenneth 49
AEI (American Enterprise Institute) 49
Afghanistan 53, 89, 145, 157, 170, 204, 239
    journalists and 92–3
    Operation Anaconda 58–62, 64–5

reconstruction 61–2
Romania and 47
al-Hakim, Abdul Aziz 108, 226
al-Hakim, Muhammed Bakr 152
al-Hashemi, Akila 202
al Keylini, Kamel 208, 211
al Qaeda 6, 12, 111, 135, 155, 162, 170, 215, 229
    Operation Anaconda and 58–9
al Sager, Mohammed 103
al-Sadr, Moqtada 233, 235–7
al-Sistani, Ali 225, 233
al-Zargawi, Abu Musal 240
Alaska 26, 216
Albright, Madeleine 114
Alexander, Anthony 194
Algeria 5
Ali, Tariq 83, 150
Allbaugh, Joe 213
Allen, Bob 122
American Hospital Group 209
ANC (African National Congress) 41–2

Andrews, Tom 96
Annan, Kofi 107, 199
anti-Communism 145
anti-globalization 23
anti-war protest 3, 75–85
Aon 230
Arendt, Hannah 10, 13, 20, 70, 121, 141
Argentina 171–2
Armenia 63
Armitage, Richard 49, 186
ArmourGroup 230
Ashcroft, John 200
Atta, Mohammed 197
Australia 5
Azerbaijan 63, 216
Aznar, Jose Maria 27

Ba'athists 232–3, 234
Bacevich, Andrew 106, 177
Bach, Pham Van 134
Bahrain 56
Baker, Cissy 94
Baker Hughes 66, 220
Baker, James 63, 66, 153, 190, 191, 215–7, 225–6, 228
    appointment to White House 220–2
Baker Potts 225
Bangladesh 173, 195
Barone, Michael 50
Bartley, Robert 50
Barzani, Masoud 108, 152
Basra 231
Baum, Dan 183, 188, 212
Bechtel 159, 168, 183, 197, 208, 211, 230
Beers, Rand 28, 162, 170
Beirut 157
Belten, Catherine 108
Bennett, Richard 109
Bennett, Robert 12
Berkeley 18

Bernard, Dick 78
bin Laden, Osama 60–1, 64, 65, 67, 155, 156, 170–1
bin Laden, Shafiq 215–6
Blades, Joan 78
Blair, Tony 54, 209, 240
Bleucher, Heinrich 121
Blitzer, Wolf 96–7
Bodine, Barbara K. 153
Bolton, John 49
Boot, Max 159–60, 182
Booz Allen Hamilton 184
Boucher, Richard 226
Boyd, Wes 78
BP (British Petroleum) 63
Brahimi, Lakdar 8
Brazil 175
Brecht, Bertolt 1
Bremer, Paul 6, 109–10, 153, 154, 156, 158, 159, 162, 174, 197, 206, 209, 213, 223, 224, 234
    Order 39 and 8
    privatization and 172–3
Brightman, Gordon 33, 35, 37–41
Briody, Dan 216
Briscard, Jean-Charles 61
Bristol Myers 1
Brown, Jock 122
Brzezinski, Zbigniew 2
Buddhism 138
Bulgaria 240
Bunnia, Mahmoud 211
Bush, Jeb 191
Bush Jr., George W. 24, 144, 161
    achievements 229
    denies 9/11-Iraq link 198
    energy policy 190–4
    Carlyle Group and 216–7
    Hume on 118–9
    NATO and 45–6

plans for Iraq 184
speech onboard Abraham Lincoln 115
Bush Doctrine 48, 69–71, 84, 86
    anticipated by Kennedy 129–30
Bush Sr., George 26, 143–4, 215–6, 189–90
    Saddam and 227
Byrd, Robert 27, 72, 86–7

Caldwell, Christopher 239–40
Cambodia 17, 53, 133, 136, 186
Cannistro, Vince 161
Card, Andrew 73
Card, Bill 75, 80
Carlucci, Frank 216
Carlyle Group 215–9, 220–1, 193
Carroll, Phillip J. 204
Carter, Jimmy 11
Casteel, Steve 224
Caterair International 216
censorship 92–5
Chalabi, Ahmed 106, 108, 207, 233–4, 235
Chalabi, Salem 213–4
Chambers, Whittaker 141
Chase, J.P. Morgan 171
Chavez, Hugo 54
Cheney, Dick 24, 66, 86, 92, 144, 156, 169,
    183, 186, 191, 192, 197, 222
    Cheney Report 64
Cheney, Lynne 187
Chevron Texaco 63
Chicago Democratic Convention (1968) 18
China 135–6, 145, 175, 216, 240
    dollar and 54
    Vietnam and 145–6
Chirac, Jacques 199
Chomsky, Noam 3
Churchill, Winston 130
CIA (Central Intelligence Agency) 48, 161
Citigroup 171
civil rights 12, 22

Clark, Vern 180
Clark, Wesley 95
Clarke, Richard 4, 9
Clarke, Victoria 93, 94, 102
Clean Air Act 194
Cleland, Max 77
Clinton, Bill 9, 11, 49–50, 218
    closure 21–2
Cockburn, Alexander 83
Coffin, William Sloane 41
Collins, Susan 75, 79
Communism 46, 141–3
Computer Science Corp. 185, 189
Conant, Charles 142
Conkey, Elizabeth 35
Conroy, James T. 232
Contract International 230
Cookes, Stoney 122
Cordesman, Anthony 25–6
corporations 22–3
Cowley, Malcolm 142
CPA (Coalition Provisional Authority)
    8, 157, 202–3, 208, 210, 212, 213, 223,
    224
    headquarters bombed 225
CPC (Caspian Pipeline Consortium) 63
Creative associates International 230
CSIS (Centre for Strategic and
    International Studies) 49
CSP (Centre for Strategic Policy) 49
Cuba 16, 17, 54, 135, 162
Cubic 185
Czech Republic 185

Dasquie, Guillaume 61
Davis, Rennie 122
Dean, Howard 14, 85
Decter, Midge 141
Defense Department Guidance 222
defense spending 10, 170–1, 212

Delay, Tom 165
Dellinger, Dave 122
Delta Airlines 209
Democratic National Convention
    (Chicago, 1966) 32–5
depression 1, 166–7, 215
deregulation 171, 194
    Carter and 11
DIA (Defense Intelligence Agency) 48
Diem, Ngo Dinh 137
Dijbouti 53
Djerejian, Edward P. 66
dollar
    undermined by corporate fraud 2
    versus euro 6, 86, 53, 107–9, 110,
        196–7
Dominican Republic 240
Dong, Pham Van 126, 127, 130–3
Dowd, Maureen 93, 206
DPB (Defense Policy Board) 167
duBay, Mark 79
DynCorp 185

Eagleburger, Lawrence 66
Eastland, James 16
Edwards, Richard 111
Egleson, Nick 122
Eisenhower, Dwight 128, 129
Eisner, Pete 187
Eliade, Mircea 134
"embedding" 13, 91–5, 109
England, Gordon 187
Englehardt, Tom 83, 100, 240
Enron 1, 23, 190
Erinys 185
Eritrea 5
Estonia 46
EU (European Union) 54
    oil and 3–4
euro 3–4, 21

dollar and 6, 27–8, 53–7, 86, 107–9,
    110, 190–1
Europe 46–7
Exxon 65
ExxonMobil 63, 209
Fallujah 7–8, 195–5, 230–7, 240
Famin, Qasim 61
Feith, Douglas 2, 9, 13, 48–9, 105, 143,
    184, 213
Ferguson, Niall 175, 181, 234
Ferguson, Tim 110
Fisk, Robert 6
FitzGerald, Frances 144
Fleischer, Ari 116–7
Fluor 230
Forsling, Elizabeth 33, 35, 36
France 173, 196–7, 209, 225
    Iraq reconstruction and 211
Franks, Tommy 59, 91, 105, 116, 153, 158
free trade 26, 29, 217–8
Friedman, Tom 151, 199, 221
Fruchter, Norm 122, 146

Gandhi, Mahatma 44
General Electric 230
Georgia 53, 145, 225
Germany 225
    Iraq reconstruction and 211
Ghorbanifar, Manchur 184
Gitlin, Todd 83–4
Global Crossing 1
Grateful Dead 20
Greene, Graham 138
Greenspan, Alan 11, 167
Greuning, Ernest 137
Gribben, David 186
Grumman, Northrop 186–7
Guantanamo 12, 239
Guatemala 162
Gulf War I (1991) 50, 66, 92, 95

Halberstam, David 95
Halliburton 1–2, 23, 53, 65–6, 73, 97,
    151–2, 159, 183, 186, 197, 204, 208,
    212, 220, 230
Hamas 4, 5, 231
Hartung, William 187
Hayden, Tom 122, 124
health and safety 23
Heckmatyar, Gulbuddin 61, 64
Henderson, Hazel 53
Hersh, Seymour 5, 93, 96–8
Hildenbrand, Mark 100
Hollinger International 97
Homeland Security 9, 11–2, 176
Honduras 239
Hook, Sidney 141
Howland, John 213
Hughes, Baker 191
Hume, Anthony 118–9
Hungary 185
Hussein, Saddam 20, 48, 50, 155, 156–8
    capture of 223
    euro and 55, 86, 107–8, 190–1

identity politics 19
IILG (Iraqi International Law Group)
    213–4
Ijaz, Mansoor 168
IMF (International Monetary Fund) 166,
    171, 208
imperialism 9–10
import controls 173–4
India 199
International American Products 230
International Criminal Court 28, 52
Iran 6, 29, 135, 162, 192, 215, 225, 229
    dollar and 53
Iraq
    attack on (1998) 50
    invasion of (March 2003) 47–8, 53,

55, 71, 72–80, 75–87, 88–9,
    156–60, 163
    compared to Vietnam 177–8, 236,
        238, 240
    condemned by diplomats 240
    economic effects 215
    Israeli advisers and 231
    military campaign 99–115
    oil and 9–11, 86, 174–5, 208, 226
    pre-planned 184, 190–4
    civil war 7
    euro and 9–11 86, 175–6
    privatization 229–30, 234, 238
    reconstruction 27, 151–5, 157–8, 174,
        186, 196, 199, 205–14, 224, 226–7,
        230–1, 238
    resistance 6–8, 153–60, 180–1, 203–4,
        204–6, 198–9
    US withdrawal 222–4
IRDC (Iraqi Reconstruction and
    Development Council) 211
Isaacson, Walter 13, 93–4
Islamism 5, 229–30
Israel 4–5, 8–9, 24, 28, 49, 49, 73, 162,
    173, 186, 192, 183, 229
    Iraq and 231
    oil and 133
Italy 3
Itera 61–2

Jackson, Bruce 169, 186
Jackson, Henry "Scoop" 14
Japan 147, 199, 240
Jenkins, Jerry 25
JINSA (Jewish Institue for Strategic
    Affairs) 49
JINSA (Jewish Institute for National
    Security Affairs) 134–5
Johnson, Lyndon B. 66, 132
Jordan 5, 53, 211, 213

Kagan, Donald and Frederick 129–30
Kagan, Robert 45, 51, 52–3, 59, 70, 90
Karzai, Hamid 61, 170, 185
Kay, David 201, 205
Kazakhstan 63, 145, 240
KBR (Kellogg, Brown and Root) 66, 97,
    114, 151–2, 183–5, 186, 188–9, 212,
    220
Keane, John 164
Kelley, Stephen F. 79
Kennedy, J. F. 30–1, 38–9, 128
    anticipates Bush Doctrine 129–30
    on defense policy 34–5
Kennedy, Edward 218–9
Kent State killings 15
Kenya 40
Kerry, John 25, 26, 28–9, 85
Keynes, John Maynard 176
Khalilzad, Zalmay 49, 61
Kharzai, Hamid 185
Khashoggi, Adnan 97
Khodorkovsky, Mikhail 216
Khrushchev, Nikita 35, 135
Kimmit, Mark 236
King, Carol 122–3
King, Martin Luther 17
Kirkpatrick, Jeanne 141
Kissinger, Henry 16–7, 131, 132–3, 206
Klare, Michael 64
Klein, Naomi 5, 7, 8, 218, 224, 227
Kopkind, Andy 16, 20, 122
Koppel, Ted 227
Korea 32
Kosovo 50
Kristol, Irving 51, 141
Kristol, William 51, 70, 86
Krugman, Paul 178, 180, 221
Kucinich, Dennis 182
Kurds 7, 20, 151, 152, 154, 203, 226, 235
Kuwait 5, 20, 53, 56

Kyoto Protocol 28, 52
Kyrgyzstan 64, 145

Lake, Anthony 31
Laos 17, 133, 136
Latif, Mohammed 231
Latvia 46
Lau, Ha Van 127, 134, 135–9, 145
Laudato, George A. 114
Lay, Kenneth 190
Leahy, Patrick 207
Lebanon 135
Lebedev, Platon 216
Ledeen, Michael 134–6, 143, 162
LeHaye, Tom 25
LeMay, Curtis E. 71
Lewinsky, Monica 50
Libby, I. Lewis 49, 69, 191–2
Libby, Scooter 143, 222
Lieberman, Joseph 202
Lippmann, Walter 36
Lis, James 112
Lithuania 46–7, 57
Lobe, Jim 221–2
Lockheed-Grumman 183, 186–7
Lopy, Joe 186
Louis Berger Group 230
Luce, Henry 36
Lustick, Ian 163
Lynd, Staughton 124

Maass, Peter 151
MacArthur, Douglas 31, 32, 182
MacArthur, John R. 92
McDonald's 209
Macdonald, Dwight 141
McCaffrey, Barry R. 106
McCarthy, Mary 123, 130, 134
McCarthy, Joseph R. 35–6, 37
McEldowney, Carol 121–7, 134–6

McKee, Robert E. 204
McKiernan, David D. 153–4, 159
McNamara, Robert 129, 132
MAD (Mutual Assured Destruction) 128
Madrid bombing 3, 27, 239
Major, John 216
Makiya, Kanan 84
Mandelbaum, Michael 46
Mao Zedong 17, 128
Maresca, Jack 60
Margolis, Eric 100–1, 233
Marquis, Christopher 182
Marshall, J. M. 221, 222
Marxism–Leninism 18
Mattheissen, Peter 84–5
MCA (Millenium Challenge Account) 171
Meacher, Michael 191
MEFTA (Middle East Free Trade Area) 172–3
Mello, Sergio Vieira de 196
Merck 1
Meszaros, Istvan 10
militarism 176–7
    as economically destabilizing 183
    censorship and 92–5
    military spending (US) 10, 170–1, 212
Mineta, Norman 187
Minh, Ho Chi 71, 137, 138
Mondale, Walter 78
Moore, Isaac 112
Moore, W. Bruce 159
Moravcsik, Andrew 159–60
Morgenthau, Hans 36
Morocco 5
Morse, Wayne 137
Moussa, Amr 103
MoveOn 14, 25, 75–78, 81–2, 86
Mubarak, Hosni 5
Muhammad, Raid Abdul Ridhar 110

Muller, Robert 86, 200
Mungo, Ray 122
Musharraf, Pervez 60, 65, 170
Muttawakil, Wakil Ahmed 59–60
My Lai 96
Myers, Richard 65, 92, 105, 155, 161, 232
    torture and 239

Nash, David J. 227
Nasser, Gamal Abdel 233
National Security Strategy (September 2002)—*see* Bush Doctrine
National Socialism 3, 13, 46
NATO (North Atlantic Treaty Organisation) 50, 46, 185
Naylor, Sean 58
Negroponte, John 5
neoliberalism 11
Netanyahu, Benjamin 51
New Bridge Strategies 213, 185
New Zealand 240
Newstadt, Richard 36
Nicaragua 240
Nigeria 41
Nixon, Richard 17, 30, 36
Niyazov, Saparmurat 62
North Korea 88–9, 106, 147, 181, 216, 225
Novak, Robert 200, 226
Noyes, Richard 140
nuclear weapons 14, 49, 88, 145
Nye, Joseph 57–8

O'Neill, Paul 224
O'Reilly, David 63
Office of Special Plans 48
Offley, Ed 102
Oglesby, Carl 18
oil 21, 27–8, 151, 173, 208
    as cause of war 62–3
    euro and 3–4

oil (cont'd)
    import price 229
    Israel and 133
    Iraq and 55–6, 86, 174–5, 226
    Saudi Arabia and 56
    Venezuela and 54
Oldham, Jim 38, 40
Oman 56, 63
OPEC (Oil Producing/Exporting
    Countries) 4, 6, 28, 73, 54, 55, 191
Operation Anaconda 58–9
opium 65
Othnan, Mahmoud 212

Pakistan 89, 170, 199
Parenti, Christian 202–3, 210
Paribas 108
Pariser, Eli 75, 77–80, 85–7
Pariser, Emanuel 75, 80
Parks, Rosa 17
Parsons Brinckerhoff 227
Patriot Act 9, 12
Pelosi, Nancy 202
Perini Corporation 230
Perle, Richard 5, 9, 13–3, 50, 50–1, 70,
    96–8, 134, 143, 169
Pfaff, William 237–8
Philippines 170
Pietropaoli, Steve 94
Pike, John 223
Plame, Valerie 200
PNAC (Project for the New American
    Century) 49, 140, 191–2
Podhoretz, Norman 13, 141
Pollack, Kenneth M. 49, 55–6, 159
Powell, Colin 63, 71, 92, 105, 107, 154,
    197, 209
preemptive strikes 9, 10, 52, 69–71, 77, 89,
    172, 174, 192, 199
    as blunder 85

    retreat from 225
privatization 171, 173, 183
    as fascist 189
    in Iraq 229–30, 234, 238
    of military 183–90
Putin, Vladimir 45–6, 108, 216

Qatar 56

Randal, Jonathan 139
Rather, Dan 93
Ray, Violet—*see* Seminon, Paul 5
Reagan, Ronald 11, 36, 48
Recknagel, Charles 55
Reichard, Lawrence 83
Renner, Charlotte 80
Research Triangle Institute 230
Rice, Condoleezza 164, 197, 206
Ridge, Tom 11–12, 187
Ridgeway, James 168, 189
Riper, Paul Van 121
Rite Aid 1
Roach, Stephen 175
Roche, James G. 186
Romania 45–7, 57, 185
Rosneft 61–2
Rothstein, Vivian 122
Rove, Karl 199–201, 225
Roy, Arundhati 3
Rubenstein, David 216
Rubenstein, Richard 95
Ruckeyser, Muriel 195
Rumsfeld, Donald 24, 63, 81, 84, 86, 89,
    91, 47, 48, 100, 104, 105, 106, 121, 141,
    147, 153, 156, 155, 158, 159, 181, 191,
    197, 198, 206
    privatization and 188
    torture and 239
Rusk, Dean 39, 70, 128, 132, 182
Russia 63, 209

Safire, William 50, 70
SAIC (Science Applications International,
   Co.) 211
Said, Edward 25
Saleem, Izzadine 240
Saleh, Jassim Mohammed 232
Salisbury, Harrison 124–5, 130–4
Sanchez, Ricardo S. 210
SAS (Special Air Services) 187
Saudi Arabia 6, 29, 56–7, 191, 216, 229
Schroeder, Gerhard 27, 108
Schulsky, Adam 13
Schultz, George 168
Schumer, Charles 240
Scowcroft, Brent 2, 70, 222
SDS (Students for a Democratic Society)
   18, 122, 124
Seminon, Paul 5
September 11 2002—*see* 9/11
Serbia 50
Seward, William 142
Shakespeare, William 22
Sharon, Ariel 4, 24, 51
Sharpeville massacre 42
Sheehan, Jack 168
Sheehan, Neil 139
Shehadeh, Salah 231
Shi'ites 7, 20, 158, 232, 233–7
Shinseki, Eric K. 105
Shohat, Orit 231
Siemens 230
Simmons, Matthew 56
Singer, P.W. 185
Sloyan, Patrick J. 92
Smith, Albert E. 187
SNCC (Student Nonviolent Coordinating
   Committee) 17
Snow, Edgar 128
Snow, Olympia 79, 80
Somalia 157

Sontag, Susan 85, 123–4
Soros, George 2–3
South Korea 88, 147, 240
Soviet Union 142–3
Spain 3, 239
Squibb 1
Steinberg, James 198
Stephanopoulos, George 81
Stephens, Philip 2
Stern, Sol 122
Stevenson, Adlai 33, 36
STRATFOR (STRATegy FORecaster)
   147, 202, 206, 214–5
Strauss, Leo 13
Subiros, Pep 165, 181, 183, 209, 216
Sunnis 230, 232, 234–5, 236–7
Syria 29, 135, 229

Tabb, William 218
Tae-joon, Park 216
Tajikstan 64
Talabini, Jalal 108, 226
Taliban 12, 60–1, 64–5, 66–8, 170
Tambo, Oliver 41–2
Task Force 121, 223
Taylor, William 156
Tenet, George J. 200, 204
terrorism 9, 11–2, 28, 49, 144–5, 162, 167,
   191, 197–9
   Bush on 46, 48
   Clinton on 49–50
   stock market and 5
   war on 2
Tet Offensive 131
Thach, Pham Ngoc 134
Thomas, Evan 132–3
Thompson, Loren 99
Total 226
trade deficit 229
Trireme 97

Trotsky, Leon 40
Trudeau, Garry 198
Truman, Harry S. 32, 39
Tunisia 5
Turkey 5, 47, 135–6, 186, 199
    Perle and 51
Turkmenistan 62, 63
Tutmiler, Margaret 153
Twain, Mark 43–4

UN (United Nations) 8, 29, 195–6,
    198–9, 208–9
unemployment (US) 26
United Arab Emirates 56
Unocol 60–2, 65, 67
Uzbekistan 53, 64, 66, 145

Vann, John Paul 95
Venezuela 53–4
Vidal, Gore 14
Vietnam 15, 17, 31, 36, 39, 38–9, 70–1,
    85–6, 120–50, 162
    China and 145–7
    compared to Iraq 177–8, 236, 238, 240
    journalism and 139–40
    Kennedy and 128–9
    US atrocities in 124–7
Villepin, Dominique de 196
violence 10
Viviano, Frank 62

Walker, David M. 190
Wallace, William S. 103
Walters, Roger "Buck" 159
Warden, John 104
Washington Group International 230

Waxman, Henry 183, 204
Weatherman 15, 124
Weinberger, Caspar 143, 168
Welch, Joseph 35–6
welfare cuts 11, 166–7, 178
Wheeler, John 139–40
Whitman, Bryan 91, 93, 105
Will, George 50
Wilson, Brian 209–10
Wilson, John 122
Wilson, Joseph 199–201, 205
Wilson, Woodrow 237
Win Without War 96, 102
WMD (Weapons of Mass Destruction)
    25, 201–2, 223
Wohlstatter, Albert 14
Wolfowitz, Paul 2, 13, 48–9, 50, 69–71,
    86, 103–4, 105, 143, 191–3, 221–2
Wolkow, Timothy 112–3
women's liberation 18
Woolsey, James 168
Word Bank 166, 171, 208–9
WorldCom 1
World Trade Center attack—*see* 9/11
Wurmser, David 49

Yassin, Ahmed 4, 5, 26, 231
Young, Marilyn 121
Young, Ron 122

Zakheim, Dov 27, 49
Zell, L. Marc 213
Zhou Enlai 131
Zinni, Anthony 105
Zoellick, Robert 172